Mission of Christian Churches in Post-Pandemic India

Mission of Christian Churches in Post-Pandemic India

Edited by
Acharya Catherine Prabhujyothi, DCP

2021

Mission of Christian Churches in Post-Pandemic India – published by Indian Society for Promoting Christian Knowledge (ISPCK) Post Box 1585, Kashmere Gate, Madarsa Road, Delhi-110006.

Online order: http://ispck.org.in/book.php

Also available on amazon.com

ISBN: 978-93-90569-45-8

Laser typeset by

ISPCK, Post Box 1585, 1654, Madarsa Road, Kashmere Gate, Delhi-110006 • *Tel:* 23866323

e-mail: ashish@ispck.org.in • ella@ispck.org.in
website: www.ispck.org.in

Contents

From the Editor

"Then I saw a new heaven and a new earth.The former heaven and the former earth had passed away, and the sea was no more. I also saw the holy city, a new Jerusalem, coming down out of heaven from God, prepared as a bride adorned for her husband. I heard a loud voice from the throne saying, 'Behold, God's dwelling is with the human race. He will dwell with them and they will be his people and God himself will always be with them [as their God]. He will wipe every tear from their eyes and there shall be no more death or mourning, wailing, or pain, [for]the old order has passed away." [Rev. 21: 1-4]

The **new order** has indeed begun to take shape in the hearts and lives of people. Just as the human body shows symptoms of various sicknesses as a sign of self-purification when it is contaminated with too much toxin, the Nature – a living organism, also has its own mechanisms to purify its body when it is burdened with too much poison. Just imagine the amount of negative waves we, the humans, the most significant organ of the body of Nature send out daily by way of every inhuman thought, word, and action! The receiving end, the Nature/the entire creation of which we, the humans, are only a small part, has become saturated with toxin beyond its capacity to bear.

The advent of Corona Virus in the form of Covid 19 and its mission on earth [still going on] is part of the inevitable and much needed purification process of the earth family. We have to humbly admit our failures and sins that contributed heavily to the ill-health of the Nature and death of the many constituent [our fellow human beings and other beings] elements the Nature is made of.

From a spiritual point of view, the Creator Governor of this world, who entrusted it to our care, was forced to intervene in our businesses as we proved to be too selfish, too greedy, too egocentric to care for 'the other' [inclusive of all the living and non-living]. In this healing process, we, the humans, are brought down to our knees, to a new awakening while God has taken control in order to re-create, renew the face of the disfigured earth and sky. See, it is impossible even for Him to manage *His* home while we claim to be in power and try to occupy the seat which belongs to Him only. It took a tiny virus to teach us, to drive us home to the awareness of this great truth. Now is the time [before it gets too late] for us to wake up, gird up the loins readying our lives to participate in the *re-creation* process for a "new creation" initiated by the Divine with an invitation to our active partnership as humans [made in His own image] in general and as *disciples* of his Son, Jesus Christ in particular.

This book in your hands is an attempt from the part of some who have heard the call from above and from within to take responsibility both individually and collectively, to move in the new direction under *the guidance* of the *Spirit of Christ* as His committed missionaries to bring out the much desired change in attitude and life. While going through the articles compiled here, I was deeply touched and even moved to tears at times by the sincerity and openness of the authors, who were bold enough to speak out and confess *our* sins *we* have committed as *Christians* and as *human beings*.

Almost every article in this manual is like 'an examination of conscience' inviting the reader to the same. The book presents a new vision and mission for Christians and Christian Churches in the post-pandemic India. It will surely help to prepare the ground for the emergence of 'a new heaven and new earth' in the post-pandemic era.

The Ecumenical Symposium held at Dharma Bharathi Ashram on 27 November 2020 on the theme '*The Mission of Christian Churches in*

Post-Pandemic India' was the fruit of the prayerful reflections of two men of God, 'Acharyasri' (Acharya-guru Swami Dr Sachidananda Bharathi, DCP) and Revd Dr Adai Jacob Cor-Episcopa. Though they hail from different Christian backgrounds with different ministries, both of them are always conscious of the one common identity (being ***Disciples of Christ***) and the common mission (bearing witness to Jesus of Nazareth the Christ) they share.

'Acharyasri' for the last 38 years has been engaged in promoting *'an Indian face of the Christian faith without religious conversion and cultural alienation'* through various activities in different parts of India. As a former Indian Air Force officer and with his lived-life-experiences in four religious traditions under four gurus, he was enabled to develop a new vision of Christianity for the third millennium. Ever since his near death experience in an air accident and his first personal encounter with the living Spirit of Christ in 1982, he has been on this mission. He has now summed up the fruits of his spiritual quests over these years in his semi-autobiographical book 'A New Creation in Christ' written during (lockdown) the initial months of the COVID 19 pandemic. He is a strong proponent of the concepts of the 'Unbound Christ' and 'Open Christianity', which are at the core and center of ***'the Indian face of the Christian faith'*** developed by him.

Revd Dr Adai Jacob Cor-Episcopa hails from the Malankara Jacobite Syrian Orthodox background. He is the Founder Principal of 'Malankara Syrian Orthodox Theological Seminary' (MSOTS), the premier Seminary to train and prepare the priests of the Jacobite Church. He did his Ph. D in Theology from Regensburg University in Germany and had occupied a number of important positions in the Church both abroad and in India. He is deeply pained by the divisions and conflicts among Christian Churches, especially among the Jacobite and Orthodox factions and has been writing and working for ecumenical unity and cooperation in building up the 'Body of Christ', the Universal Ecumenical Church in which the different Christian Churches in the world are unique and important parts with specific functions to perform in the plan of God.

Though both Acharyasri and Cor-Episcopa are rooted deep in the rich spiritual traditions of their own respective Christian Churches, they also share the common mission of regenerating the Christian Churches based on the **'Cross of Christ'.**

Many of us too, I am sure, are deeply pained by and ashamed of the disunity and fights among us Christians in Kerala. Dharma Bharathi Ashram is committed to promote a culture of unity and peace and is located in central Kerala, the stronghold of the two rival factions, the Orthodox and Jacobite Churches. When the tension between these two Churches rose to maximum pitch in 2019 following the Supreme Court Judgment, as a member of Dharma Bharathi Ashram I felt we should do something to bring peace and unity among them. But I had no idea how to work on this huge and seemingly impossible task. It was during my 50-day silence retreat held at Jeevan Dhara Ashram, Jaiharikhal in the Himalayas in 2019 (Easter Season), I was inspired to work for ecumenical unity and harmony through silence prayer and fasting. On my return to the Ashram, with the encouragement and whole-hearted support of Acharyasri, I have been regularly doing it on a specific day [Friday] every week, since 21 June 2019.

I also requested some of my close friends, who are men and women of prayer to join me in prayer at the specific time [from 12:00 to 03:00 pm] from their own places. I left the expected result entirely into the hands of God without making any demands. It has been a token of my love for the Body of Christ, which we call 'the Church', of which I too am a part. I simply responded to the promptings of the Spirit within me and allowed It to work in and through me. That's all.

As the prayer and fast continued, slowly and steadily there emerged a small ecumenical prayer group at the Ashram without any conscious efforts from our part. They gather every Tuesday evening at the Ashram for prayer and table fellowship. The Kingdom of God is like a mustard seed growing into a tree or like the yeast that leavens the wheat flour when mixed with. So is the presence of a ***disciple*** of Christ or of a group of them gathered in His name in the world. I am fully convinced that the Spirit of Christ is at work here as It is everywhere. God is ***the Doer***, not *us*. But we need to *allow* Him; the rest will be taken care of. This is my experience in my spiritual quest.

The National Ecumenical Symposium held on 27 November 2020 was also the fruit of the combined spiritual quest of all of us. It was a source of great joy for us to host this Ecumenical Symposium. This book in your hands is the fruit of that National Symposium.

The first Article is a comprehensive concept paper by Acharyasri on the mission of Christians in post-pandemic India. Secondly, Revd Dr Adai Jacob Cor-Episcopa provides the New Testament foundation for the mission of Churches in the post-pandemic India. Revd Dr George Samuel of Marthoma Church, the Director of DBSFR [Dharma Bharathi School of Forgiveness and Reconciliation], provides the much-needed theological and Christological perspectives to the mission. The Article by Friar Bobby Vadakkal, the Coordinator of DBSFR is included next. This is followed by the Article by Sri Thomas Varghese on Peace and Sustainable Development perspectives. These are the authors who were the Resource Persons and Speakers in the National Symposium.

H. E. Timotheos Mathews Metropolitan was kind enough to inaugurate the symposium. He has also kindly contributed an article for this book. All articles are included in the order they were received.

I hope and pray that this book will be made good use of by all Christian Churches in India, especially by the Seminaries and Formation Houses as a study material.

May God bless the Christian Churches and Mother India!

May a new heaven and new earth emerge for the human race during the post-pandemic era!

Acharya Catherine Prabhujyothi, DCP
Mataji, Dharma Bharathi Ashram
General Editor

Preface

The COVID-19 pandemic has become a 'turning point' in the evolutionary growth of human consciousness. We have a very challenging mission at this critical juncture in the history of humanity. We are called to work together with all people of goodwill on earth for rebuilding the pandemic-devastated world on a peace and sustainable development paradigm.

A unitive spiritual consciousness which will inspire us to see the spiritual unity underlying all physical diversities in the world should provide a strong foundation for such a peace and sustainable development paradigm. This book is being published for promoting such a peace and sustainable development paradigm and unitive spiritual consciousness in post-pandemic India in which the Christian Community is called to play an important role.

A National Ecumenical Symposium on 'The Mission of Christian Churches in Post-Pandemic India' was held at Dharma Bharathi Ashram on 27 November 2020. It has provided the basic inspiration and core contents for this book. This book also includes Articles on various interrelated themes written by leaders/ thinkers/teachers/activists from various Christian Churches in India.

The first Article by Acharyasri (Acharya Dr Sachidananda Bharathi, DCP) presents an ecumenical mission termed 'Navasrushti India Mission' that can be made their own by Christian Churches in post-pandemic India. I have had the pleasure and privilege of working with Acharyasri in some of the experimental initiatives through which he has developed the vision, ideology and action plan that are being presented as constituents of the Navasrushti India Mission which can give an 'Indian face' to the Christian faith. Promoting an Indian face of the Christian faith without religious conversion and cultural alienation is the task that Acharyasri has taken up as the mission of his 'second life'.

The post-pandemic era calls for a millennium leap forward in the evolutionary growth of human consciousness. Because of her Earth Family Consciousness and her incessant quest for God, truth and non-violence, India has a call and a mission to help humanity take this millennium leap forward. But she is unable to respond creatively to her destined call and mission because of the widespread poverty, unemployment, corruption, casteism, communalism, illiteracy, ill health and criminalism that have afflicted her national life. With the COVID-19 pandemic, these destructive forces have gained greater strength. They have now become serious problems facing the nation.

Poverty, casteism, corruption, communalism, criminalism and other evils existing in India today are only the external symptoms of an internal cancerous moral decay that has afflicted the soul of India. This cancerous moral decay has spread to all vital organs of India's national life. Liberating India from this moral degeneration is more of a religious and spiritual mission than a political and economic task. In the multi-religious and multi-cultural context of India, this is a long term interreligious and socio-spiritual mission calling for an Integral Renaissance of India encompassing the religious, political, economic, social and ecological dimensions of her national life. It will need a great deal of sustained and collective prayerful efforts and voluntary sacrifices.

An interreligious and socio-spiritual mission is the crying need of the hour for achieving the two interrelated objectives of liberating India from the cancerous moral decay afflicting her soul, and of rebuilding the post-pandemic India on a peace and sustainable development paradigm based on a unitive spiritual consciousness.

The historic mission ahead of the Christian Churches presented in this book is a creative response to this two-fold task ahead of the post-pandemic India. This book is meant to serve as an ecumenical mission manual for the Christian Churches in post-pandemic India for achieving the above-mentioned two interrelated objectives.

After the deluge in Kerala during August 2018, we had formed a Kerala Integral Renaissance Action Forum (KIRAF) to promote an Integral Renaissance of Kerala, which was formally inaugurated on 15th December 2019 by Sri. Arif Mohammad Khan, the Hon. Governor of Kerala, at POC, Palarivattom, Kochi.

The COVID-19 pandemic has motivated us to expand the Kerala Integral Renaissance Movement as a New Creation Movement for an Integrated World Order based on a peace and sustainable development paradigm and a unitive spiritual consciousness.

The erstwhile KIRAF is now integrated with 'Dharma Rajya Vedi' (DRV) which is an interreligious organization to promote the New Creation Movement. The Navasrushti India Mission presented by Acharya Sachidananda Bharathi in this book as an ecumenical mission for Christian Churches in post-pandemic India is being promoted by DRV as an India-specific mission within the New Creation Movement.

The Kerala Integral Renaissance Movement is now integrated with the Navasrushti India Mission. A Kerala pilot project of Navasrushti India Mission is also being promoted by Dharma Rajya Vedi under the name 'Navasrushti Kerala Mission'. With such a solid background, the Navasrushti India Mission stands on a very strong foundation.

With great pleasure I recommend this book to the Christian Churches in India to be used as an Ecumenical Mission Manual for the mission ahead of them in post-pandemic India.

I also recommend the Navasrushti India Mission as an interreligious mission for a culture of peace and sustainable development in this ancient land of religions.

KP Fabian
Professor, Symbiosis University, Pune
Former Ambassador of India to Italy

Introduction

A National Ecumenical Symposium was organized on 27 November 2020 at Dharma Bharathi Ashram on the theme ***'The Mission of Christian Churches in Post-Pandemic India'***. This was a prayerful effort to find a creative response to the crises facing the post-pandemic India from a Christian point of view. This book is the fruit of that prayerful effort.

A. Organizing Partners

The National Ecumenical Symposium held at Dharma Bharathi Ashram at Mulanthuruthy near Kochi in Kerala on 27 November 2020 was organized jointly by Malankara Syrian Orthodox Theological Seminary (MSOTS), Disciples of Christ for Peace (DCP) and Dharma Bharathi School of Forgiveness & Reconciliation (DBSFR). It was sponsored by Dharma Bharathi Foundation (DBF). Brief descriptions of these three organizing partners and the Sponsor are included below:

1. Malankara Syrian Orthodox Theological Seminary

Malankara Syrian Orthodox Theological Seminary (MSOTS) located at Vettikkal near Mulanthuruthy is a Theological Seminary for training the priests of the Jacobite Syrian Church. Very Revd Dr Adai Jacob Cor-Episcopa is the Founder Principal of MSOTS. With his dedicated service and under his enlightened leadership MSOTS has been developed into a premier training academy for training the priests of the Malankara Jacobite Orthodox Syrian Church. The initiative for the National Ecumenical Symposium came from his prayerful reflections.

2. Disciples of Christ for Peace

Disciples of Christ for Peace (DCP) was founded in 1998 by Acharya John Sachidanand (now Acharyasri Dr Sachidananda Bharathi, DCP) as an Open Consecrated Society within the Catholic Church for *'Unity and Peace through Sahana Yoga'* in India through interreligious dialogue and joint action based on the Fundamental Duties of Indian citizens given under Article: 51-A of the Indian Constitution. DCP was registered as 'an ecumenical communion of love' with a global coverage in 2009 (Reg. No. IV–72/2009) to promote *'abiding peace within individuals and families inspired by the Gospel of Lord Jesus Christ and guided by the living Spirit of Christ'* without religious conversion and cultural alienation. Dharma Bharathi Ashram at Mulanthuruthy near Kochi in Kerala, founded in 2003, functions as the Registered Office, Spiritual Home and Coordinating Center of DCP.

3. Dharma Bharathi School of Forgiveness & Reconciliation

Dharma Bharathi School of Forgiveness & Reconciliation (DBSFR) was founded in 2006 by Acharyasri (Swami Dr Sachidananda Bharathi, DCP) for providing residential gurukul model training for future visionary-missionaries of DCP. The Coordinating Office of DBSFR functions from Guru Bhavan in Dharma Bharathi Ashram.

4. Dharma Bharathi Foundation

Dharma Bharathi Foundation (DBF) was created and registered in 2001 as an Educational, Scientific, Cultural and Charitable Trust for a civilization of love, unity and peace in the world. DBF is also dedicated to God for an Integral Renaissance of post-pandemic India.

B. Aim of the National Ecumenical Symposium

The aim of the National Ecumenical Symposium was to bring out an Ecumenical Mission Manual that can be used by the various Christian Churches for the mission of rebuilding the post-pandemic India on the strong foundation of the Gospel values and of a socio-spiritual sustainable development paradigm through interreligious cooperative action.

C. Contents of this Book

The readers will find the various articles written by Christian leaders/ teachers/activists from different Churches in India that are included in this book very inspiring and enriching. The authors, through their articles, share with the readers not only their knowledge and expertise on the subjects, but also their years of experience in their areas of work. Hence, most of the articles can also be very useful for various Christian Communities and Institutions in their planning and training. That is also the hope with which this book is being published.

The first article is by Acharyasri. This is the expanded version of the Keynote he had delivered at the National Ecumenical Symposium. It presents an ecumenical vision and mission that can be shared by Christians and the Christian Churches in post-pandemic India.

1

The Christian Mission in Post-Pandemic India

Acharyasri *

After many years of mission work in the North Indian States, I had returned to our Dharma Bharathi Ashram, Mulanthuruthy, on 25th November 2017 (my 71st birthday). I also wanted to undergo Ayurvedic treatments for Arthritis and other age-related sicknesses of my physical body.

The deluge in August 2018 devastated Kerala. I saw the deluge as a 'wake-up call' for this State which is the cradle of Christianity and Islam as well as of communism, consumerism and materialism in India. I wrote a book titled *'SAMAGRA NAVOTHANA MAHAYAJNAM: An Integral Renaissance for Peace & Sustainable Development of the Flood-ravaged Kerala'*. The Kerala Integral Renaissance Action Forum (KIRAF) was formed to take the mission forward.

The 'Kerala Integral Renaissance Movement' was formally inaugurated by Sri. Arif Mohammad Khan, the Hon. Governor of Kerala, at POC, Kochi, on 15th December 2019. While working to develop the Kerala Integral Renaissance Movement, I was invited to Delhi in February 2020 for undertaking a 'forgiveness and reconciliation mission' there in the lines of the one I had undertaken in UP during 2013-2016 following the communal violence at Muzaffarnagar in 2013.

The Delhi violence was not exactly a communal violence among Hindus and Muslims, but had serious political issues behind it. Hence, I could do nothing much there, and I returned to Dharma Bharathi Ashram on 09 March 2020.

A. COVID-19 Pandemic

The COVID-19 pandemic has confined me to Dharma Bharathi Ashram ever since my return from Delhi. This is an Ashram initiated by me in 2003 to promote an Indian face of the Christian faith without religious conversion and cultural alienation.

The forced confinement in the Ashram gave me enough time to reflect prayerfully over the mission of my 'second life' that had begun with an air accident and my first personal encounter with the living Spirit of Christ in 1982 while serving as an officer in the Indian Air Force. I was also inspired to write a book under the title 'A New Creation in Christ' which presents the story of my 'second life' beginning with my first personal encounter with the living Spirit of Christ in 1982. The book was dedicated to God through Sadguru Jesus Christ at a function held in Dharma Bharathi Ashram on 08 July 2020, the 38th anniversary of my air accident and first personal encounter with the living Spirit of Sadguru Jesus Christ, my Divine Master.

The COVID-19 pandemic has brought great pain, agony, death and devastation to humankind. It has convinced me of the solidarity of humankind, the unity of all lives, and the interdependent organic nature of planet Earth. It has also revealed to me the role that the *disciples* of Sadguru Jesus Christ are called to play in the post-pandemic world to promote these three core realities of our very existence in this world. It has further revealed to me the great role that *India* is called to play in the post-pandemic era to rebuild the pandemic-devastated world on an eco-spiritual sustainable development paradigm and Earth Family Consciousness.

Based on my convictions strengthened by the lessons taught by the pandemic and inspired by the revelation of India's mission in the post-pandemic world, I was motivated to expand the Kerala Integral Renaissance Movement, to contextualize the New Creation Movement and integrate them into one mission for an Integral Renaissance of India under the name 'Dharma Rajya Mahayajnam' which was initiated from Dharma Bharathi Ashram on 02 October 2020.

The National Ecumenical Symposium organized in Dharma Bharathi Ashram on 27th November 2020 on *'The Mission of Christian Churches in Post-Pandemic India'* inspired me to transform the Dharma Rajya Mahayajnam into 'Navasrushti India Mission'. It is presented to Christians and Christian Churches in India as an interreligious nation-building mission in the post-pandemic era with an inclusive vision, eco-spiritual ideology and a comprehensive action plan. It is briefly outlined in this comprehensive concept paper which is also an expanded and modified version of the Keynote that I had delivered at the National Ecumenical Symposium.

With effect from 02 October 2020, I have entered into the final stage of the mission of my 'second life'. This is envisaged to be a stage of integration. Hence, I have also changed from saffron to white dress with the simplified name 'Acharyasri'.

I was initiated into spiritual life under the guidance of my Christian guru, Revd Fr Bede Griffiths, OSB Cam, with the name 'John Sachidanand' on 25th November 1984 (my Air Force name was Sqn. Ldr. N. V. John). I left the Indian Air Force in 1989 at the age of 42 to devote myself fully to my new mission. As a preparation I had undertaken 3 months of *'mauna vrata'* (silence and prayer) in Saccidananda Ashram near Kulithalai in Tamil Nadu, where my guru was living at that time. I had also written a book *'Pratyasa Dharma*

Samhita' during this period of silence and prayer. I had outlined in it the vision and mission of my second life in a seminal form. At the end of my '*mauna vrata*' I was given 'Acharya diksha' on 18 January 1990 by my guru with a specific ministry of *promoting an Indian face of the Christian faith without religious conversion and cultural alienation.*

I had renounced family and private property, and ventured out as a '*parivrajaka*' (homeless mendicant) on 3rd July 1996, the feast of St Thomas, with the written permission of my wife who was at that time an Additional Commissioner of Customs and Central Excise (IRS, 1974 Batch). I had entered into 'Sanyasa' in 2001, also with her permission.

As a 'Sanyasi', clad in saffron dress I had lived a life of renunciation from 25th November 2001, my 55th birthday. I had also initiated the '*Bharathi*' *Chaturashrama Sanyasa Parampara* on 8th July 2003, the 21st anniversary of my first encounter with the living Spirit of Christ and took the name 'Swami Sachidananda Bharathi'. After 19 years of leading a life of renunciation, I felt the inner call for integration in the spiritual quest of my 'second life'.

B. The New Indian Renaissance

What India urgently needs today for enabling herself to play her destined role in the post-pandemic world is an Integral Renaissance that can bring about a moral and spiritual regeneration of the religious, economic, political, social and ecological dimensions of her national life. In order to understand this historic mission ahead of India in the post-pandemic era, it will be worthwhile to have a glimpse into the history of the birth and growth of the renaissance spirit in the Indian soil. This begins with Raja Ram Mohan Roy (1772 – 1833) and the 'Brahmo Samaj' Movement.

The 18th century is referred to as the 'Dark Age' in Indian history. The evils of sati, child marriage, polygamy, caste system, polytheism, immorality, injustice and corruption flourished in India at that time. Raja Ram Mohan Roy fought against these evils. He also advocated equal inheritance rights for women. He adopted and applied an enlightened religious approach to fight against the social and moral evils afflicting the Hindu society in India at that time. The first thing he did was to promote monotheism with a concrete moral code for the Hindus. The 'Brahmo Samaj' was the fruit of his labour of love. It was born from a 'marriage' between the Hindu social realities with the Christian morality that expressed themselves through his personal life and mission. Raja Ram Mohan Roy died of meningitis in Bristol, England, on 27 September 1833.

By his tireless and fearless efforts through the Brahmo Samaj, Raja Ram Mohan Roy was able to bring about a renaissance of the Hindu society during the Dark Age by abolishing sati, child marriage, and polygamy. He had thus earned the name, 'The Maker of Modern India'.

The following four insights gained from the successful efforts of Brahmo Samaj can be used effectively by all those who are working for meaningful and non-violent social transformation in the Indian society:

1. Religion has always remained the most powerful motivating force in India throughout her history. Nothing in India really succeeds unless it touches the religious sense of the Indian people. This has to begin with an understanding of the one true God and His saving grace ever active in human history.

2. In the multi-religious context of India, we need to build our mission on an integral vision of life and reality and a synthesis of science and spirituality with a concrete action plan to fight the various evils afflicting the nation.

3. The cancerous social evils of the dehumanizing caste system, the all-pervasive corruption and the growing communalism eating into the soul of India as well as the economic, political

and ecological crises facing the nation can be fought effectively only through an enlightened pan- India interreligious mission.

4. One has to begin any divine mission in India with a sincere effort to bring about a moral and spiritual renaissance of religions in India. This has to begin with one's own life and with one's own religion.

The four insights mentioned above were the motivation for us to organize a 3-day National Interreligious Seminar from 29 September to 02 October 1990 at Renewal Center, Kaloor, Kochi, Kerala, on the theme *'Emerging Integral Vision of Reality & Religious Response'*. This historic National Interreligious Seminar had given birth to 'Dharma Rajya Vedi' (DRV).

The divine mission entrusted to DRV was to promote a 'New Indian Renaissance' based on an integral vision of life and reality and a synthesis of science and spirituality (Ref. Experimental Initiative No. 6, chapter-4, of my book 'A New Creation in Christ' for details of the birth of DRV). DRV had undertaken a number of projects and programmes at different parts of India over the years in its quest to realize its vision and mission as can be seen from the various Experimental Initiatives mentioned in my book 'A New Creation in Christ'.

DRV had finally initiated a socio-spiritual movement named 'Dharma Rajya Movement' in 2018 for transforming India into a spiritually awakened, morally regenerated, economically prosperous and politically strong 'Bharatiya Dharma Rajya' based on my book *'Bharatiya Dharma Rajya: Vision of Kingdom of God in India'*. The book and the Dharma Rajya Movement were dedicated to God and Mother India at Raj Ghat, New Delhi, on 02 October 2018, as part of the celebrations of the 150th birth anniversary of Mahatma Gandhi as mentioned under Experimental Initiative No. 38 in chapter-4 of 'A New Creation in Christ'.

I have realized through years of my experiments and experiences that what we needed for the fruitfulness of the New Indian Renaissance was a liberative spirituality of forgiving, enduring and self-sacrificing love that can provide a much-needed soul force and inner dynamism to it. This liberative spirituality was already made available to humanity by Sadguru Jesus Christ two thousand years ago. Such a liberative spirituality had already made an entry into Indian history through Mahatma Gandhi.

Bringing the living Spirit of Christ into the source and center of the New Indian Renaissance was found to be an essential prerequisite for the success of the mission of DRV. Developing and promoting an 'Indian face of the Christian faith' without religious conversion and cultural alienation became a historic imperative for the success of the New Indian Renaissance.

C. An Indian Face of the Christian Faith

Dharma Bharathi Ashram at Mulanthuruthy near Kochi in Kerala was inaugurated on 17 December 2003 to promote an 'Indian face of the Christian faith' without religious conversion and cultural alienation.

'Christian faith' is an abiding faith in the one true God revealed to humanity by Sadguru Jesus Christ (John 1: 18). It is also the faith that accepts and acknowledges Sadguru Jesus Christ as the 'Word of God' incarnated in human history (John 1: 14). Christian faith also implies accepting and acknowledging Sadguru Jesus Christ as the 'human face of God' (John 14: 9) and as 'the way, the truth and the life' in humanity's eternal quest for God (John 14: 6).

Christian faith has acquired a number of 'faces' in its evolutionary growth over the last two millennia. The first was the 'Jewish face' which had presented Jesus of Nazareth as the 'Lamb of God who takes away the sins of the world'. This Jewish 'face' was given to Jesus of Nazareth based on the Old Testament narrative of the 'fall and redemption' of humankind and the concept of 'original sin'.

Then came the 'Roman face' which had proclaimed Jesus of Nazareth as the 'Saviour' of humankind and the 'King' of the Jews. The Jews were under the Roman subjugation at that time and they were eagerly waiting for a liberator to liberate them from the Roman subjugation. Many of his disciples and followers saw in Jesus of Nazareth such a liberator.

However, it was the 'Greek face' that had enabled the Christian faith to open up to the non-Jewish world by proclaiming Jesus of Nazareth as the *'Christos'* and *'Logos'*. The Greek word *'Christos'* implies the 'anointed one of God'. The English word 'Christ' comes from this Greek word. The Greek *'Logos'* implies the 'Word of God'. In Indian terms, it implies the Primordial Word, *Sabda Brahman* or *Adi Shabda*.

After a few centuries there emerged the exclusive and violent 'Colonial face' of the Christian faith that proclaimed Christianity as the 'only true religion' and the Bible as the 'only true Word of God' and Jesus of Nazareth as the 'only true God'. Such exclusive claims led to conflicts and violence. Saving the souls of 'pagans' by converting them to the colonial version of Christian faith became an obsession for the European Christian missionaries and their counterparts and followers all over the world. This exclusive and violent 'Colonial face' which satisfies the religious ego of its proponents is the most widely spread face of the Christian faith in the world today. This is because the European colonial powers had conquered and ruled over a large number of countries in the world. Christian missionaries with the help and support of these colonial powers succeeded in spreading the 'Colonial face' of the Christian faith all over the world.

The latest face of the Christian faith is the 'Commercial face'. It has its roots in a competitive consumerist culture. This 'Commercial face' proclaims Lord Jesus Christ as the Lord of health and wealth, and as the giver of all good things in life. It makes 'preaching the

Gospel' a highly commercial and competitive proposition with a great deal of sound and fury. Kerala, the cradle of consumerism in India, is a very fertile ground for this version of the Christian faith. One only has to visit any of the many Charismatic Retreat Centers and Pentecostal Prayer Houses in Kerala or read their journals to understand this truth.

The Christian faith that is being promoted in India today by various Christian Churches is based on one or more of the above five 'faces' acquired by it over the centuries of its evolutionary growth. Unfortunately, none of these five faces of the Christian faith appeals to the religious-minded and educated Indians because these are not in harmony with India's religious genius that has ever been seeking for God, truth, and non-violence incessantly with an open mind.

Dr E Stanley Jones, one of the great American missionaries who had understood both India's spiritual worth and the power of the Gospel of Christ well, had pointed out that *'the religious genius of India is the richest in the world. The forms that it has taken have often been the most extravagant, sometimes degrading and cruel. Those forms are falling away, or will fall away, but the spirit persists and will be poured through other forms. As that genius pours through Christian moulds, it will enrich the collective expression of Christianity. But in order to do that the Indian must remain Indian. He must stand in the stream of India's culture and life, and let the force of that stream go through his soul so that the expression of his Christianity will be essentially Eastern and not Western. This does not mean that Indian Christianity will be denied what is best in Western thought and life, for when firmly planted on its own soil it can then lift its antennae to the heavens and catch the voices of the world. But it must be particular before it can be universal. Only thus will it be creative – a voice, not an echo.'* Like Dr Stanley Jones, many disciples of Sadguru Jesus Christ in India, including me, have felt the need and urgency for an Indian face of the Christian faith.

Indian spirituality and India's religious quest have also been emphasizing the need for interiority and silence in prayer and for a culture of simplicity and renunciation in the lifestyles of religious leaders and spiritual masters. The pomp and show of many Christian leaders and the sound and fury of many Christian prayer groups as well as the consumerist culture of many Christian communities are totally alien to the religious genius of India and to India's spiritual culture.

India urgently needs a Christian faith which is in harmony with her rich cultural and spiritual traditions and insights. It must be expressed in terms and symbols that can be easily understood and assimilated by the religious-minded people of India. 'Knowing the one true God and Jesus Christ whom He has sent' is the source and condition of eternal life taught by our Divine Master.

The Theology, Christology, Missiology, Spirituality and Philosophy of the Indian Church must be in harmony with the revelations in the New Testament and with the enlightened spiritual insights and cultural traditions of India. This is an urgent requirement for the Christian faith to bear abundant fruits in the Indian soil. I have been involved in the task of developing such an Indian face of the Christian faith ever since my first encounter with the living Spirit of Christ in 1982. Following the example of Meister Eckhart (1260-1328), the German mystic and theologian, I was also forced to ask the question *'what is it to me if the Son of God was born to Mary, unless He is born in me, in my time and in my culture?'* My efforts to find an answer to this question also motivated me to seek for an Indian face of the Christian faith.

I have come to realize that in order to be able to develop an Indian face of the Christian faith, the Christians and Christian Churches in India will have to first of all adopt and undergo the following five important paradigm shifts in their own individual and collective lives. I have found these paradigm shifts very effective in my own life and mission.

1. A paradigm shift from sacraments and membership of the Church to meditation and discipleship of Christ.
2. A paradigm shift from loud vocal prayers to saints and saintly mediators to gentle contemplative prayer direct to God the Father in the name of Lord Jesus Christ.
3. A paradigm shift from a stagnant 'repetitive loyalty' to the Word of God to a dynamic 'creative fidelity' to the Spirit of God.
4. A paradigm shift from preaching the Gospel and converting people to Christianity to building up the 'Government of God' (kingdom of God) on earth in collaboration with all peace-loving people of goodwill belonging to the different religious traditions of humankind without any 'hidden agenda' of religious conversion and 'saving the soul'.
5. A paradigm shift from the self-centered consumerist culture of competition and the divisive materialistic philosophy of 'success' to an other-centered socio-spiritual culture of cooperation and a holistic eco-spiritual philosophy of 'fruitfulness'.

With these paradigm shifts in their individual and collective lives, the Christians will also be able to overcome the moral decay and spiritual apathy that have afflicted their lives and their Churches today. Such a five-fold paradigm shift will lay a strong foundation for developing and promoting an Indian face of the Christian faith without religious conversion and cultural alienation.

We have also developed the two important core concepts for the Indian face of the Christian faith. These are the 'Unbound Christ' and 'Open Christianity'. These two core concepts are explained briefly below.

1. 'The Unbound Christ'

The term 'Unbound Christ' implies the 'Word of God' that existed before creation. This Word was with God and was God. All things were created through Him (John 1: 1-3). This Word of God is present in all religious traditions and scriptures of humankind in varying degrees and measures.

Jesus of Nazareth was the incarnation of the Word of God in human history. His disciples identified him as 'Christ, the Son of the living God' (Matt. 16: 16). However, the Word of God cannot be limited to the historical person of Jesus of Nazareth alone. He is 'the way, the truth, and the life' in humanity's quest for God (John 14: 6). Hence, Christianity and other religious traditions of the world are only 'pointers' and witnesses to God and to the Word of God.

Christianity by virtue of being founded on the Word of God incarnated in, with and through Lord Jesus Christ, has a very important role to play and a great responsibility to fulfill in helping humanity to come to a deeper understanding and experience of the one true God and His incarnated Word. Knowing the 'one true God and Jesus Christ whom He has sent' is the basis and prerequisite of 'eternal life' (John 17: 3).

The knowledge of the one true God and His Word is not confined to or bound with Christianity and the Holy Bible alone. Other religions and their scriptures are also pointers to and custodians of such a redemptive knowledge of the 'Unbound Christ'. All that is needed to understand this truth is to develop a 'Christ Consciousness'.

By the term 'Christ Consciousness' we mean the divine Consciousness which had incarnated in Lord Jesus Christ and which had enabled him to live and work in this world with deep and abiding love for God and humanity. It is that Consciousness which had enabled him to accept willingly the suffering death on the cross by submitting himself fully and unconditionally to the 'Will' of God, whom he had addressed as his 'Father'.

Lord Jesus Christ had an intimate personal relationship with God as a beloved son with his ever loving and ever forgiving merciful father. He was 'the beloved Son, with whom God was well pleased'

(Matt. 3: 17). He also enjoyed the status of being the *"only begotten Son that whoever believes in Him should not perish but have everlasting life"* (John 3: 16).

The Christ Consciousness is also being referred to by us as 'Unitive Spiritual Consciousness' which will enable us to see the spiritual unity underlying all physical diversities in the world. It will help us to understand the all-pervasive nature of God, the solidarity of humankind, the unity of all lives, and the interdependent organic nature of planet Earth. It will also enable us to experience the truth of the dictum, 'God in All & All in God'. The departing prayer of Lord Jesus Christ was for an abiding unity among his disciples and among all those who believed in him (John 17: 20-26).

Through the Christ Consciousness we will also come to experience the truth of the Pauline revelation, *'we live, move and have our being in God'* (Acts. 17: 28).

It is upon the strong and deep foundation of such a Christ Consciousness/Unitive Spiritual Consciousness that humanity is called to build its future. An Integrated World Order built on this Unitive Spiritual Consciousness alone can withstand the trials and tribulations of history, and usher in a culture of abiding peace and sustainable development on the earth. This will also provide a strong socio-spiritual foundation for the Kingdom of God/ 'Government of God' on the earth.

2. 'The Open Christianity'

The term 'Open Christianity' implies a way of life rooted in Christ Consciousness and guided by the teachings of Lord Jesus Christ as recorded in the four Gospels, especially in the 'Sermon on the Mount' (Matt. 5, 6 & 7). The source and center of this Open Christianity is a living and loving relationship with the person of Lord Jesus Christ who is the same yesterday, today, and forever (Heb. 13: 8). 'Open Christianity' also implies living one's life inspired and guided by the Christ Consciousness dwelling within one's own self.

All peace-loving people of goodwill in the world, irrespective of their religious, cultural, linguistic, geographical, ideological, ethnic and gender differences, can live happy and fruitful lives based on the concept of Open Christianity, and be enriched and enlightened by it. The various Christian Churches in the world are to be seen as various autonomous communities of the people of goodwill living this Open Christianity in their own time-space contexts, united to one another with an abiding love as embodied and exemplified by their Divine Master, Lord Jesus Christ (John 13: 34 – 35; 15: 12-13) and guided by his teachings.

The various Christian churches/communities in the world may have different physical and cultural expressions from time to time and from place to place, but all of them share the same spiritual experience of the one true God and His Word-incarnate. The Open Christianity will be like a large tree with many branches. It is the vision of a Global Ecumenical Church inspired by the Unbound Christ and rooted in the Christ Consciousness. Every Christian church/community in the world will be seen as an important and unique organ of this 'Mystical Body' of Christ, the Global Ecumenical Church, with a specific and unique function to perform in the post-pandemic world.

Every disciple of Lord Jesus Christ and every Christian church is an important constituent of the 'Mystical Body' of Christ. But they can remain so only as long as they are united to one another through an abiding love inspired by the Christ Consciousness, and are guided by the teachings of Lord Jesus Christ. "By this all will know that you are my disciples, if you have love for one another" (John 13: 35). Unity among his disciples was the prayer of the Lord (John 17: 21).

Many Christians and Christian churches in India today are scandals to Christ. More people are alienated from Christ in India by Christians preaching Christianity without practicing the Christian values in their own lives. This brand of Christianity must die, so that a new vision of Christianity built on the strong foundation of an Indian face of the Christian faith can emerge in the post-pandemic world. The post-pandemic era will be an era of the Indian face of the Christian faith.

Just as the institutionalization of Christianity had begun from the West with Rome as its center, the spiritualization of Christianity must begin from the East with India as the center. Within India itself, it is Kerala, the cradle of Christianity in the Indian subcontinent that has to be the seedbed and role model of the Indian face of the Christian faith in the post-pandemic period. The troubles and tribulations facing the Christian churches in Kerala today are preludes and prerequisites for the much-needed death and resurrection of these churches. A new vision of Christianity is impatient to be born in Kerala.

I for one see Kerala as a 'second Israel'. The first Israel gave to the pre-pandemic world the Crucified Christ, the Savior of humanity from sins, sinful tendencies and sinful structures. The message of this crucified Christ is drowned in the cacophony of the various Christian churches today. The second Israel has to give to the post-pandemic world the Risen Christ, the giver of abundant life and abiding peace. This message of abundant life and abiding peace of the resurrected Christ will break through the barriers of institutionalized 'Churchianity' and will lead to the Open Christianity of our vision.

D. The Integral Renaissance of India

As seen above, the post-pandemic India requires an Integral Renaissance encompassing the religious, economic, political, social and ecological dimensions of her national life based on a synthesis of science and spirituality. We have also seen that such an Integral Renaissance of India needs the living Spirit of Christ to provide the necessary soul force and inner spiritual dynamism to it. This is possible only if the Christian faith is given an Indian face without religious conversion and cultural alienation.

The interreligious theology termed *Prabhu Parameshwar*, the advaitic Christology termed *Sadguru*, the kingdom of God missiology termed *Dharma Rajya*, the liberative spirituality of love termed *Sahana Yoga* and the holistic philosophy of peace termed *Dharmodaya* developed by us as the basic constituents of the Indian face of the Christian faith are now presented by Dharma Rajya Vedi as the five foundational constituents of the Integral Renaissance of India. (For details of these basic constituents, please refer to chapter-7 of the book 'A New Creation in Christ'.

E. Navasrushti India Mission

The Navasrushti India Mission with its Kerala pilot project termed 'Navasrushti Kerala Mission' was formally inaugurated at Dharma Bharathi Ashram on 30 January 2021, the 73rd anniversary of the martyrdom of Mahatma Gandhi, and the first anniversary of the outbreak of the COVID-19 pandemic in India. This also marked the inauguration of an interreligious Christian mission for the Integral Renaissance of post-pandemic India.

Dharma Rajya Vedi (DRV) initiated in 1990 for a New Indian Renaissance, as mentioned elsewhere in this comprehensive concept paper, is responsible to provide the necessary organizational support and human resources for the Integral Renaissance of post-pandemic India and its Kerala pilot project. The 'Disciples of Christ for Peace' (DCP) initiated in 1998 for peace and unity in India based on the Fundamental Duties of Indian citizens is made responsible to provide the necessary 'soul force' to DRV and to the Integral Renaissance of post-pandemic India and its Kerala pilot project. DRV & DCP are also being given new shapes and forms in the post-pandemic era. New Constitutions are adopted for DRV & DCP on 30th January 2021 which will come into effect from Pentecost – 2021. The original Malayalam name *'Christusishya Shanti Sangham' (CSS)* is also being used for DCP hereafter.

'Navasrushti India Mission' is an interreligious and socio-spiritual mission through which the much-needed Integral Renaissance of post-pandemic

India will be given concrete practical expressions based on an inclusive interreligious vision of a great new India termed *'Bharatiya Dharma Rajya'*, a holistic eco-spiritual ideology termed *'Bharatiyata'* and a comprehensive action plan. These three constituents of the Navasrushti India Mission are briefly explained below.

1. *Bharatiya Dharma Rajya*

The vision of a great new India adopted and promoted by DRV for the Navasrushti India Mission is termed *'Bharatiya Dharma Rajya'*. This is an inclusive interreligious vision of a great new India built on the deep and strong foundation of the *Prabhu Parameshwar* theology, *Sadguru* Christology, *Dharma Rajya* missiology, *Sahana Yoga* spirituality & *Dharmodaya* philosophy developed for the Indian face of the Christian faith.

a. The 'Fundamental Duties' of Indian citizens presented under Article: 51-A of the Indian Constitution will provide a strong Constitutional foundation for the 'Bharatiya Dharma Rajya'.

   'Responsible citizenship' based on the Fundamental Duties of Indian citizens is the crying need of the nation today. 'We, the People of India' still carry a 'subject mentality' and expect the Government officials and political leaders to create a good, prosperous and happy nation for us to live in peacefully forever. This is a totally immature and irresponsible approach and attitude. A 'responsible citizenship consciousness' based on the Fundamental Duties of Indian citizens alone can help us to realize our vision of a 'Bharatiya Dharma Rajya'. Political leaders and Government officials are there only to help the citizens to build a great new India of justice, liberty, equality, and fraternity based on the much-needed responsible citizenship consciousness.

b. A decentralized democratic system based on the Panchayatiraj - Nagar Palika Acts 1992 will provide a strong political foundation for the 'Bharatiya Dharma Rajya'.

'Democracy' is defined as the government *of* the people, *by* the people and *for* the people. Unfortunately, the Indian democracy today has become a 'government of the party, by the party and for the party'. Political parties in India today are also highly influenced by the rich and the powerful people and by the rich business/industrial houses in the country. Practical application of the Panchayatiraj – Nagar Palika Acts, both in letter and spirit, can help to make democracy in India strong and truly citizen-centered.

c. An economic system based on cooperation and principles of partnership/trusteeship, instead of competition and monopoly/private ownership will provide a strong economic foundation for the Bharatiya Dharma Rajya.

d. The concept of *Sarvodaya* (Welfare of all) cherished by India since long will provide a strong social foundation for the Bharatiya Dharma Rajya.

e. An Earth-Family Consciousness which upholds the solidarity of humankind, the unity of all lives and the interdependent organic nature of planet Earth that is at the core of Indian thought and culture will provide a strong ecological foundation for the Bharatiya Dharma Rajya.

f. Discoveries of modern science pointing to the interdependent organic nature of planet Earth and unity of all lives will provide a strong scientific foundation for the Bharatiya Dharma Rajya.

g. The Gandhian vision of *Gram Swaraj* and the Gandhian *Talisman* which calls upon the leaders and decision-makers in the country to make their decisions with the aim of empowering the last and the least in the country will provide a strong Gandhian foundation for the Bharatiya Dharma Rajya.

h. Emperor Ashoka the Great and his Dharma Chakra which is at the center of India's National Flag will provide a strong historical foundation for the Bharatiya Dharma Rajya.

The divine mission of Christians and Christian Churches in post-pandemic India is to work tirelessly, fearlessly, prayerfully and incessantly to transform the post-pandemic India into the Bharatiya Dharma Rajya as envisioned above. DRV invites all like-minded organizations, institutions, civil society groups, political parties and religious communities in the country to work together with it as autonomous collaborating partners to transform India into the Bharatiya Dharma Rajya of our vision with the grace and truth as well as the power and wisdom of God.

2. *Bharatiyata*

A holistic eco-spiritual ideology termed *Bharatiyata* is developed and promoted by DRV to provide a strong ideological foundation for the Navasrushti India Mission. *Bharatiyata* is based on the following four insights drawn from the 'Sanatana Dharma' tradition of India. These four insights will constitute the four pillars of *Bharatiyata*.

a. *Pragyanam Brahma* (Aitareya Upanishad): This implies that *Brahma* (God), the Source of all being and Ground of all existence, is *Pragya* (Consciousness). We live, move, and have our being in this Universal Divine Consciousness. Everything is created through, with, and from this Universal Divine Consciousness. Everything exists *in* this Universal Divine Consciousness and *because of* this Universal Divine Consciousness. This is the deepest insight into the nature of the Ultimate Reality experienced and taught by the enlightened saints and sages of ancient India. This Universal Divine Consciousness is the 'Word of God', the Christ - Consciousness that was with God and that was God, and through whom all things are created (Jn 1: 1-5). The 'Word of God' took flesh and incarnated in human history as Jesus of Nazareth through whom grace and truth came to humankind (Jn 1: 14-17).

b. *Ekam Sat Vipra Bahudha Vadanti* (Rig Veda): This implies that the Ultimate Truth is One but the saints/ the wise people in the world call it by various names. However, this Ultimate Truth, God, is beyond all names, forms and attributes ever comprehended and comprehensible by human intellect. Yet, every human person can develop an intimate personal relationship with this one true God, following the example of Sadguru Jesus Christ. Hence, it is foolish to fight or argue in the name of God and religion. The Self-revelations of God within individuals and in scriptures and religious traditions of humankind are bound with time and space, and are determined by the context and the level of consciousness of the person/ community/ society/ religion concerned.

c. *Isa Vasyam Idam Sarvam* (Ishavasya Upanishad): This implies that God pervades the whole creation. We live, move and have our being in God (Acts 17: 28). Creation is the Self-expression of God bound with time and space. Hence, the whole creation is sacred. Every human person, every living being, and Mother Earth as a whole, need to be treated with respect and caring love. Everyone and everything is unique and important in the creative plan of God. The human spirit is created in the image and likeness of the Divine Spirit. Hence, it is holy and eternally divine. All discriminations in the name of religion, nationality, party, language, ethnicity, gender, caste, class, colour, creed etc. are crimes against God and humanity. Damages to ecological harmony and environmental health are also crimes against God and fellow living beings.

d. *Vasudhaiva Kutumbakam* (Maha Upanishad): This implies that all living beings inhabiting our planet Earth together constitute one large Earth Family bound with a common destiny. The Covid-19 pandemic has taught us this truth in

> a very painful manner so that we might never forget it. The varieties of trees, plants and creepers; all species of animals, fishes, birds, reptiles etc. and the humankind as a whole together form this Earth Family. The human species constitute the most advanced species among all living beings on earth. Human beings are called to live like 'elder brothers and sisters' to all other living beings. Hence, we are also called to take loving care of all living beings inhabiting our planet which is our 'Common Home'.

The above four Sanatana Dharma insights are truly Indian and truly universal at the same time. They are also truly Christian. These are together termed *Sanatana Dharma Chatushtayam.*

The *Sanatana Dharma Chatushtayam* will enable 'We, the People of India' to rebuild the post-pandemic India on the strong foundation of an Earth-Family Consciousness.

Practical applications of this holistic eco-spiritual ideology of *Bharatiyata* constituted by the *Sanatana Dharma Chatushtayam* will help us to spiritualize economics and politics, and rebuild science and technology on a new foundation of *love.*

Economics and politics are interdependent and interrelated as two sides of a coin. All economic decisions are political decisions, and all political decisions are influenced by economic considerations. The spiritualization of economics and politics is the crying need of the modern era which is being enslaved by a competitive consumerist culture and self-destructive materialistic philosophy.

Spiritualizing politics and economics and rebuilding science and technology on a new foundation of love will constitute the two-fold challenging task ahead of the post-pandemic world. India, especially the Church in India, has an important role to play in this challenging task.

3. A Comprehensive Action Plan

A 7-point Comprehensive Action Plan (CAP) is presented by DRV for the Navasrushti India Mission.

The first action programme in this 7-point CAP is termed ***'Tyagarchana Jaiva Samrudhi'***. It is also the membership condition for joining the Navasrushti India Mission. It involves two things:

- Sacrificing something one likes every day and saving a minimum amount of Rs. 10/- daily from such sacrifices.
- Using this amount and doing a minimum one hour of physical labour daily to produce organic vegetables, fruits and other food items for one's own family through one's own initiatives.

Tyagarchana Jaiva Samrudhi is meant to make one self-sufficient in one's own food requirements through one's own physical labour. This will make India a self-sufficient and healthy *'Jaiva Samrudha Bharat'* within a short period of time without any support from Government Agencies, Political Parties or Banks. This is the first step towards realizing the vision of the *'Bharatiya Dharma Rajya'* based on the ideology of *'Bharatiyata'* of Navasrushti India Mission as presented above.

Membership of Navasrushti India Mission is open to all peace-loving people of goodwill in India who love Mother India and are committed to the welfare of all her children irrespective of their religion, caste, colour, class, party, gender, language, culture etc. Members only have to take up the *Tyagarchana Jaiva Samrudhi* and make it their very own. There is no other membership conditions. There are also no Membership Fees, no Membership Forms and no Membership Registers. Individual initiative and commitment are the only conditions.

Similarly, all Civil Society Groups, Residential Associations, Governmental & Non-Governmental Organizations, Religious Communities, Political Parties, Social Service Societies, Clubs,

Educational Institutions etc. in India can also become autonomous collaborating partners of DRV in Navasrushti India Mission by taking up and making *Tyagarchana Jaiva Samrudhi* their own and promoting it among their members and in their own surrounding areas, residential colonies, villages, towns etc.

The other 6 action programmes within the 7-point CAP of Navasrushti India Mission are:

a. A Christ-centered meditation termed *Shanti Yajna Meditation* for forgiveness, reconciliation and inner peace.

b. An interreligious sadhana termed *Tyagarchana* for spiritual unity and purification of India.

c. A five-point interreligious programme termed *Pancha Sutra* for the moral regeneration and non-violent social transformation of India.

d. An interreligious programme termed *Bharatiya Dharma* for responsible citizenship and national integration based on the Fundamental Duties of Indian citizens.

e. An interreligious campaign termed *Khushhaal Bachpan Abhiyaan* for happy and healthy childhood for children in India below 18 years of age.

f. An interreligious movement termed *Gram Swaraj Andolan* for empowering the local self-governing bodies based on the Panchayatiraj - Nagar Palika Acts.

Members can take up one or more of these 6 action programmes and promote them in their own families/areas.

(NB: For details of these programmes please refer to chapter-7 of my book 'A New Creation in Christ'.)

Navasrushti India Mission with its inclusive vision, socio-spiritual ideology and comprehensive action plan presents an interreligious mission for the Integral Renaissance of post-pandemic India. This mission can be taken up and made their own by all peace-loving and responsible citizens of India, especially by Christians and Christian churches in post-pandemic India.

The Dharma Bharathi School of Forgiveness & Reconciliation (DBSFR) and the Navasrushti Academy of Integral Renaissance (NAIR) functioning from Dharma Bharathi Ashram will provide the necessary training for members and leaders of the Navasrushti India Mission.

Conclusion

The best things in life are got at the cost of great pain. A new plant grows only when the seed falls into the ground and dies. A great mission will need a great amount of voluntary sacrifice and suffering. All citizens of India, especially the Christians and Christian churches in India, are lovingly invited to unite and work together with mutual respect for rebuilding the pandemic-devastated country through the Navasrushti India Mission presented in this comprehensive concept paper.

The interreligious vision, ideology and action plan of Navasrushti India Mission are akin to 'seeds' to be sown in the hearts and minds of the citizens of the country, especially of the Christian citizens, in the post-pandemic era. We will also have to initiate and undertake non-violent struggles for transforming India into the 'Bharatiya Dharma Rajya' of our vision and for making Kerala an inspirational prototype of this vision through an integral renaissance of this most literate and politically conscious State in India based on the vision, ideology and action plan of Navasrushti India Mission. We are called to achieve our goal and accomplish our mission with the power and wisdom of God in Christ.

May God, the ever merciful and compassionate Parent of all humankind, bless Mother India and all her children, and the whole

Earth Family. May God bless all religions, religious communities and political parties in India. May God bless the Christians and Christian churches in post-pandemic India with His power and wisdom, and with His grace and truth revealed through Sadguru Jesus Christ, the Prince of peace and Lord of love.

Jai Bharat... Jai Vasudhaivakutumbakam.....
Om ..... Shanti... Shanti..... Shanti.....

---

* **Acharyasri** (formerly Acharya-guru Swami Dr Sachidananda Bharathi, DCP) is a former atheist Indian Air Force Squadron Leader turned an ardent disciple of Sadguru Jesus Christ and a promoter of an Indian face of the Christian faith without religious conversion and cultural alienation. An encounter with death in an air accident and the subsequent personal encounter with the living Spirit of Christ in 1982 was the 'turning point' in the life of Squadron Leader N V John. He was initiated into spiritual life in 1984 with the name 'John Sachidanand'. He received *'Acharya diksha'* in 1990. Acharya John Sachidanand renounced family and private property in 1996 with the written permission of his wife (She was an IRS officer from 1974 Batch). He received *'Sanyasa diksha'* in 2001. He initiated the *'Bharathi' Chauturashrama Sanyasa Parampara* in 2003 and took the name 'Swami Sachidananda Bharathi'. He has lived-life experiences of four religions – Christianity, Hinduism, Islam & Sikhism, and a fairly good knowledge of all other religious traditions.

He is the Founder and Acharya-guru of Disciples of Christ for Peace (DCP) and Dharma Rajya Vedi (DRV) as well as a number of other Organizations, Institutions, Ashrams and Missions in India. He has travelled widely and has authored more than 20 books. He was awarded a honorary Ph D by Concordia University. He has also received a number of Awards for his selfless service and dedicated leadership. He was one of the delegates who represented India in the *Millennium World Peace Summit of Religious and Spiritual Leaders* organized by the United Nations in New York in August 2000. He was also a signatory to the 'Commitment to Global Peace' in this Summit.

With effect from 02 October 2020, he has entered into the *'Ativarna Ashram'* and is now dedicated to an integration of his life and spiritual quest. He has changed from saffron to white dress and has taken a simple name 'Acharyasri' from that day. Presently he resides in Dharma Bharathi Ashram, Perumpilly, Mulanthuruthy, Kochi, Kerala-682314. (Mobile: 8281874941/6238488650 & E-mail: swamisachidananda@gmail.com & URL: www.navasrushti.org)

2

The New Testament Perspectives of the Mission

Revd Dr Adai Jacob Cor-Episcopa *

Introduction

From the 1st century onwards the Christian Church was growing day by day and the Christian faith was spreading beyond the boundaries of Palestine. The Christian message reached in every nook and corner of the world. Gradually the Christian Church became one of the most powerful and prominent institutions in the world. When the Hierarchical Institution of the Church became very powerful, in the same ratio, the powerful Christian message was diluted and became powerless and the Churches in the world began to deteriorate. This deterioration radically affected the Churches in the world in the 20th and 21st centuries. For example, in Europe there was a time, when more than 90% of the people believed in Jesus Christ as Son of God and Saviour, but now more than 90% do not know Jesus Christ at all.

According to H.G. Wells – the most prominent historian of the world,"Jesus Christ was the most powerful and vehement spiritual revolutionist the world has ever seen". Jesus Christ opened and revealed the right path towards the salvation of the human race. Nobody till now has denied and denounced the path opened by Jesus Christ and his path is till now the true and real path for lasting peace and harmony (in the world) of the human race.

The life and message of Jesus Christ is for the whole humanity and he transcends all the boundaries. Even then real doubt remains whether the powerful Christian Churches in the world locked Jesus Christ in their own iron cages hindering access to other peoples in the world. If we ponder over the situation in the 1st century: the apostles were proclaiming Jesus Christ to the Jews, gentiles and to everybody and everywhere, suffering all sorts of persecutions. They were led by the Spirit of Christ. Jesus Christ the incarnate Son of God is for the whole humanity. If we confine Jesus Christ, his life, and message inside the walls of the Church, then it is against the last will of Jesus Christ expressed in Lk 24:47.

1. Jesus Christ and the Kingdom of God

Jesus Christ came to this world to establish the kingdom of God. His life and message was aimed at establishing the kingdom of God. He called God as His Father and revealed the true God through his life and teaching. God is revealed as the loving and merciful Father, who considers the human race as his own sons and daughters. The universal brotherhood of human race where the self-sacrificing love and mercy rule over the citizens as guiding principles in the kingdom of God is envisaged by God. His Son, Jesus Christ, is sent to the world to realize this will of God. Jesus was born in Bethlehem and brought up in Nazareth among the Jews. Perhaps 99% of the Jews, who faced Jesus, considered him as a simple human person, as son of Joseph and Mary. But the disciples were able to recognize him as Son of God and Messiah (Christ).

For the above mentioned universal brotherhood of the whole human race, we have to build upon the basis of the Spirit of Christ which awakes in human race a unitive spiritual consciousness. "The unitive spiritual consciousness will help us to understand the all – pervasive nature of God, the unity of all life and the interdependent organic nature of the planet Earth". How can a man called Jesus of Nazareth positively influence the human race and establish the kingdom of God? This question is answered through putting another question. How can a tiny invisible Corona virus negatively influence the whole human race? To rebuild the pandemic devastated world the Churches in the world have a great role to play.The world and the humanity need the Spirit of Christ - that means the self-sacrificing love and mercy – and mutual co-operation and help.

2. The New Message Given by Jesus for the Salvation of the World

In the history of humankind nobody influenced the history so positively and radically like Jesus Christ. What was the new message given by Jesus Christ to humanity?

According to the Bible, man is created in the image of God (Gen 1:27; 2:7). Image does not mean outward appearance, but inner constitution. Creation of man in the image of God implies that the essence a human being has to be sought in God. God is revealed in Jesus Christ and only through Jesus Christ we will be able to know the essence of God. In the fullness of time God revealed through Jesus Christ the hidden mysteries about God. The death of Jesus Christ on the cross was the climax of the earthly ministry of Jesus. The essence of the character of God is revealed on the cross. Jesus Christ embraced crucifixion out of his selfless and self-sacrificing divine love towards humanity. Jesus Christ – the Son of God, is the embodiment of self-sacrificing divine love. This divine love is the essence of the character of God. Therefore, to know the character of God, we have to look at the crucified Jesus Christ. Out of immense love towards humanity he sacrificed his life on the cross. This is the new message Jesus Christ through his self-sacrificing love has given to the human race for their salvation. Therefore, the Kingdom of God is a Kingdom of self-sacrificing love. After deeply understanding the essence of Jesus Christ, the Son of God, the beloved disciple tried to define the essence of God in simple words and said: – God is love (1 Jn 4: 8). The path of the divine love is the path of every Church and each individual. The Churches in the world have to come back to the path of self-sacrificing love shown by Jesus Christ.

Because man is created in the image of God, the essence of the character of man also must be the selfless and self-sacrificing love revealed by Jesus Christ. This is the way of God shown by Jesus Christ for salvation. Pride, greed, and selfishness are the way of Satan and that is the reason for all types of problems and evils in the world.

3. Cross – the Sign of Universal Salvation

The cross represents the sum and substance of the teachings of the scripture. What is the sum and substance of OT and the Ten Commandments? 'Love your Lord God' and 'Love your neighbor' are the two commandments in which all other commandments are included. The vertical line represents the love towards God and the parallel line of the cross represents the love towards fellow beings. When we look at the cross we must be able to understand that the cross is the symbol of the main two commandments of God and thus also the sign of salvation.

The cross, on the other hand, the principle and living way of life, is indebted to be adopted by all the Christian Churches. It seems that the Churches have forsaken the cross and adopted the materialistic and consumerist way of life during the last centuries.

4. Return to the Cross of Christ

I would like to emphasize the idea expressed by Acharyasri Dr Sachidananda Bharathi, DCP in his keynote address. According to Acharyasri, the institutionalization of Christianity with great patriarchal centers like Rome was the first stage in the Redemptive mission of Jesus Christ. With Covid 19 Pandemic the first stage has come to an end and the new stage in growth has begun.

Let me quote from Acharyasri's keynote address: "A spiritualization of Christianity by returning to the cross of Christ is the crying need of the post pandemic era. I believe that such spiritualization will constitute the next stage in the evolutionary growth of Christianity. This has to begin with the Individual disciples of the Divine Master in the post pandemic era, who are prepared to share the redemptive mission of their Lord through the path of his cross, which is the path of forgiving, enduring, and self-sacrificing love. I have termed this path of the cross of Jesus Christ as *Sahana Yoga*".

According to Acharyasri 'Sahana' means to suffer and 'Yoga' implies communion with God. I think returning to the cross of Jesus Christ is returning to the original unpolluted Christianity. Acharyasri explains the problem of Christian Churches: let me quote: "The Christian Churches in the world today have lost this mystery of the cross. The task ahead of the Christian Churches in the post-pandemic world is to rediscover this lost mystery of the cross of Christ".

5. The Church as Continuation of Incarnation

Through the book 'Acts of the Apostles', Luke gives a picture of the situation after the time of Jesus. After the death, resurrection and ascension of Jesus Christ, there emerged the Church as the Body of Christ and the Holy Spirit came upon the Church to give guidance and leadership. Jesus Christ started the work of salvation and after him came the Church and the Holy Spirit to continue the mission of Jesus Christ and therefore, the Church is the continuation of the incarnation. Following the footsteps of Jesus Christ, the apostles continued the mission of Jesus Christ and thus the Gospel began to spread and the Christian Church began to grow.

The description of the life style of the 1st century Christians in Acts is also very much inspiring for Christians today and it is described in Acts 2: 42-46. Here we can see the summary of the life style of the 1st century Christians and we can distinguish the following four aspects of the daily life of the Christians:

a. Hearing the words of the apostles

b. Keeping fellowship and unity among the members of the Church.

c. Celebration of the Holy Eucharist to bring to the present the Christ incident

d. To be devoted in daily prayers.

Through the above mentioned life style the Christians experienced the presence of the Risen Christ and of the Holy Spirit in their daily lives.

Another important aspect of the life of the 1st century Christians was the keeping of absolute economic and social equality among the members of the Church. All the believers were of one heart and one soul. The Christians sold their properties and laid the proceeds at the feet of the Apostles. It was distributed among them according to each one's need. Nobody claimed any private ownership of property.

In the history of the human race pure socialism with economic and social equality was never practiced except in the 1st century Christian Church. A comparative study of the lifestyles of the 1st century Christians and that of the present members of the Church will help us a lot to correct the deviations in the life style of the Christians today.

6. The Incarnation and Self-emptying Character of God

Jesus Christ was Logos – the eternal Word of God. He was with God and was God and was enjoying all the glories in heaven. But he emptied himself and came down from heaven and took the form of a servant. He was born as a man and was fully obedient and humbled himself and became obedient unto death (Phil 2:5-11). This self-emptying principle practiced by Jesus Christ is a living example for all Christians. The institutionalized Churches in the materialistic and consumerist world are not ready to adopt the self-emptying example shown and adopted by Jesus Christ. The Churches try to accumulate and amass wealth and try to become rich in temporal matters. Natural consequences are the discarding of spiritual matters and deviation from the right path of Jesus. The Churches have to come back and follow the great Master Jesus Christ by accepting this self-emptying principle.

St Paul interprets incarnation of the Son of God in Phil 2:5-11. Here we get a very crucial and important revelation and idea behind the incarnation of the Son of God. Through the Son of God, who became a human, we the human beings were able to know and experience the nature of God. For the salvation of the human beings, God is ready to humiliate himself and empty himself, forsaking all His glories as Lord and Creator of the whole Universe. His birth in the manger of cattle was the humblest form of birth. The family of Jesus was one of the poorest and also insignificant for Jewish community and society. As an adult human being, He never tried to project himself or boost himself as an important person. Three years of his public ministry was an untiring task for fulfilling the responsibility entrusted to him.. He preached the Word of God to the common people and thousands of meek-hearted people repented from their sins and began to follow his footsteps. He called twelve disciples to accompany him and they considered and called Jesus as teacher and Lord. Beyond the expectations and contrary to the social and normal practices prevalent in the society, the teacher knelt down before his disciples, laid aside his garments and girded himself with the towel and washed their feet. This towel of Jesus is the symbol of self-emptying, service and humility. Then Jesus said to his disciples "You call me Teacher and Lord; and you are right, for so I am. If I then, your Lord and teacher, have washed your feet, you also ought to wash one another's feet. For I have given you an example, that you also should do as I have done to you" (Jn 13: 13-15). The self-emptying character of the Son of God is evidently revealed from the beginning till the end of His life.

The apostles were fully engaged in fulfilling their mission and responsibility to establish the Kingdom of God following the self-emptying path and example of Jesus Christ. The members of the Hierarchy of the Christian Churches are expected to be successors of the apostles of Jesus Christ, who are indebted to adopt and follow the example of Jesus Christ in service and in self – emptying. Selfishness, self -boosting, greed, pride, luxury etc. are not the path of Jesus, but contrary to the example of Jesus.

Not only the leaders of the Church, but also all the faithful, are expected to follow the path of Jesus Christ in self-emptying and selfless service to God and to fellow beings.

7. The Ecclesiastical Paradox of Selfishness, Self-boosting, Pride and Greed

In the institutionalized Churches, many of the leaders in hierarchy have the tendency for self-boosting and develop the mentality to be proud, selfish and greedy in relation to others. Selfishness, self-boosting, pride and greed are contrary to the example of self-emptying mode of life adopted by Jesus Christ to fulfill his mission of the salvation of humanity. The episcopal Churches in the world have attributed special dress code to leaders of the Church, because they are elected shepherds appointed to look after and serve the sheep or the people of God even sacrificing their own life (Jn 10: 11). The common people give high respect and honour to the ecclesiastical leaders. With their special garments such respect and honour should not be expected and demanded like the scribes and Pharisees because such an attitude is vehemently criticized by Jesus Christ (Mt 23: 1-39). On the contrary, the leaders of the Church have to put into practice the virtues of humility, simplicity, and meekness in their lives and must be with the people of God as its inseparable part. Self-emptying and self-sacrifice are the ways shown by Jesus Christ for all the Christians and especially for all the leaders of the Church to establish the Kingdom of God.

If the leaders of the people of God seek in their lives selfish private earnings, self-security, undisturbed luxury, earthly joy and happiness, instead of selfless dynamic service and ministry, they really forsake the self-emptying path of Jesus. Jesus called the multitude and his disciples and announced very clearly the qualification of a person who wanted to follow Jesus. It is clearly reported in the Gospel of St Mark: "And he called to him the multitude with his disciples and said to them, "If anybody would like to follow me, let him deny himself and take up his cross and follow me. For whoever would save his life will lose it; and whoever loses his life for my sake and for the sake of the Gospel will save it" (Mk 8: 34-35).

Self-denial or self-emptying is the qualification to follow Jesus Christ. The real followers and disciples and the successors of the disciples of Jesus Christ who lead the Christian Church are indebted to adopt the path of Jesus Christ. An explosion of a spiritual revolution in the whole Christian world is vitally necessary in order to revitalize the path of Jesus Christ to establish the kingdom of God for the salvation of the human race. The Christ-Spirit revealed in Jesus Christ has to be embraced by every human being. Jesus Christ can thus transcend the boundaries of the Christian Church and all other religions in the world and can remain as "Unbound Christ" without any wall of separation (Acharyasri Dr Sachidananda Bharathi's keynote address).

8. The Cross of Christ as the only Way to Establish the Kingdom of God.

The Son of God emptied himself and became a humble human being in order to establish the kingdom of God through his earthly ministry. In the very beginning of his public ministry Jesus expressed his aim and said: "The time is fulfilled and the Kingdom of God is at hand; repent and believe in the Gospel" (Mk 1: 14). The life and ministry of Jesus was aimed at establishing the kingdom of God. The climax of the life and ministry of Jesus Christ was his death on the cross. His call to the human race is to follow him taking up their cross themselves. In order to be a true follower of Christ, one has to grasp the crucial and deep meaning of the Cross of Christ.

a. The Cross of Christ Means Self- sacrifice, Suffering and Death

We have already seen that the incarnation of the Son of God was an act of self-emptying of The Almighty God for the Salvation of the human race. The process of self-emptying reached its climax, when the Son of God suffered and died on the Cross. This is the path chosen by Jesus Christ to establish the kingdom of God. St Paul was the greatest missionary the world has ever seen. He preached the Gospel in different places travelling far and wide and converted thousands to Christian faith. St Paul himself reveals the theme of his Gospel: "But we preach Christ Crucified, a stumbling block to Jews and folly to Gentiles, but to those who are called, both Jews and Greeks, Christ the power of God and the wisdom of God" (1 Cor. 1: 23). According to Paul, the great power of God that brings the human race to salvation flows from the cross of Christ. "For Christ did not send me to baptize, but to preach the Gospel, and not with eloquent wisdom, lest the cross of Christ be emptied of its power. For the message of the cross is folly to those who are perishing, but to us who are being saved, it is the power of God" (1 Cor 1: 17-18). The message of the Cross of Christ is self-sacrifice, suffering and death, which has to be adopted by each and every human being to establish the Kingdom of God and to enter into the salvation of God.

b. The Cross of Christ as Self-sacrificing Love

The highest form of love that has to be adopted by each human being is revealed on the Cross of Christ. If anyone sacrifices his life for the sake of the one whom he loves, then that is the greatest form of selfless love (Jn 15:13). The divine love revealed on the cross was selfless and self-sacrificing love. The followers of Jesus Christ have to practice this love in their lives. In the old commandment given by God to Moses, the central points were love towards God and love towards fellow beings. Jesus gave a new interpretation to the old commandment of love on the basis of the Cross of Christ and distinguished this commandment as a new commandment.

Jesus said to his disciples: "A new commandment I give to you, that you may love one another" (Jn 13: 34). The leaders of the Churches as successors of disciples are invariably indebted to follow this new commandment of Jesus Christ. A new revolution in the thinking of the Christians in this world is necessary in order to put into practice the selfless, self-sacrificing love of Jesus Christ. A new revival of Christianity on the basis of the new commandment of Jesus Christ is absolutely necessary.

c. The Cross of Christ and the Essence of the Nature of God

I have already mentioned above that in the incarnation of the Son of God itself the self-emptying nature of God is revealed and this fact is clearly explained by St Paul in Phil 2: 5-11. The aim of God in Self-emptying is salvation of the human race. To achieve the aim the Son of God never ceases with self-emptying, but goes to the maximum. The incarnated Son of God also as a human being, went maximum up to his death, which we call the Cross of Christ. St Paul interprets baptism as participation in the death, burial, and resurrection of Jesus Christ (Rom 6:3-4). Every baptized Christian is thus empowered to participate in the nature of God through self-emptying and self-sacrificing love. Through Jesus Christ a great revelation about the true nature of God took place: for the salvation of the human race, the Son of God emptied himself and he is the embodiment of self-sacrificing love. As the image of God, every human being has to adopt the above nature of God and if the human race adopts this nature and character of God, then a global revolution will take place leading to everlasting peace, justice, and harmony. Selfishness, self-boosting, self-security, pride, and greed are contrary to the above mentioned path of God.

d. The Cross of Christ as the Unique and Divine Way to Establish the Kingdom of God

There is a clear cut difference between the Kingdom of God and a worldly kingdom. To establish a worldly kingdom primarily one needs an army and external physical force to protect the kingdom and a police force to keep the internal discipline. But the life and example of Jesus Christ reveals the idea of a divine universal Kingdom, in which the unity of the human race is envisaged and the heart of each individual is filled with selfless and self-sacrificing love and at the same time throw away his selfishness, which is the root cause of all conflicts. According to Acharyasri, what we need in the post-pandemic era is a spiritualization of Christianity and this process of spiritualization must be begun in Kerala. The time of the institutionalized Christianity is over and now from Kerala the spiritualized Christianity has to be spread to the rest of the world. I appreciate very much Acharyasri's vision of "A Global Ecumenical and Interreligious Center" called 'Viswa Shanti Peetam' ". The most suitable place according to Acharyasri for such a centre is Kerala, because it is the cradle of Christianity and interreligious harmony. Other establishments under Viswa Shanti Peetam like Global Ecumenical & Interreligious Parliament House, Global Eco-spiritual Open University, and Global Headquarters and coordinating offices of Dharma Rajya Vedi, Inner Peace Meditation Centre are all divine insights given to Acharyasri. The beginning of big things is always simple and small. Here at Dharma Bharathi Ashram, a small circle of open-minded disciples of Christ is being formed and depending upon God's mercy we visualize realizing the global dream of unity and brotherhood of the humankind.

Conclusion

In the coming post – pandemic era the Churches in the world, especially the Churches in India can play a pioneering role in rebuilding India and other nations, if we are ready to take up the challenge. Our first and foremost challenge is to recognize our great

Master Jesus Christ correctly and to follow his footsteps. As followers of Jesus Christ, we have to work hard to realize the dream of the Kingdom of God proclaimed by Jesus Christ. For that we must be ready to adopt the self-sacrificing divine love revealed by Jesus Christ in his life especially through his sacrificial death on the cross. Therefore, the urgent call to all Christians is to return to the Cross of Christ in order to continue the true and real mission of Jesus Christ.

Jesus Christ, as the Son of God, is not simply the God of Christians only, but God and Savior of the whole human race. The Church as continuation of the Incarnation is entrusted to continue the mission of Jesus Christ. The self-emptying principle is the unique way adopted by Jesus Christ to fulfill his mission of human salvation. Selfishness, self-boosting, pride, and greed are clear-cut deviation from the path of Jesus Christ. It is antichristian and such types of life style will destroy justice, peace and harmony, and above all the unity of the human race.

---

* **Revd Dr Adai Jacob Cor-Episcopa** is the Founder Principal of 'Malankara Syrian Orthodox Theological Seminary' (MSOTS) which the premier Seminary to train and prepare the priests of the Malankara Jacobite Syrian Orthodox Church. He did his Ph. D in Theology from Regensburg University in Germany and had occupied a number of important positions in the Church both abroad and in India. He is deeply involved in ecumenical unity and interreligious dialogue and have been writing and working for building up the 'Body of Christ', the Universal Church in which the different Christian churches in the world are unique and important parts and organs with specific functions to perform in the plan of God.

3

The Mission of the Christian Church in the Post-Pandemic India: Considering a Revised Christology Relevant to the Mission in Indian Context

Revd Dr George Samuel *

Introduction

The world today is going through an unprecedented damage because of the sporadic outbreak of Covid 19. This has brought in tremendous changes in the society and we termed it as New Normal. In this context we are constantly being forced to rethink and redefine the very core concepts of social institutions and political organizations and their functioning. Some definite questions have been raised on the relevance of religious notions and faith practices prevalent for long years. Certain level of criticism has been there on the significance of social practices and rituals we held unalterable as part of our religious affiliations. Some have also been undergoing transitions in today's life and death situation. This seems the new context of humans engaging with unforeseen reality of a Pandemic.

We have to engage in a process of understanding anew and redefining the mission and work of the Church as a community among others.

Theologically speaking the Church is considered as the people having specific call from God for being a community accountable to God and to the people around. The term Ekklesia denotes the process by which God called it out as a community (Ek= out, Kaleo – Called). Literally it means an "assembly", "Congregation" or "meeting". A similar term was used in the Old Testament referring to gathering of People of God, "the Lord's Congregation" or "meeting before the Lord". It is important to note that in the New Testament no built structure ever called "Church." The term always referred as Peoples' community which had congregated according to the call of God. This community is having obligation to humanity to render an account on the commission implicit in its faith and the way it is fulfilling that commission.[1]' The mission of the Church has been derived on the basis of Church's commitment towards humanity and to God, who has given the commissioning of being the Church in the world.

In the Bible we see in the first book Genesis, 'God in the beginning 'called' this world into existence (Genesis Ch. 1; John Ch.1) through God's word. God called the world out of nothingness (Chaos) to the cosmos through the Word (Logos). The creation narrative in the first book of the Bible is the earliest story of creating the material world and humans into a community. That was the first community God created, an inclusive one of all created beings, which was the oikoumene[2]- the inhabited world as God's created community. The first narrative ascribes God having intimate connection with the created world and maintained closer relation with them. In Genesis chapter 3 we find God coming to meet with them in the garden, calling "Where are you?"(ch. 3. 9) This suggests that God wanted to maintain stronger connection and wished being together with them in the garden. The first narration speaks on the 'image of God' but the second account says something on God's intention of having fellowship with the created world particularly with humans.

Jack Miles suggests that "If in the first account of creation God made humankind because he wanted an image, the Lord God, in the second account, seems to have made human beings because he wanted company."[3] So the biblical theology proposes strongly that the Community was God's deliberate intention about the world, God is also being a part of it. Humans have the primary role of maintaining the community spirit keeping harmonious relations with one another and social amity as Oikoumene of God. The various communities we find in our land today, definitely have this responsibility of keep going the togetherness on the basis of the oneness of being God's created being to take care of one another and to protect the world in peace and harmony. This is the point where we have to think of the significance of a community termed "Church" among diverse communities with multiple origin and cultural divergence. God has called the entire creation for being the community of God fulfilling the purposes given to them. This aspect is the implied mission of God accomplished in a definite context for which the communities have to be partners with God's will and purpose.

An inevitable interaction of Christian faith addressing the living context of the people is the subject of Christian Theology in India today. Social life here is explicitly intertwined with powerful spirituality and appalling poverty. The social scene is even today in the first part of the third millennium, overarched by destitution and subjugating communalism, which leads to deplorable caste divisions. So the Church here is challenged to transcend every parochial conceptualization and rise above the constriction of simply being a community practicing the wide spread communal exercises among other communities in India. Here now the mission of the Church is as a transformed community it should redefine and redraft its Ecclesiology and Missiology so as to engaging contemporary challenges in India today. The basic affirmation of the Church is that it is a community called out as participant in the saving act of God in this world as commissioned by God in Jesus Christ for being a transformed/transforming community within the larger community. The content of the call given is not for being an isolated community but rather a community in relation with other peoples around with broader vision and greater mission for creating a New Humanity. The acknowledgment of the Spirit of Jesus Christ working in the world is transforming humanity from within our religion to which we are adhered to. This aspect explains a new Christology which envisages the transforming power of Jesus Christ encounters all religions, including Christianity. In this perspective ecclesiology obviously becomes anthropological, where common humanity is addressed and understood in the light of the divine humanity explained and revealed in Jesus Christ. The concern of the Church in this context is not to safeguard it as an institution but rather a mission in Christ making humans truly human, standing against every force of dehumanization. Here the Church is compelled to redefine its mission and formulate a new theology of community of humans which ascertains the importance of the community always challenged by the gospel of Jesus Christ as foundation.

The ecclesiological challenge now is for redrafting Christology for a revised ecclesiology open to other communities strengthening human relations, despite all diversities that prevail among them. We have to seek for new paradigms of Indian ecclesiology relevant to our living context. The method adopted is essentially a *Secular mediation* of the Gospel, which does not ignore other faiths and ideologies. As Dr M. M Thomas, the famous Indian Christian theologian had proposed, a theology of *humanization* is the ground for having dialogical engagement with other faiths. In this process Church has to consider different ideologies that have serious engagements on human issues in our country today. The goal of this process is that people of divergent faiths and ideologies might join together for the total liberation of humanity responding to the challenges of gospel of Jesus Christ. In the final analysis the attempt is to redefine the significance of the Church from within for being a people of God among *God's people outside the boundary walls of the institutional*

Church. The *Ecclesia* is an open community relating to humans with whom Christ has already been in relation transforming them from within. *Ecclesiology* ***takes a turn realizing the activity of the Spirit of Christ in communities other than the Christian Church, thus the "ecclesia" of God may be formed wherever 'humans' respond to God's purpose revealed in Jesus Christ.*** The Church must be instrumental in transforming the human communities at the same time being transformed in its response to the challenges of the gospel of Christ. In this the Church becomes the *sacrament of God for the world*. So the Church is the community of God in solidarity with the suffering people as a sacrament of bearing the pains and struggles of the poor and the marginalized.

Christian theology deals with human interaction with the divine as well as human relation with one another and human participation in the continuing creative act of God. So doing theology is inevitably connected to human life situations. This is the basic dimension of doing 'local theology' responding to the 'living context' of the people. Thus theology must have to be local and contextual. Since the Church can never ignore the living context, it should have to focus its attention to the struggle of the people in the pandemic situation.

Ecclesiology primarily deals with the spiritual aspects of the people, but at the same time when the Church takes life situation of the people, it deals with the human conditions of living, such as poverty, subjugation and natural calamities and humanitarian crises. Indian theologizing points to both aspects of theology and anthropology seriously to redefine the spiritual inwardness of humanization connecting it with salvation. Dr M. M Thomas explains it as theology of humanization envisages the Church's commitment for social action capable of challenging dehumanizing situations and structures and of working for social transformation. In this process has been recognized the meaning of social revolutions informed by the gospel of Jesus Christ which liberate people from demonic spiritualities. It is the Church's involvement in the suffering of the world as response to the call given to the Church for being in solidarity with deprived people. So the commitment of the Church is to recognize the Christ, who is actively present in the midst of the people and to participate with him in the transforming mission.

Responding to and participating in the activity of God is the new mission dimension. This will involve being part of the struggle for just, participatory and sustainable community. The significant aspect here is that spirituality takes on new anthropological dimensions which are significant to the 'sociality' of the Church. The 'sociality' of the Church essentially points to the 'communality' of ecclesia for being a community 'Called-out' for the sake of others. This realization of God's purpose constitutes the central core of the Church's mission today. Hence, the Mission focuses on others, rather than catering to self-interested mission projects. Missions start from God and find final goal in fulfilling God's purpose. So the important matter in the Church's mission theology is the realization of this theological aspect of being a participant in God's mission, which is open, inclusive, and transforming.

The above connection influenced in constructing a relevant ecclesiology in the present context of increased cultural and religious interactions, ecclesiology needs to take cultural engagement seriously and positively. This cultural engagement is an important aspect of the mission in India. For this the Church needs to get out from its cultural bondage to 'imported' elements. In this process, the gospel of Christ must be 'incarnated' into the cultural matrix of the people, transcending culture and religion as such.

Here the Christian Church has to redefine its Mission and as community to relocate itself in the current scenario as 'a community among Communities' in India. Here today the Church is getting a "New Call" for being a community of God to help humanity to engage the turmoil situation with a new self-understanding and with a new Mission perspective. So the Church has the obligation to redraw its Shape and redefine its Functions in the very new situation as humanity engages new struggles in the journey to future.

Christology for a Contextual Ecclesiology

In the pluralistic religious context of India, it is rather debatable emphasizing the Centrality of Christ in exclusive terms. It may be interpreted the same as the traditional Christian aggressive assertion of the uniqueness of Jesus Christ over against other living faiths. The Indian Christian theologians always tried to redefine Church's proclamation on Christ as the Lord and Saviour taking into consideration various Christological perspectives in Church's approach to other faiths. It is obvious that these Christologies have been developed outside the traditional frame of Christian theology. The attempt was to find neutral position affirming certain common elements in each religious faith for enabling fruitful interaction with one another.

When Christian theology is convinced about the fact of God's intervention into history in Jesus Christ, it has to develop its theology based on Christology. In a pluralistic context, theology replaces 'Christ-centeredness' with 'Theo-centric' views to have a point of contact for progressive dialogue with living faiths. However, theologians like Dr M.M. Thomas develops a Christ-centred theology of religion in the wider context of India for evolving an integrated human community giving emphasis to the humanity of Jesus Christ.

In Christ the divinity and humanity blended together as the character of God. Christologically, both these aspects are significant. However, the humanity of Jesus Christ is the ground, where people can join together for advancing towards new humanity expressed in him. If the dialogue progresses in communion with others, the principle of common humanity would necessarily emerge and the principle of new creation with wider dimension with Christ as the centre will be the result. The Church must explicitly be clear about this conviction, not by making certain exclusive confessions, which do not have any significance for those who are living outside of the Church. In this process humanity can meet together and exchange views on each one's faith commitments and also engage with 'humanity of God' explained in Christ. Since humanity is a common denominator to both Christians and others, it can be the common ground for being together, with wider goals to be achieved for the common good of humanity. Implied in this Christology is a paradigmatic shift away from the traditional Christology founded on Creedal affirmation and absolutism of the Christian Church. [4] The significance of Christ being incarnated could vary in distinct cultures, where the meaning of human existence could be understood over against the ongoing struggles of dehumanization, disintegration and degeneration of life. It is made clear that the humanity of Jesus Christ is the ground of knowing God and human condition as well. So the centrality is the common ground where humans come together initiating a common journey searching for meaning of human existence and recognizing the significance of human spirituality. A shift evident in this is that Christ being liberated from the traditional Christian doctrinal bindings and dogmatic defining. The core mission of the Church is to bring out the challenging relevance of the gospel to the human context[5]. So the Christological task in India today is to find a common ground for humans to meet together and move forward with a common goal. It is a move basing on the humanity of Jesus Christ working together for "the glorious liberty of the Children of God" and for the "deliverance of creation from degeneration."[6]

Christology in Transition

The Christian Church in each generation had to reconstruct Christology in accordance with the historical necessities. It doesn't mean that Christology has been changed according to the changes that take place in the world, but that the understanding of Christ and his ministry have been changed. So the changed life situation may be meaningfully comprehended, and the questions raised may be relevantly addressed. These transitions influenced the Church's approach to other faiths and also in drafting the theology of mission according to the new awareness received. For example the early Church in the Gentile mission confronted the popular polytheistic notion, however affirmed strict monotheism. Reconciling this monotheistic faith conviction of the early Christian confession of Jesus Christ the Son of God, the deity of Jesus Christ became central to theology for the early Christian community.[7]

The Christological challenge in the Indian ecclesiology today is, whether Christology could be limited to the framework of traditional or contemporary theology. How could the Church redefine the correlation of Christology with other people's God experiences? Is it the Church could possibly construct a more open and inclusive Christology based on the knowledge of the person and work of Christ in line with the socio-cultural context making the message of the gospel of Christ relevant to the situation today.

Acharya Guru Dr Sachidananda Bharathi proposes "*Sadguru Christology*" in the socio-religious context of India inspired by the qualities of the Sadguru Jesus Christ.[8] He finds it as the 'foundation of the Indian face of the Christian faith, and deals with the knowledge and experience of the divinity of Christ and its practical applications in the lived context'[9]. In this search for relevant Christology linked with one person brought him to the understanding of *Advaitic* (non-dual) Christology.[10] What he suggests here is the possibility of contextual Christology in India that can endorse the idea of the Church as a community interacting with other communities according to the will and purpose of God for humanity's sake.

I would suggest certain other Christological propositions relevant today in the Indian context of pluralism and diversity of religious perspectives.

Vedantic Christology

The Universality of the person of Christ has been emphasized in Indian Christology by ***Vedantic*** categories, which envisages a universally common factor of ***human interiority and mysticism.***

'Sanadhana' is implicitly having connection to every other and so there must be no difficulty in integrating other in to it. So 'Sanadhana Dharma' has space for Jesus Christ into its vast inclusive space in the process of the 'Hinduization of Jesus Christ'[11]. In every sense Hinduism is viewed distinct from Christianity as a religion. But the primary concern here in this discussion is how Jesus Christ could possibly be comprehended and interpreted within reformed Hinduism. The basic affirmation is that Christ and his person be understood in the Vedantic framework is entirely different from the Christ pictured within Christian dogmatic perspective of the Church. The Vedantic or Universal Christ acknowledged in the 'particularity of Indian spirituality' is the one who is liberated from narrow historicism of the West and is made available as 'unbound.'[12] It was an attempt to see Christ in the context of the mystic idea of oneness with the Absolute. Christ is viewed as part of *Sanadhana Dharma*[13]. Vedantic Christology can be understood properly only through Vedantic Anthropology. Generally, Vedantic view shows disregard to the material world and history, but principles and precepts are considered more significant than the history of the person. So it views Christ freed from all historical limitations in order that he may be realized everywhere as 'principle.' So the Christ ideal, the 'Christ-principle', or Christhood is important as Raimond Panikkar exposes this in 'The Unknown Christ."[14]

Keshub Chandra Sen explains how Christ was already present in India though in unrecognized manner. "The holy word, the eternal Veda dwells in everyone of us.., Go into the depth of your own consciousness, and you will find this indwelling Logos… The real recognition of Christ has taken place in India… only the nominal recognition remains[15].

He had never denied the historical person of Christ, however, he tried to see Christ in *Vedantic* categories of *asceticism and yoga.*[16] The problem with Vedantic Christology regarding the personhood is that the notion of 'Concrete personality' has been seen as a limitation of the universal principle. Personality normally is equated with *ego or self.* Being liberated from this confinement is termed as *Jivanmuktha* as those who are absolutely selfless and in principle having no personality. It is real transcendence. Swami Vivekananda explained this, "Jesus had our nature; he became the Christ; so can we and so must we. Christ and Buddha were the names of a state to be attained. Jesus and Gautama were the persons to manifest it"[17].

Two aspects have to be considered of Indian Christology from a Vedantic anthropological perspective:

(1) Though the *Vedantic anthropology* considers the 'person' as degrading limitation, Christology affirms the "person" in history as responsible being to fulfill the ultimate purpose of God. Primarily the Christological task in India today is to clarify this in the social context of poverty and struggles various groups of people in India face.

(2) The matter of privatizing religion where confines the person to mere individualistic piety. This would demean the idea of human community and eventually would lead humans into isolation. Christian piety oriented to individual salvation having no regard to the historical relevance of human life encourages a piety of detachment. The interesting thing is that while Raimundo Panikkar searches for *the* Unknown Christ of Hinduism, concern was the search for *the Mystic Christ* and *the Christ Principle* in the *Vedantic* Category. However, M.M. Thomas *acknowledges* the Christ in the renascent India, envisages the *historical person* affirmed in concrete expressions of humanity. M. M Thomas' focus is to discern how Christ confronts the heart of India, which is the basis of Churches' mission and core of Missiology.[18] Drafting Christology is contextual or in another sense situational, which would derive "*the Challenging*

relevance" of the gospel of Christ to the context it was preached. R. Panikkar reiterates basically Hindu-Christian meeting together for peaceful co-existence of people of diverse religions possible only through positive dialogues and interaction.

Swami Abhishiktananda finds the importance of a meeting in "*the cave of Heart*," where Christ is already present. It is the transcendent platform, which should have to be made concrete meeting places, discerning the unknown presence of Christ in the heart of India. Implied in it is the important aspect of heart meeting heart on the level of spirituality. Raimundo Panikkar affirms that "the Universal Christ is the Mystery of God, eternal Christ, who is already present in Hinduism and in all other religions even before the appearance of Jesus of Nazareth and is present in the world, both implicit and explicit."[19] In order to address the *Vedantic* questions, R. Pnaikkar thinks, ***the universality of Christ*** may be used as the base for theological discussions for better understanding.

CHRIST BEING ACKNOWLEDGED- Christology

In Indian Christology there is the recognition of the presence of Christ outside the Church as the life principle. This idea has been explained, "He (Christ) is the embodiment of Divine Grace who leads every human to God; there is no other way but through him. Is not this what Christians call Christ? It is he who inspires the prayers of human and make them 'audible' to the Father; it is he who whispers any divine inspiration and who speaks as God matter, what for a person's faith or thought may have. Is not he the light illumines every human being coming into this world?"[20]

Such a Christ can never be confined to the limits of Christianity. And this Christ can be seen being present in and among people of other faiths. Panikkar explains further that a Christ who was not with every least sufferer, a 'Christ who did not have his tabernacle in the Sun, a Christ who did not represent the *Cosmotheandric* reality with one Spirit seeing and recreating all hearts and renewing the face of the earth, surely would not be…the Christ of the Christian.'[21] This is in a way explaining the expression 'unknown Christ' over against the notion of 'hidden Christ' in other religions. He gives stress on the presence of the one mystery (not necessarily the 'same' mystery) in both traditions.[22] The basic idea is that, although the Christ-mystery is present in both Indian tradition and the Christian, it is understood differently as it was said in **R'gveda** that (God is) **ONE** (though) the sages call it by **Many** names.[23] It has been explained further that the name 'Christ' is a common name standing for a ***universal divine mystery,*** while the name 'Jesus' is a ***particular name*** for a particular people as the embodiment of the '*universal Christ-principle.* So the name 'Jesus' cannot be translated, but Christ can because the '*Christ–principle*' can be embodied and expressed in names other than Jesus.' The scope of a new Christology here is to translate Christ in the Vedantic anthropology framework without losing its content.[24] However, he emphasizes that historical name should never be confined to the historical Jesus. For S J Samartha this Christ is 'unbound' and he is beyond the limits of Christian theology and understandings and may be understood as the unknown Christ of Christianity.

Iswara Christology

The Christology has been further explained through the concept of *Brahman* and *Iswara.* The *Brahman* is the absolute, with no quality (*nirguna*), unknown and unknowable. The Vedanta explains that even inside this *nirguna Brahman,* there are qualitative contents, which is called *Saguna Brahman* (Brahman with attributes/quality). This is also called *Iswara*, the Lord, and the Creator God with personal attributes. R. Panikkar sees *Iswara* as the personal aspect of the supra-personal *Brahman.* He/She/It is the link between Brahman and the world, and is responsible for the liberation of world from the bonds of *Maya*. *Iswara* is distinct from the Absolute; and is the expression (Hebrews1. 3) 'the reflection of God's glory and exact imprint of God's very being, and he sustains all things by his powerful word'. And he is the image (2 Cor. 1.15), the revealer (Jn. 1.14, 18; 3.18, 6.46); it is equal in nature, but distinct in substance and personality.[25]This interpretation has problem when applied to Christian tradition, since it cannot think about a Godhead whose transcendence and absoluteness could be understood as univocal 'relationlesness' to the creation. Christologically, it should be understood as to indicate a way to what Christian tradition calls God the Father through God the Son.

Perspective on History and Person in History

The question of historicity of Christ has been a matter of discussion in Indian Christology. Swami Vivekananda sees 'un-historicity' as the sign of a perfect religion. In his famous address in the 1893 World Parliament of Religions in Chicago he said, "Vedanta alone, under some form or another, is fit to become the universal religion of man. For, while all the other great religions of the world are based on the lives of their founders, Vedanta alone is based on principles. It is absolutely impersonal. Its authority is not affected by the historicity of any particular man."[26]

Vedantic Christology suggests that the historical particularities of 'Jesus' have no special relevance for those who live in other geographical, cultural and historical contexts. Mahatma Gandhi also held similar position. He wrote in 1940 in his work, "*The Message of Jesus Christ*', "I may say that I have never been interested in a historical Jesus. I should not care if it was proved by someone that the man called Jesus never lived and that what narrated in the Gospel was a figment of the writer's imaginations. For, the 'sermon on the Mount' would still be true for me.[27]

Here the critique of western Christology is on its over exaggerated historicism, as though historicity is the main element of reality. In contrast to a narrow emphasis on historicism sees Jesus Christ solely as the centre of human history, placing stress on the man Jesus. But Church's consideration is that Jesus is the unique Son of God, the second person of the Trinity, the universal theandric mystery. The intention is to minimize emphasizing the historicity of Jesus Christ and focusing the universal and meta-historical *Christ –Iswara –* Principle revealed or represented in Jesus Christ.

However, M. M. Thomas emphasizing the historical person of Christ centred on the humanity of Jesus searches for a common humanity in a definite anthropological frame. In it he finds a common ground for inter-religious and inter-ideological dialogue, looking for concrete historical expression of the divine-human interaction, rather than doing theology by being away from daily human experiences. While emphasizing the historicity of Jesus, there is the realization of the ongoing action of God in human history through Jesus Christ. So the Christology here sees God who participates in human affairs as human, calls for human participation in historical reality sharing the life predicaments of people. Historical particularities are not important but Christology moves away from the philosophical or meta-historical plane to the realm of theological anthropology. It primarily deals with the fundamental questions that disturb humanity in living situations. Recognizing the Spirit of Christ working outside the traditional Church, stress must be given on the humanity of Jesus and also to the realm in which the Spirit pervades is the common ground for the search for the meaning of life.

Liberation Christology

In contemporary theology we find a definite blend of a theology of religion with a liberation motif for addressing concrete issues humans face today. This is very evidently seen in the writings of Paul F. Knitter.[28] In this we have to consider various ideologies prevalent today in the process of broader dialogue, which emphasizes the liberation praxis. Knitter formulates Christology in the context of inter-religious dialogue aiming the emancipation of humans, whereas M. M. Thomas finds the liberation of humanity as the ground of being together in the process of living in harmony. Dialogue is a practice for emerging the truth and sharing the space being together experiencing that truth is understood differently by various peoples. Knitter endorses "Doing before Knowing" as a religious imperative.[29] We see here a shift from *Theocentrism to Soteriocentrism* on a definite liberation axis. Knitter finds in theo-centrism a moving away from the definition of the divine from a particular pointer to wider universal one, going beyond the limits of the particular. "Christ has value only in so far as Christ points us to God."[30] The underlying thrust is the definite anthropological orientation of Christology, starting from the humanity of Christ and moving towards God. It is in another sense a move from the particular to the global and then to the Ultimate. This is a collective goal of searching for a **new humanity**, which should be the significant agenda of religions and ideologies today. In this context, Dr M. M. Thomas considers a search for meaningful human living in this world, which is very much essential and thus recognizes ***Salvation*** in ***humanization***[31] and which has the connection of soteriology with anthropology. Here, Christ is seen as the one who provides meaning to human life directing people to God by empowering them facing the trials and struggles in day to day living. Christ as historical person seems significant in this view. Salvation has been defined not as an otherworldly affair, but as human engagement of struggles in the present, in which the cry of all people is the same despite their religious understandings and faith allegiances. Hence the saving act of God revealed in Jesus Christ includes all others, either as anonymous, cosmic presence within them or as the goal of final fulfillment. Therefore, a theo-centric model of *relational uniqueness* for Jesus Christ has been attributed. It is the affirmation that Jesus is unique by the relational capability to include or to be included-by other unique religious figures. Such a view of Jesus Christ is not exclusive or normative but a theocentric, universally relevant manifestation of divine revelation and salvation.[32] The New Testament understanding of the Kingdom of God progressively shifted to Son of God perceptions. It is evident all titles attributed to Christ and the confession on Jesus have their origin in the salvation experience of individuals and communities.

Hence the Christological issue is obviously that of distinguishing the experiences from interpretations. In the New Testament there is 'pure' Christ-experience without interpretation of the faith communities. The experience with this 'Human' made them realize the power of God, which enabled them to feel, understand, respond, and act differently in their own context. Thus the saving experience in Jesus was an experience of salvation.[33]

What is outside the living realities of the people confronting the tragedies of terrible pandemic? The concern for the social wellbeing of the poor and the suffering may be the starting point for us to have a dialogue and respectful interactions. So the emphasis here is of orthopraxis over orthodoxy for being faithful to the great tradition we uphold. The primary purpose of Church's confession is to form a new pattern of life, not a bundle of beliefs and work for Jesus' kingdom, but for sharing the love of God which had been explained to humanity in and through Jesus Christ.

The Cosmic Christology and Questions Regarding Nature and Environment

Before I close this elaborate discussion on the Christological questions and propositions suitable for evolving a space for humanity coming together to face the challenges of the times, let us have a look at the Cosmic Christology. The early understanding of Cosmic Christology found Christ the redeemer confronting with the world of powers and principalities. Currently, it has been seen that the same Christ confronted with Nature, which humans have disfigured into chaos through exploiting its resources unethically and contaminating with poisonous wastes. So, it is essential for humanity to deliver the Nature from desperate self-annihilation and preserve her from eternal destruction. J. Moltmann looks into the Cosmic Christology in the light of the contemporary ecological issues, and says "A new Cosmic Christology must end the historical Christology of modern times, not abolishing it but gathering it into something more which will overcome its limitations and preserve its truth."[34] Implicit in it is a search of faith 'to discover the therapeutic powers of Christ in the world's present situation and allow them to be experienced.[35]

The anthropocentric Christology emphasizing the idea of human salvation only, ignored the questions of 'abandoned Nature' and 'disastrous exploitation' of mother earth. The increased awareness of the ecological catastrophes leads to the recognition of the limitation of a Christology focusing exclusive human salvation and thereby directed to a Cosmic Christological search. Since the Asiatic religions are "Nature Religions", this opens the necessity of Christological thoughts informed by the Asian religious perspectives addressing the crises the world faces relating to Nature and environment. Theologically, in Christ humanity confronts God as responsible partners, most of all, good stewards under the divine purposes revealed in Jesus Christ. So being responsible partners with God in Christ is a definite call for being protectors of the environment and Nature.

In 1961, at the 3rd General Assembly of the World Council of Churches in New Delhi, Joseph Sittler[36] the famous Lutheran theologian explained the unity agenda as the unity of humanity not simply the unity of the Churches. Stepping out of the regular ecumenical thinking, he asserted 'Cosmic Christ' as the foundation of this proposed unity (Col. 1.15-20). For, Christ is the foundation of all things living and non-living. The redemptive act of Christ is for all things and for the entire universe. Against the general dualism of good and evil, Paul proclaims that 'everything is claimed for God and everything is related to Christ. Here the doctrine of 'redemption' seems revolving the doctrine of 'creation'. Joseph Sittler was critical of the dualistic perceptions of the Western Church that separates Nature and grace, for it does not do justice to the cosmic vision of Christ in the New Testament.[37] It is essential to confront the threat to Nature with a Christology of Nature in which the power of redemption does not stop at the level of human hearts and human moral living, but extends to the realm of the whole of Nature. Hence, Nature is the scene of grace and the sphere of redemption just as much as history.

So a Christology that has a cosmic dimension will increase 'passion for the threatened earth.'[38]

Christology of New Humanity

Paul D. Devanandan (1901-1962) was an Indian protestant theologian, ecumenist and one of the pioneers in interreligious dialogue in India, in the 3rd Assembly of the WCC in New Delhi emphasized three aspects of the Church's witnessing the gospel of Jesus Christ. In the first place, the reality of the New Creation in the Risen Christ is the determining factor in the world history, which provides history meaning and significance despite all confusion and disorder. This new creation is the destiny of the 'entire creation' for which the whole creation and history waits for (Roman. 8: 19- 24).

Secondly, the core of the message is that in Jesus Christ, God is reconciling the world to God. This divine act brings humans to be in peace with God and helps to discover the wholeness of human personality. This work of redemption is manifested in human history in the life, death, and resurrection of Jesus Christ.

Thirdly, in the message of the kingdom of God, there is the hope that the whole creation will be transformed into a totally different realm of being, where the will of God becomes a reality. This is a continuous act of God even today in the Spirit of the Risen Jesus Christ, recreating humanity in the world.[39]

So the mission of the Church becomes a cosmic process in three interconnected aspects: (1) A Divine Enterprise (2) An Historical Reality and (3) A Peoples' Movement.

The cosmic dimension of the redemptive act of God in Jesus Christ is the creation of new humanity aiming at the recreation of the whole cosmos (Colossians 1.16-20). "We are coming to realize that the total sweep of the good news envelops God's entire creation. The ultimate end is a new heaven and new earth, which means a New Creation.[40]

Conclusion

In a recent book *A New Creation in Christ,* Acharya Swami Sachidananda Bharathi attempts to explain the practical dimensions of the New Creation experience in our life. This is a wonderful possibility of the Grace of God and Swamiji explains it basing on his own life experiences in relation to Satguru Jesus Christ. He says "Developing a new vision of Christianity for the third millennium based on these constituents that could transform the world into a New Creation in Christ…"[41] which means that the new creation is an ongoing act of God's grace in the world at present and for tomorrow too. What is expected of the humans is to be partners with God in the divine act whatever manner possible. Swamiji vividly describes how one can connect oneself with the divine purpose (Will of God) that is pervading through the entire globe for the preservation of the fullness of life. However, we should keep in mind the truth that the theology of history not only relates to human history alone, but to the movement of the entire created universe as well. So the very idea of new creation or new humanity is definitely the outcome of human participation with God and the divine purpose implied in it. In Christ, God deals with the whole people. 'The redemptive purpose of incarnation is all inclusive'. The whole creation in all its being is already redeemed by the work of Christ'.[42] This should never be understood or interpreted as an exclusive claim of Christianity as a religion, but it is intended by God for the whole humanity and the entire created world. Since the Gospel of Christ is primarily the good news of the new order God establishes, calling everyone to accept for what they already are, and to discern the purpose of God while living in this world for being truly humans. What we are attempting in this search of variant dimensions in Christology, is for asserting a ground for an open interaction of the Church in India with different communities of faiths around it. This brings the entire humanity in the position to recognize the reality of an 'objective redemption' or refusing to recognize it. If this recognition could be possible, it provides an opening for the people in our nation to understand each other and to respect other peoples' religions and culture. The recognition of the universal reality may take many forms, not necessarily that of Christian religion. This kind of an affirmation may raise many questions about the exclusive role of the Church in the world and the significance of it as a community of humans acknowledging the saving act of God in the world. This provides new impetus for the Church to broaden its vision and redraft its mission theology for experiencing within the power of God's grace, becoming a new creation in God's world to have very positive interaction with people who have the same experience in a different form and manner.

---

* **Revd Dr George Samuel**, Kottarakkara, Kollam District, Kerala (Mobile: 9446166078 & Email: gsachen@gmail.com).

Clergy of Mar Thoma Syrian Church (1980 – 2021); holds a PhD in Systematic Theology from the University of Chicago Consortium, Chicago, USA; former General Secretary of the Christian Education Department of the Mar Thoma Syrian Church; ministered as Minister for various parishes in India and abroad; served in organizations such as CSSM & SU, MTE Association and Youth Movements (Mar Thoma Missionary and Educator).

Endnotes

[1] J. Moltmann *The Church in the Power of the Spirit- A contribution to the Messianic* Ecclesiology, (England: SCM Press 1977).

[2] ***Oikoumene*** Greek word literally means "inhabited" used to denote the entire inhabited world dating from antiquity. In the Roman Empire it was used to term ***civilization*** as well as the secular and religious imperial administration. In 20th century Christian church used the term to refer to unified Church which is the ultimate of *Ecumenism.*

[3] Jack Miles, *God A Biography* (New York: Vintage Books,1996) 36. The first creation account is found in Genesis 1. 1- Ch 2.4; the second creation account can be seen in Genesis Ch 2. 5-25.

[4] Jacob Thomas, "Insights from M. M. Thomas for an Ethical Christology in India" in *Christian Witness in Society* (Bangalore: BTE & SSC, 1998), 204.

[5] Ibid, 205.

[6] Romans Ch. 8: 19-21.

[7] W. Pannenberg, *Systematic Theology,* Vol. II, (Grand Rapids Michigan, 1991) 278. Christology has been categorized as "high Christology" or "Christology from

above," emphasizing more of the divinity of Christ, while certain others known as "low Christology" or "Christology from below" emphasizing the humanity of Jesus Christ. Christology "from above" had been always the accepted typology in Christian Theology.

[8] Swami Dr Sachidananda Bharathi, *A New Creation in Christ- Story of My Second Life*, (Dharma Bharathi Ashram, Mulanthuruthy Kochi, 2020) 264.

[9] Ibid.

[10] Ibid 263.

[11] Mathew Vekathanam, *Christology in the Indian Anthropological Context*, (New York & Bern: Peter Lang, 1986), 161. *Hinduization here means an uncritical re-interpretation of the mystery of Christ so that it may fit into the frame of Hinduism, not intending to sort out the differences. Diversity in Hindu thought is the expression of the reality which cannot be critiqued just on the basis of differences.Difference seems positive and acceptable.*

[12] S. J. Samartha, *The Hindu Response to the Unbound Christ,* (Madras: CLS, 1974), 100-01.

[13] Mathew Vekathanam, *Christology in the Indian Anthropological Context*, 173.

[14] Raimond Panikkar, *The Unknown Christ Of Hinduism*. New edition, (London: Darton, Longman and Todd, 1981) 45.

[15] Keshub Sen, *Keshub Chunder Sen's Lecture Vol,2.33* He was a Bengali Philosopher and social reformer attempted to incorporate Christian Theology within the frame work of Hindu thoughts (1838- 1884) He was influenced by RamaKrishna and found "New Dispensation" inspired ny Christian thoughts and Vaishnav Bhakti.

[16] M. M. Thomas, *The Acknowledged Christ of the Indian Renaissance* (London; SCM press, 1969), 60-61.

[17] Swami Vivekananda, *The Complete Works of Swami Vivekananda,* (Advaita Ashram, Belgaum, 1947), Vol.7.20.

[18] M. M. Thomas, *The Acknowledged Christ, xiv.*

[19] R. Panikkar, *The Unknown Christ of Hinduism*, 24-25.

[20] Ibid. 49 R. Panikkar cites references from Vedantic texts on human quest for the ultimate mystery.

[21] Ibid., 20.

[22] Ibid., 26.

[23] Ibid. 13, 23.

[24] R. Panikkar., *The Unknown Christ.*, 26.

[25] Ibid., 156.

[26] Geoffrey Parinder, *Avatar and Incarnation* (New York: Barnes and Noble inc. 1970), 233-34.

[27] M. K Gandhi, *The Message of Jesus Christ* (Bombay: Navabharath Publishers, 1940), 35.

[28] Paul F. Knitter was a Divine Word Missionary and later assumed a position at Xavier University Cincinnati as a professor of Theology. He received the Licentiate in Theology from the Pontifical Gregorian University in Rome and studied under Karl Rahner before earning a Doctorate in Theology.

[29] Mark Hei, *Salvation: Truth and Difference in Religion* (Maryknoll, NY.; Orbis Books 1995), 75.

[30] Ibid.

[31] M. M. Thomas, *Salvation And Humanisation: Some Crucial issues of the Theology of Mission in Contemporary India.*, (C L S, Madras:1971).

[32] Paul F, Knitter, *No Other Name: A Critical Survey of Christian Attitude Toward World Religions* (Maryknoll, N Y. Orbis Books 1985), 171-72.

[33] Ibid. 175.

[34] J. Moltmann, *The way of Jesus Christ,* 275.

[35] Ibid.

[36] Joseph Sittler, " The Emergence of A Theme, " in *Essays On Nature and Grace,* (Philadelphia: Fortress ress, 1972) 7-9, 62.

[37] Orthodox theologians like Irenaeus and Gregory of Nyssa see nature and grace and mutually connected. Delinking of nature and grace led to the contempt of nature which resulted in the subjugation of nature. Gradually it reached to the point of irresponsible handling of nature and exploitation of natural resources.

[38] J. Moltmann. *The Way of Jesus Christ*, 277.

[39] M. M. Thomas. *Risking Christ For Christ Sake.* (Geneva: World Council of Churches, 1987), 86-87.

[40] P. D. Devanandan. *Christian Concern In Hinduism*. (Bangalore: Christian Institute for the Study of Religion and Society 1961) 118-20 cf. Revelation 21: 1-4 the presence of God with humans and there will be the consolation from the divine for having the fullness of hope.

[41] Swami Dr Sachidananda Bharathi, *A New Creation In Christ: The story of My 'Second Life*, (Mulanthuruthi: Dharma Bharathi Ashram 2020) 249.

[42] P. D. Devananda, *Christian Concern in Hinduism,* 108.

4

Time for Fruition of Ecumenism: A Catholic Perspective

Friar Bobby Vadakkal *

A non-living invisible genetic material named novel Corona Virus has shrunk the world as never before into isolation and fear. The global village has proved to be true in a totally unexpected way by Covid 19.

Are we in a defining moment of history? We have been witnessing changes to which people are adapting fast. The new normal is affecting how people perceive prayer and other religious practices without crowding in massive structures of worship as in earlier days.

With announcement of vaccines, the old habits and practices may or may not return. It is good for Churches who pressed pause button to the time-old traditions to make use of this opportunity for some serious rethinking.

RE-IMAGINING CHURCH

In recent times, health has moved to the central stage of concern with lifestyle changes, increasing conflicts in persons, families, communities faced with migration and cultural transitions, digital communication, and finally the pandemic. Both poor and rich alike have come under unprecedented threat. Health today is understood not merely as absence of disease but as wellbeing.

The biblical notion of *Shalom* in Hebrew which means wholeness, completeness and welfare, points to harmonious and peaceful existence. It is a matter of equilibrium of five dimensions - physical, mental, social, emotional and spiritual wellbeing. So, healing is restoring wholeness of body, mind and spirit. A true mission of healing includes caring, curing, restoring, forgiving, and reconciling.

The urgent call for solidarity raised by Pope Francis in *Fratelli Tutti*[1] is a timely reminder not only to Catholics but to all Christians and Disciples of Christ. The image used by the Pope of ***Church as field hospital*** in 2013 is relevant to indicate the urgent response needed of Churches during the pandemic.

"I like to use the image of a field hospital to describe this 'Church that goes forth'..... it is not a solid structure with all the equipment where people go to receive treatment ..."[2]

"... it is necessary to go out: to go out from the churches and the parishes, to go outside and look for people where they live, where they suffer, and where they hope."[3]

"The Church does not exist to condemn people, but to bring about an encounter with the visceral love of God's mercy. We need to enter the darkness, the night in which so many of our brothers and sisters live... make contact with them and let them feel our closeness, without letting ourselves be wrapped up in that darkness and be influenced by it."[4]

A challenging mission of merciful love without reservations! A very urgently needed life giving task it is for our times indeed. If Christian Churches share this common mission of healing, the world will hear the Good News lost in the divisive noises that have drowned the message of hope. To take it up, Churches have to surmount the contempt of other Churches born out of unhealthy presumptions.

Pope with a sick man St Peter's Square Nov. 20, 2013

Credit: Evandro Inetti/ZUMAPRESS.com

FROM SELF-REFERENCE TO RECONCILED DIVERSITY

The Catholic Church's attitude reflected in Satis Cognitum (1896) and Mortalium Animos (1928) towards ecumenism was one of reluctance. It flowed from a self-understanding that the unique Church founded by Jesus Christ is the Catholic Church and that the unity was possible if only other separated Christians returned to its fold. Those outside the Catholic Church were termed schismatics or heretics.

The Secretariat for promoting Christian unity established on 05 June 1960 by Pope John XXIII as one of the preparatory commissions for the Vatican Council marked a new course of thinking. Thanks to its good work, Vatican II inaugurated a new era admitting that, "Many elements of sanctification and of truth are found outside the visible confines of the Catholic Church" (LG, art. 8). With the issue of Decree on Ecumenism Unitatis Redintegratio (Restoration of unity) in 1964, there was openness to communion with other Christian Churches. The document admits that responsibility for the division of the Body of Christ exists on both sides and calls for a change of heart to make ecumenism possible.

It is noteworthy that the final solemn act of the Ecumenical Council of Vatican II was at once a healing of historical memories, a mutual forgiveness, and a firm commitment to strive for communion[5]. Both the leaders – Pope Paul VI and Patriarch Athenagoras admitted that this gesture of justice and mutual pardon was just an initial step. The ecumenical activity to be accomplished through prayer, dialogue, charitable co-operation and interior reformation (conversion of heart and ecclesial practices) was taken up seriously since then.

Pope Paul VI (1963-78) continued his predecessor's commitment to renewal and reunion, making a permanent department charged with the application of the council's directives on ecumenism. "From polemical opposition among the different Christian denominations, we have moved to mutual respect, dialogue and a measure of practical collaboration. But, if unity is to be sincere, it cannot yet be realized. Human goodwill is not enough to accomplish this miracle," Pope Paul VI's address at the Angelus of 17 January 1971[6] indicated the progress.

In 1972, Roman Catholic Church decided not to seek WCC membership because of the disparities between the structure, self-understanding and size of it and the WCC and its members. Although Roman Catholic Church is not a member of the World Council of Churches, there is official cooperation at various levels including a Joint Working Group set up in 1965 for exploring collaboration, cooperation, and participation as full members in the WCC's faith and order commission, as well as the common preparation of the Week of Prayer for Christian Unity.

In May 1980, addressing an ecumenical gathering in Paris, Pope John Paul II, insisted that "our personal and community memory must be purified of the memory of all the conflicts, injustice and hatred of the past. This purification is carried out through mutual forgiveness, from the depths of our hearts"[7]. Ut Unum Sint of 1995 reiterated that the Catholic Church is committed irrevocably to following the path of the ecumenical venture. Not only John Paul II wrote the first papal encyclical on ecumenism, but also accomplished many prophetic gestures of visiting countries of Orthodox traditions - Romania, Georgia, Greece and Ukraine. John Paul II read diversity as providential to discover the untold wealth in Christ's Gospel and promoted ecumenical dialogue as exchange of gifts and not mere exchange of ideas.

"I cannot possess Christ just for myself; I can belong to him only in union with all those who have become or who will become his own. Communion draws me out of myself towards him and thus also towards unity with all Christians. We become "one body" completely joined in a single existence," Pope Benedict XVI mentioned in Deus Caritas Est (Art 14).[8] He also introduced a note of caution on the evolving teaching of some Churches of the west on matters of sexuality as barriers on the path towards full communion.

"Catholics and Evangelicals feel we are becoming closer, living in harmony with our differences. We are looking for a reconciled diversity… I do not think we can at the moment consider uniformity or complete union, but we can consider a reconciled diversity that implies walking together, praying and working together, and together seeking unity in the truth."[9] The statement of the present Pope when he was Archbishop of Buenos Aires, in an interview published in Spanish as El Jesuita in 2010 indicates the Catholic position today.

> The concept of "unity in reconciled diversity" goes back to the Protestant theologian Oscar Cullmann (1902–1999). Cullmann summarized this model in his book *Unity through Diversity*, in which he wrote, "Every Christian confession has a permanent spiritual gift, a charisma, which it should preserve, nurture, purify and deepen, and which should not be given up for the sake of homogenization."[10]

In June 2015, Pope Francis held a historic meeting with the Waldensians in Italy. At their invitation, he was a guest at their church in Turin. It was the first time a Roman pontiff had visited a congregation of the Waldensian Church, which had a history of suffering at the hands of the Roman Catholic Church. Speaking to them Pope said, "On behalf of the Catholic Church I ask your forgiveness. I ask your forgiveness for unchristian-like and even inhuman attitudes and conduct which, historically, we have had against you. In the name of the Lord Jesus Christ, forgive us!" Eugenio Bernardini, the moderator of the Church leadership ("Tavola") of the Waldensian Church, for his part, made an explicit request to the Pope, especially given the Reformation anniversary of 2017, to reconsider Roman Catholic Church ecclesiology and to no longer think of Protestants as being "half churches." [11] The papal visit was reciprocated to the Vatican on 5 March 2016, by a Waldensian delegation received by pope. After the audience, Pastor Bernardini said, "The meeting has encouraged us all to continue the journey, as well as to promote cooperation and fellowship between our Churches, in spite of the distinctive differences, and sometimes divergences, between us."[12]

As the Pope replied to the question in an Anglican church on 26 Feb 2017, "ecumenical dialogue cannot be done in laboratory, it is done in journeying together responding in service to the needs of the world."[13]Pope Francis has stressed time and again that his own Church needs to free itself from being too self-referential and return to its central task of witness to Christ and the Christian message. The present urgency has gifted the Churches and especially the Catholic Church to realise its universality bringing together Petrine, Pauline, Johannine and other dimensions within a concrete reconciled diversity.

ECUMENISM AND CATHOLIC CHURCH IN INDIA

Experiments in uniting Churches in India were made by Christo Samaj in Calcutta, National Christian Alliance in Western India and the National Church in Chennai in the context of Indian national movement. Anglican, Lutheran, Congregationalist, Baptist and Methodist missionaries organized South India Missionary Association. The United Mission Tuberculosis hospital at Arogyavaram and the Christian Medical College, Vellore were the outcome of their cooperation. The National Missionary Society founded in 1905 drawing together Indian Christians from different denominations led to the formation of The United Theological College, Bangalore in 1910. The National Missionary Council formed at the YWCA Calcutta in 1914, became National Christian Council and later in 1979 became National Council of Churches in India (NCCI).[14]

After Vatican II, the ecumenical openness of Roman Catholic Church received concrete expression in India. It has full members at the national and regional councils of Churches. The Catholic Bishops Conference of India and NCCI have partnership in the areas of inter-faith dialogue, dalit concerns, unity week celebrations, and united action towards political situations especially violation of minority rights. NCCI convened a large meeting in 2002 of the leaders of NCCI, CBCI, and Evangelical Fellowship of India, at its Nagpur campus. A celebration of the Prince of Peace was held from Nov 14-17, 2002 at Talkatora stadium, New Delhi which was jointly organized by all the three. These three bodies formed the United Christian Forum which speaks on behalf of the Indian Christians only based on common issues.[15]

Local Roman Catholic churches are encouraged to become members of local, national and regional councils. However, any ecumenical action has to be "in conformity with the teaching" of the Roman Catholic Church. The local church's ecumenical collaboration should be confined to dialogue commissions, joint working groups/committees, and should not extend to further ecumenical commitments - Theological associations, Biblical associations, Church history associations, Exchange of professors, common endeavors like new translations of Bible, an ecumenical comprehensive history of Christianity in India and ecumenically published periodicals.

The Roman Catholic insistence of "communion with Rome", the centrality of the "Eucharistic Sharing" for the Orthodox Church, and the protestant emphasis on the "conciliar nature" have been roadblocks in ecumenical dialogue.[16] Too much of concern about dogmatic and structural unification have not led to fruitful communion.

CORRECTION OF MODELS

When we realize that **there is much more that unites us than divides us,** a commitment to look beyond divisions and consider one another from the perspective of unity for the common mission will follow. The journey to unity is made possible by Christ, who heals all wounds and memories, and transforms the pain of past experiences to the gift of reconciliation.

The transforming power of the gospel defied the worldly logic as the early Christians proved. It became a hidden but active leaven of change. It was the grace of the Spirit of the Risen Christ that was at work. "*Jesus reminds us: 'Without me you can do nothing.' He is the one who supports us and encourages us to seek ways to make unity an ever more evident reality.*"[17]

The moratorium imposed by the Covid pandemic brings a time for Christian leaders to think out of box and not to get isolated in their islands of Churches. The old maps which Churches hold need update to correspond to the changed territories of people's lives.

In the view of Hans Urs von Balthazar, a Swiss theologian, Church is inherently a complex, multi-dimensional network.[18] According to him the earliest Church, in its period of origins, had diverse centres of authority, adjudication and service. The unity of Church has the model of relationship Christ establishes in New Testament. Balthasar identifies a number of individuals and groups in the New Testament and amplifies their symbolic significance as foundational archetypes within the Church: Mary, Joseph, Mary Magdalene, Martha and Mary, the Jews who were sympathetic to Jesus (Nicodemus, Joseph of Arimathea, Simon of Cyrene), Judas Iscariot, John the Baptist, Peter, the Twelve, Paul, the Beloved Disciple, James, and so on.[19] This can serve as the constitutive principles of universality in every age and guide the journey towards fruitful ecumenical dialogue.

In Evangelii Gaudium of 2013, Pope Francis shows a new model of polyhedron replacing the model of concentric sphere with which Catholic Church has been looking at ecumenical dialogue. This is a welcome shift that gives a model of unity in which the identity of different Churches is preserved without losing the identity of the whole, where each seek "to gather the best of each."[20]

OPENING HEART SPACES

The Franciscan church at Bukit Batok in Singapore has a hall called Art Space where an artist welcomes persons who want to express themselves through paint, or drawing on paper. One need not be good at art to do this. Anyone who goes there is helped to express themselves in lines, forms, shapes and colors. The artist assists you to listen to your inner self with these expressions. I was fortunate to be introduced to her by the friars who considered it an important part of their ministry. She showed me the works of two persons- a Sri Lankan refugee and a traumatized missionary from East Timor. Then came a remarkable revelation! These persons after going through a healing process through artistic exercises were encouraged to exhibit their works! It has enabled not only others to enter the healing process, but tuned them to become wounded healers! The ripple effect it has created brought the name HEART SPACE to this art space!

The clergy in all Churches are used to pulpit preaching and not so much to listening. They are accustomed to the performance of liturgy where they are the center of focus. They are not used to empathic attentiveness. The confessionals in Catholic church, where some sort of listening takes place, is not a place for dialogue. It has been reduced to a ritualized personal laundry without any interpersonal application or social significance. The cry of the world today is for spiritual accompaniment. This implies a shift from monologue to dialogue, listening to each other and arriving at learning together God's will.

People are looking for inner compass to orient themselves and navigate in the fast-changing terrain. Instead of evacuation plan for the next world, Christian Churches will do well to get involved in creating safe spaces, where persons can listen to their inner selves, to each other and to God. Acquiring ability to listen in turn to understand others, will result in a shift in the model of communication in the churches. The existing pastoral/priestly church leaderships are not used to it. If healing and reconciliation become the focus, other kinds of ministries and leaderships have to find their rightful place. It is good to remember that much of the ecumenism happened through dialogue of life from the ranks of the churches in front of situations they faced together. The missionaries from Asia and Africa, the lay persons who founded YMCA, YWCA and SCM pioneered the way to practical ecumenism responding in faith to the common challenges faced in their respective societies.

SERVANTS OF BEATITUDES

"Despite his religious garb and his almsgiving, he was still, even though he had no weapons, the representative of a feared foreign administration of which everyone was suspicious. In the eyes of the people, he represented power." And then a very significant event marked the life of Charles de Foucauld which transforms him into the Universal brother:

On that day, he had nothing left and was able to do nothing. And it was precisely at the moment when he was reduced to total powerlessness, with nothing left to say, entirely dependent upon his neighbors and totally vulnerable to their power that they felt responsible for him and entered his life. It took illness to reduce him to such a state of weakness in order for his hosts to approach him and offer him something on an equal footing. They shared their wealth with him: a bit of milk to save his life. They offered their knowledge and what they knew would be best for him. They did what they were able to do within their limited means. They didn't think about it, didn't calculate the effect that it might have. They simply did what was normal to save his life.[21]

Do not the Churches in India find themselves in similar predicament? Aren't they too powerful? Haven't they made themselves unapproachable? Could the pandemic be a period of moratorium to re-examine and discern how to discover strength in weakness? Any sincere search for true solution requires humility and openness to appreciate the gifts God brings through others. Being better informed need not help in reaping what Spirit has sown as gifts for all.

Lund Principle[22] formulated by WCC is a reminder to all Churches: Christians should act together in all matters except those in which deep differences of convictions compel them to act separately. Co-operating in shared ministries, pooling resources, coordinating efforts in pastoral care for sick and dying in hospitals, prisons, among the displaced, and migrants are some of the areas, where joint service is possible.

During the time of lockdown, I had the privilege to serve various persons at risk, through tele-counselling: persons in quarantine, stranded abroad, health care workers, sick and dying, couples on the verge of divorce, youth in uncertainty, jobless, migrant workers, alcoholics, those in anxiety, depression, and panic attacks. An unexpected offer came from a non-church going friend from another denomination! He arranged accommodation and office space with *wifi* support. A social psychologist who worked in different parts of the world, he considered that health care needed to go hand in hand with soul care. He had already opened his homestay as a safe space for receiving and caring those in distress. Today we form an ecumenical team to serve as psycho-spiritual care givers responding to the need of the hour.

When we are open and receptive to what the Holy Spirit offers, we are led to creative means to minister in response to those in need. It leads us to deeper understanding of the source of mutual enrichment and promptings of the Spirit. It calls us to depart from the trodden path and rise to a new level of consciousness! It brings dynamism and growth in the life of the Spirit which leads to the secret of the kingdom of God.

Sincere seeking of healing brings us closer to each other and closer to God. It is such a joint search that can respond to the changed situations. The time of difficulty has led us to a time of re-establishing ourselves on the essentials of the Christian faith. Has the Unity week observed every year led Churches to act in unity? It is time for prayers to become persons in action and celebrate liberating faith. The hall mark of this freedom is receiving and giving forgiveness which leads us to compassionate companions towards a reconciled diversity.

CONCLUSION: TIME TO RELEARN TOGETHER

Calamities such as the pandemic can be a threshold experience dividing one era from another. The signs of the times invite the Churches to take this moment to rethink their priorities and commit to God's concerns than their petty domestic business as usual. There has not been a more appropriate time to give shape to the hope of common understanding and expression of Christian faith than during this world-wide crisis. Churches have to move out from their entrenched positions to take part in it.

To answer God's Call to respond in a joint mission, Christian Churches have to go beyond being exclusionary country clubs with membership rules. If they accept, they are mere containers to share the content ie., the Spirit of Christ, the healing mission has a chance to unite them for a significant contribution.

A street philosopher Eric Hoffer[23] had the following wisdom: *"In times of great change, learners inherit the earth, while the learned find themselves beautifully equipped for a world that no longer exists."* Could the Christian Churches receive this critical phase in history as graced moment to shed their self-righteous ways, be open to listen and relearn humbly from the sources of their origin? Would they embrace the docility required of the Christ-bearers to remodel themselves on the complex multi-dimensional network of earliest Christian tradition so that the light of the gospel can shine?

For ecumenism to bear fruit, the work of Christian unity need to listen God's Spirit in their own hearts, in other brothers and sisters and beyond. As I write this, a new book ***Let us Dream: the Path to a Better Future*** by Pope Francis has come out, stating that "we cannot let the current clarifying moment pass by."[24]

May we be privileged instruments to realize the better future finding pathways to Peace!

---

* **Friar Bobby Vadakkal** is a monk who chose to follow the path of St Francis of Assisi. He joined the Order of Friars Minor (OFM) in 1983. He was ordained a priest on 15 August 2000. After his studies in Philosophy and Theology in India, he did a Licentiate in Sociology at Louvain University, Belgium, as part of which he did a research in homeless poor in Brussels.

He has taught University level Courses and has produced Documentaries. He has been an active advocate of peace and social justice. He took part in World Social Forums in Porto Allege, Brazil and Mumbai.

He served as member of Exec. Committee of OFM Justice & Peace Commission (2000-2003) and as Coordinator of OFM Justice and Peace in South Asia-Oceania (2004-2007). He has organized Franciscans' International Training on Advocacy for Human Rights in Pune & Bangalore (2006).

He is known for his contributions towards Formators' Training for Asia-Oceania OFMs (2009 in Banglaore & 2012 in Manila). His last International service was to OFMs in Papua New Guinea during 2014-2016 as the Delegate of the OFM General. He has been living as a wandering monk since 2017 in India.

Having spent time in meditation and dialogue at Thiruvannamalai, Amarkantak, Bodh Gaya, Ajmer, Rishikesh, Dharamshala, and the ancient monasteries in the cold desert of Spiti in the Himalayas, he returned to Kerala.

With his hermitage in the valley at the base of Murugan Mala, Vagamon, he associates himself with Earth-related healing projects and collaborates with Narayana Gurukula (Varkala, Kerala) in interfaith programmes.

Friar Bobby Vadakkal also extends his services to Dharma Bharathi School of Forgiveness & Reconciliation (DBSFR) as one of its Coordinators and Resource Persons.

Endnotes

[1] The encyclical "We are all brothers" i.e official teaching of Catholic church which came out on 03 October 2020.

[2] Pope at Audience: Church a 'field hospital' that cares for sick - Vatican News 2019/08.

[3] Same as above.

[4] Same as above.

[5] Ut Unum Sint §52.

[6] Doc.Cath.,68,1971, pp.109.

[7] John Paul II: Diagnostician of Divisions, Doctor of Ecumenism – Catholic World Report.

[8] Catholic Ecumenism: Towards an Integration of Faith, Hope, and Charity - Homiletic & Pastoral Review (hprweb.com).

[9] Sergio Rubin and Francesca Ambrogetti (eds), *Pope Francis: Conversations with Jorge Bergoglio* (New York: Putnam›s, 2013), 227–28.

[10] Oscar Cullmann, *Unity through Diversity* (Minneapolis: Fortress Press, 1988), 9.

[11] Pope Francis and Ecumenism - Bräuer - 2017 - The Ecumenical Review - Wiley Online Library.

[12] Same as above.

[13] Pope explains ecumenical dialogue - YouTube.

[14] William Carey: An Indian Perspective on Ecumenism Sunday - Indian Catholic Matters.

[15] A Historical Survey of Ecumenism in India.doc (live.com).

[16] Historical Survey of the Concept of Ecumenical Movement its Model and Contemporary Problems (sapub.org).

[17] Pope: Christianity can change the world if the Gospel is lived - Vatican News.

[18] Von Balthasar and the Office of Peter in the Church (theway.org.uk) p.99.

[19] Same as above p 100.

[20] Pope Francis and Ecumenism - Bräuer - 2017 - The Ecumenical Review - Wiley Online Library.

[21] http://charlesdefoucauld.be/other/JourneyToTam_Chatelard.pdf p 135

[22] https://en.wikipedia.org/wiki/Lund_Principle#:~:text=The%20Lund%20 Principle%.

[23] Eric Hoffer - Wikipedia.

[24] https://www.theguardian.com/books/2020/nov/29/let-us-dream-by-pope-francis-review.

5

Advancing Peace and Sustainable Development in the Post-Pandemic India: The Role of Christian Churches

Thomas Varghese *

It is with great hope and gratitude that I present this paper on 'Peace and Sustainable Development in the Post-Pandemic India' and outline the scope and role of Christian Churches in it. At the outset, let me clarify the position of this paper upfront, that the efforts to advance peace would not yield the results that we seek, unless it is underpinned by the principles of sustainable development. The terms sustainability or sustainable development have gained currency over the past three decades since the advent of the report 'Our Common Future', also called the Brundtland Report, published in 1987. In this report, sustainable development was defined as "development that meets the needs of the present without compromising the ability of future generations to meet their needs".[1] Though the term sustainability is often associated with or perceived within the limited frame of environmental considerations, the concept as such is far more inclusive, as it advances a development model that integrates the environmental, social and economic dimensions. What this means is that all the three dimensions are equally salient, and must be attended to, while envisaging and implementing development programs. For example, while pursuing economic growth, if the environment is jeopardized through gross exploitation of nature or through rampant pollution of the living environment, then such economic growth cannot be classified as sustainable. Likewise, if the pursuit of economic growth is accompanied by rising inequality, where wealth is concentrated in the hands of a few, while the majority are left impoverished, dispossessed and displaced, such a model cannot be termed sustainable, for it impinges on people's ability to access basic necessities and lead dignified lives.

In this paper I posit that a healthy nexus among the social-economic-environmental aspects sets the foundation for peace. It would be futile to preach peace to people who are marginalized, hungry, and malnourished and face various morbidities. Likewise, it is difficult to envisage a peaceful world, if the air we breathe, the water we drink, and the food we eat are rendered toxic, unfit for consumption, leading to poor health. We are at the threshold of making this reality pervasive as the economic model pursued strikes at the very root of our planet's life supporting systems through rampant pollution of air, water, and soil. Profit motive and capital accumulation, embedded within the neo liberal economic model promoted rigorously over the past decades, has corroded the planet's life supporting systems through mindless exploitation of natural resources, perpetuating greed and selfishness,ignoring the suffering and deprivation of the great majority. Climate change, natural disasters, poverty, rising inequality, hunger and disease - the vexing challenges of our time, are the result of a development trajectory that is out of sync with the principles of sustainability. Though there is growing awareness of the perils of the economic growth centred development model and its implications for the very survival of our species, the efforts to transition to a development model built on the pillars of sustainability have been found wanting. That is, an economic model that is in harmony with the laws of Nature and is responsive to the basic needs of the people, vis a vis food, housing, education, health and livelihoods is still a distant reality. Globalization and the rapid uptake of technology with the sole focus on multiplying profits, increases unemployment and disempowers the majority from gaining access to decent livelihoods and acceptable standards of living. Economy is not just about the production of wealth, and ecology not merely about the protection of Nature, instead both these dimensions need to be perceived from the standpoint of contributing to harmonious social development, which holds the key to sustainable human wellbeing. Only such a development paradigm can set the foundation for peace. In common parlance, peace has been perceived as a situation, where wars and conflicts are absent. But peace is a multi-layered reality, and the absence of war or conflicts is only one of the layers, though a crucial one. A healthy balancing act among the social, economic, and environmental aspects plays a pivotal role in creating conditions for fostering peace.

The secular world through its multilateral organizations such as the United Nations, civil society organizations and governments have promoted an intellectual understanding of sustainable development. On closer observation, this discursive understanding of the integration of social, environmental, and economic dimensions precludes, or does not mandate a deeper fellowship, both between people and between people and the planet. An intellectual understanding of sustainable development has not brought in the 'soul force' required (to borrow a Gandhian term) to unleash the collective power of humanity in effecting this transition. It is into this space that the Churches and its laity can contribute to providing a spiritual basis and a moral force for the wider uptake of the philosophy and practice of sustainable development both within and beyond its community. Churches need to move out of the narrow boundaries of doctrinal and denominational thinking and embrace a vision that responds to the human predicament and reflect the genuine aspirations of the people. The kingdom of God on Earth must be wrought through an interconnected and holistic view of reality, where the early Christian call for social justice rooted in the Jewish prophetic tradition, now begins to lend equal attention to economic and environmental justice.

Within this schema, the Churches need to make a conscious move to viewing and presenting the created world as sacred and its stewardship as a sacred duty. The modern narrow Biblical interpretation of "Be fruitful and multiply and fill the Earth and subdue it" (Genesis 1:28) has unfortunately been wrongly perceived as a covert license for humans to exploit Nature and consider the same as their legitimate right. But nothing can be farther from the truth. Early Christian writers present a different reality, where Nature and Scripture are two mediums that reveal divine truths and reflect God's glory. The writings of St Ephrem the Syrian, a Doctor of the early Church, venerated across denominations, make this resoundingly clear. Ephrem says, "The presence of the hidden power in the natural world lends to the natural world itself a sacramental character, which in turn requires that the natural world be used with reverence."[2] In a similar vein in the Hindu tradition, the sacrality of the created world is presented in the opening verse of the Isha Upanishad – *Om Isa-vasyam-idam sarvam* (All this – whatsoever moves or moves not in this universe is indwelt by the Lord.[3]). The world is God's creation and the divine is ever present in the manifestation. Peace emanates from a deep connection with the people, who inhabit the world and the world which supports this co-habitation. Division and exploitation must be replaced by unity and oneness, extending beyond the boundaries of Churches and even religious differences, by embracing the entire created order. This is the formula for peace that the Churches should advocate while building a post pandemic India. Within this, Churches must initiate collaboration with sister

Churches and even with other religious traditions to advance a sustainable development model to advance lasting peace in our society. Such collaborations also have the added advantage of highlighting the intersecting points of common concern intra and inter-religious, thereby vivifying similarities and watering down differences that breed suspicion, distrust, hatred and violence. Love and forgiveness, the centralpiece of Christ's teachings, must be preached and tested in the social laboratory which is our living Earth community.

There was something deeply instructive about the lockdown during the initial months of COVID-19 in India. Nature was seen going through a period of purification made possible through a temporary suspension of human activity. Many media reports mentioned clear skies, improvement in air quality, rejuvenation of lakes and rivers. Taking a cue from this, when people go about their economic activity post-pandemic, the stewardship of the Earth and the environment must become an intrinsic feature of their worldview and behaviour. The Churches should align its mission to caring for the created world and awaken people to the beauty of creation and the bounties it offers, where pure air, water and food are viewed as sacred gifts. Any exploitation or treatment of these gifts without concern for their conservation ought to be considered sacrilegious. This would to a certain degree help reverse trends of rising environmental degradation and climate change.

Likewise, the Churches have a role in promoting an alternative to the economic growth centred development model, whose sole yardstick is the measurement of wealth, which overlooks the harm caused to people and the planet. The Church has a role in setting the model for imitation in our society, and often Churches and its leadership are seen pleasing the rich and powerful, ignoring the needs of the deprived and marginalized. This needs to change based on a renewed thrust on economic justice, where proponents whose enterprises are sensitive to equity and conservation, and exemplify high moral and ethical standards, are brought to light and celebrated. This can help shape the narrative of success, setting the standards for future generations to follow.

Practical initiatives that are in line with the ideas presented above would go a long way in advancing the mission of peace and sustainable development. In this vein, a few suggestions are provided below which the Churches in India can initiate:

1. **Reducing Inequality:** Promote the uptake of cooperatives, such as through organic agriculture and dairy farming in Churches that have uncultivated land. Such projects have solid potential to meet the goals of sustainability as it contributes to local and equitable economic development through employment generation, without compromising the environment. In an age of unequal growth, distribution and access to resources, instead of, or in addition to the Church sermonizing to the rich to share their wealth with the poor, the Churches should present alternatives which hold the potential for collective and equitable growth. Cooperatives need not be restricted to the field of organic farming and dairy development alone, but can venture into other areas that can add value by providing goods and services that contribute to local economic development in an equitable manner. Local economic development is an effective counter to the disturbing trends of outmigration of rural folks to cities. Images of migrant workers walking hundreds of kilometers from cities to their native villages during lockdown without rest or access to food and water is a poignant memory that continues to haunt many in India.

2. **Environmental Awareness and Resource Conservation:** Follow green protocol in Church festivities - To counter the menace of the 'use and throw', 'disposable', 'littering' culture, ensure reusable utensils during church feasts and festivities. It is pitiable that churches generate huge quantities of waste by mindlessly using disposables for feeding thousands who attend church feasts. Churches need to adopt and

advocate through practice the principles of 3R – Reduce, Reuse and Recycle and make it part of the mission of the Church. This can help set the trend for wider change in community attitudes towards waste, natural resource conservation and clean-living environment.

3. **Peace and Communal Harmony:** Promote communal harmony by inviting speakers from other Christian denominations and religions during church festivities. I had the good fortune to visit an annual festivity of a church in the name of St Mary in Thevalakkara, Kerala a few years back, of which the highlight was that the speakers included religious representatives from the Hindu and Muslim communities, which clearly underscored the common aim of upholding peace, shared by all religious communities. Such avenues for joint declaration have been shrinking, while the decibel levels of religious bigotry and communal polarization have been rising. If many more churches, both within and across denominations, proactively promote such healthy exchanges, distrust and discord between communities can be mitigated and, in its place, communal harmony and peace can be promoted.

I conclude this paper by stating that the above practical initiatives, which are by no means fully exhaustive, yet are pointers for setting a new direction for the mission of Churches in India will go a long way in designing a constructive response to building the kingdom of God on Earth. There has been a poverty of ideas in responding to the hegemonic approach of the ruling elite who advance corporate interests through divisive politics. There is a crying need to exercise the constructive faculty latent in humans in mounting a response, even if, at the outset, it appears to be small. Such small heartfelt steps can eventually lead to greater movements which can unseat unjust and insensitive power structures. Speaking against these agents of division and destruction alone is not enough, but must include a presentation of alternatives through constructive work and cooperative action. I urge the Churches across India to rise up to the occasion both in light of the vexing challenges that threaten peace and sustainable human well-being, and also in light of the eternal message of Jesus Christ centred in love of the neighbour.

---

* **Thomas Varghese** is a Freelance Development Consultant, living and working in Kochi, India. He has wide experience in the field of sustainable development, working across research, consultancy and advisory roles with Governments, International Organizations and Non-Profits. Between 2013 and 2015, he worked in the Environment and Sustainable Development Division of the United Nations Economic and Social Commission for Asia-Pacific, Bangkok, where he was involved in implementing projects that advance sustainable development goals, especially in the waste sector, in countries spanning South and South-East Asia. Thomas is a graduate of St Stephen's College, Delhi and has completed two Master's degrees from Erasmus **University, Netherlands and Harvard University, U.S.A in Development and Religion respectively. He can be reached at thomas9varghese@gmail.com**

Endnotes

[1] United Nations Educational, Scientific and Cultural Organization, Roadmap for Implementing the Global Action Programme on Education for Sustainable Development (Paris, France: United Nations Educational, Scientific and Cultural Organization, 2014), 10.

[2] Sebastian Brock, The Luminous Eye, The Spiritual World Vision of St Ephrem the Syrian (Kalamazoo Michigan: Cistercian Publications, 1995), 165.

Joseph E. Stiglitz, Globalization and Its Discontents (New York: W.W. Norton and Company, 2002), 10.

[3] Swami Chidananda, The Quintessence of the Upanishads, (Uttarakhand, India:The Divine Life Society, 2016), 18-19.

6

Evolving an Eco-theology for Christian Mission in Post-Pandemic India

Revd Dr M.J. Joseph *

Basic Eco- perceptions

In an Indian Eco-theology, the first step is to initiate an in-depth search for the meaning of the interconnectedness of life in the pluralistic context of India. As plurality is integral to Reality, any search for the meaning of ecological pluralism in India and its impact on human life must be based on "pedagogy of encounter". There is a challenge before us to live with the knowledge of unity in diversity. The riddle of the philosophical question of the "one and the many" can only be answered through the keeping of *oikos* concept at the grassroots level. It involves recognition, appreciation, assimilation and comprehension so as to celebrate life at its best. In the Indian scenario of the Covid pandemic, ecology creates a common platform for dialogue among the religions and secular movements in the country towards evolving a common future or a better tomorrow.

I would like to list out the following basic perceptions for ecological sensitivity in God's universe whether in India or elsewhere. i) Recognition of the web of life in God's order of creation. ii) Ecological plurality as integral to the very core of human existence on this planet. iii) Stewardship of human beings as parents of God's creation. iv) Living in peace with nature. v) Establishment of ecological values of life as eco-dharma (ethics) which makes the Kingdom of God visible and affirmative in life on earth. vi) Recognition of solidarity with the five elements of the universe. These basic assumptions compel us to search for an eco-theological mission paradigm for the Church in post-pandemic India.

Kofi Annan, the former Secretary General of UNO, had rightly remarked on the world scenario: "All of us have to share the earth's fragile eco-systems and precious resources and each of us has a role to play in preserving them. If we are to go on living together on this planet, we must all be responsible for it. Let us be good stewards of the earth we inherited".

"The earth is the Lord's and all that is in it." The whole creation is facing innumerable dangers and it is on the verge of extinction to a certain extent. There is a re-thinking on the part of all concerned across any religious divide as how we have to handle Nature. The time has come for us *to search for a common thread* among the Holy Books of all religions and other secular movements for the protection of the environment. 'Weaving community of hope in India' can be realized through a dedicated search for the integrity of creation, as "*the earth is a shared inheritance*" (Pope Francis).

In Search of a Green Spirituality: Global Scenario

According to the Oxford Dictionary, the word "integrity" means, "the quality of being honest, fair and good"; "the state of being whole and unified". A religious response to climate crisis or climate injustice is now being explored at the universal level of debate. The interpretation of Religious Scriptures is being recognized as integral to the evolution of a culture of peace and eco-justice. In the Colombo Consultation of URI (Jan 31-Feb.4, 2015) on the topic "Holy Books and Eco-Spirituality," it was concluded that there is a common thread among the Holy Books of the Religions of the World as a divine mandate for the protection and preservation of Nature and its diminishing resources. The Encyclical by Pope Francis (June 18, 2015) under the title, "*Laudato Si*" (I praise Thee) speaks of the need to care for the earth and the climate justice issues. The Pope called for a bold cultural revolution to correct what he described as a "structurally perverse economic system *where the rich exploit the poor, turning Earth into an "immense pile of filth" (The New Indian Express, 20-6-2015). (For a detailed discussion of the Pope's Encyclical, Laudato Si, see National Catholic Reporter, A reader's guide to Laudato Si by Jesuit Fr Thomas Reese, July 2015.)* The encyclical is indeed an eco- capsule for the care of our Common Home.

The 9th Assembly of the WCC in Brazil (2006), under the theme, "God, in your mercy transform the world" had shared very explicit concern over the abuse of the environment. The 10th Assembly of the WCC at Busan (2013) under the general theme, "God of life, lead us to justice and peace" also speaks of a Theo-centric understanding of Eco-justice in the world today.

As life is the gift of God, there is a divine mandate to preserve and promote life at its best in the whole world. In such an attempt, there comes a hymn of praise in the order of creation as the Psalmist perceived and interpreted it in Ps.150: 6: "Let all that breathe praise the Lord".

In search of a Green Spirituality, the humans encounter the divine as Moses experienced it in the burning bush or Adam in the Garden of Eden. All the religions of the world speak of the integrity of creation "as a cosmic vision in nature". In Ps. 66:4 we read "All the earth worships Thee; they sing praises to Thee, sing praises to Thy name".

A sustainable future for all is a vision to be realized through the combined effort of all the religious people and others with secular ideologies. The Clean India movement (*Swach Bharat*) of the Government of India today is a call to live by the precepts of the Eco-dharma. Flora and fauna are in birth pangs due to the rape of the Mother Earth and our violation of moral laws in eco-ethics. The contributions of the Nobel Laureates Al Gore and Pauchuri have confirmed this.

Climate crisis is attributed to *the wanton human intervention in the rhythm of nature.* A purely anthropocentric attitude to nature makes the earth sick as the prophet Isaiah rightly said long ago: "The earth dries up and withers, the world languishes and withers, the heavens languish together with the earth. The earth lies polluted under its inhabitants, for they have transgressed laws, violated the statutes, and broken the everlasting covenant" (Is. 24:4-5).

The charm of religion is that it can evoke a kind of response that is different from scientific and technological reasoning. We have been warned by researchers that the ecological crisis of today is not simply about climate change and global warming, "*but is about us, our lives,* and the planet and the way the powerful and the rich of the earth have dominated and kept destroying nature for centuries to accumulate private wealth."

The polluting life-style of the rich is to be understood as "*an undeclared war on the poor*" largely due to the destruction of our bio-wealth. We need to remember that *"defending the earth is not a project, but a way of life"*.

The prophetic words of Jurgen Moltmann are worth recalling: "We shall not be able to achieve social justice without justice for natural environment. We shall not be able to achieve justice for nature without social justice". "Return to nature" is an urgent prophetic call of *ecological ecumenism* after the recent Fukishima Tragedy and the Covid pandemic.

Eco-Justice: A Divine Imperative

In the web of life, eco- justice is a celebration of relationship- *being fair to all forms of life.* In an eco-vision of the earth community 'giving what is due to each component of the whole', is a divine mandate to establish just relationship which is the *raison d'être* of just peace. This is well stated in Gen.2:1 where we read that Adam is created out of *adama* (the ground/soil). The relation between man and the ground is deep and intense. As human body is made of *panchaboothas* -earth, water, fire, air and space- there exists a kinship in the wider spectrum of life.

A harmonious existence of the symbols of life could be called prevalence of just peace in God's creation. Any kind of imbalance/ disorientation is a state of alienation. The petition in the Lord's Prayer, "*your kingdom come on earth as it is in heaven*" (Matt.6: 10) urges us to make a meaningful relationship in God's order of creation. Anything that disrupts or disregards the bond of a uniting tie in Creation is to be considered as injustice to its core.

Paulose Mar Gregorios writes: "We have so become accustomed to the scientific-technological stance that we have lost the faculty of addressing reality as a whole, of seeing in it the Source and Sustainer of life, of responding to it with reverence and receptivity, and of surrendering ourselves to it in all fulfilling love. We have lost the capacity to respond with our whole being to the being of the Wholly Other who presents Himself to us through the created universe ('The Human Presence: An Orthodox View of Nature', Geneva, WCC, 1978, P. 87).

Ecological Management: The Search for Eco-spirituality

In an anthropocentric attitude to life, ecological management is addressed to human beings. Man and Nature could be conceived in terms of a functional relationship, which could be termed as *interrelatedness, interdependent and independent.* Any disruption of relationship in the order of creation is to be considered as sinful, unjust and mismanagement of God's resources. All sinful situations carry a wave of injustice. The polluting life-style and attitude of humans make earth groaning for its redemption-(Rom.8:19-21).

The groaning of creation that we continue to hear from the wounded and the tortured humanity is a helpless cry of the victims waiting for the ecological messiahs to intervene and redeem them. The groaning of creation is *a public protest* that exposes the sinfulness and injustices prevalent in our social and ecological relations.

There is a correlation between the distress of the earth and social injustice. Groaning is a public display of the inherent sinfulness of the prevailing order and the resilience of the victims to transform it. In Jer.12:4, the covenant people are asked to respond to the divine call to repent as there are several unjust attitudes to the land. "How long will the land mourn, and the grass of every field wither"?, says the prophet. One may notice such violations of the land by the rich and the powerful in a globalized world. There are ecological activists who consider that the market system is destructive of the eco-system. There are innumerable examples to support it from the Asian scenario.

The pleasure sports of the rich and the affluent have destroyed forest and paddy lands in several countries. The grazing fields of the cattle have been turned to golf play grounds! In this context, the Church is called upon to include *an ecological audit* in its mission concerns and to stand for a counter culture against the market giants. In a recent statement of the WCC Central Committee on Climate Justice, it has rightly said "ecological debt-audit in partnership with the civil society is the need of the hour". Whether it is in the context of economic globalization or ecological crisis, the Church is called upon to pursue its mission in Christ's way so as to speak about the spirituality of religion.

Ecological sins such as air pollution, water pollution, noise pollution and light pollution have social resonance and therefore they should be viewed seriously. It is indeed significant that Pope Benedict the 16th in an encyclical had warned the faithful to be deeply conscious of the ecological sins in the world today. The increasing 'level of Carbon footprints in the atmosphere (390 ppm) has created unresolved problems for the future generation.

The impact of climate change on the indigenous/ aboriginal people of Asia's coastal regions has already being felt or experienced through the cyclonic storms and Tsunami tidal ways of 2004 and consequently the destruction of flora and fauna and human lives in a very high magnitude. The temperature in the Indian cities is soaring high. According to a statistical data 10 crores trees were cut down for widening roads and high ways during the last decade, whereas we were able to plant only a lakh trees. *Denial of a bright future for the future generation is an unjust situation in our midst.*

Ecological responsibility is a call to live with ecological sensitivity remembering the *Lakshmen rekha* of the divine mandate (to till, to subdue and to keep) for a sustainable future. *It is widely held that 'global warming' is due to the unbridled human intervention in God's created order of the universe.*

Act Now; Not too Late

One should remember that the climate crisis is not really about climate, as remarked by Mausam. It is not about rising the sea levels and the melting arctic ice, dead seals and polar bears facing extinction. It is about us, our lives and the planet- and the way the powerful and rich of the Earth have dominated and kept destroying them for centuries to accumulate private wealth". *In this respect, eco-injustice appears in the form of greed and consumerism.* "There is enough for the need of man and not for his greed"(Mahatma Gandhi). But *'how much is enough'* is a million dollar question!

In the Lord's Prayer, the word, "We/ours" takes over the word "I" and "mine", and also "my bread" by "our bread". The depletion of biodiversity has also contributed unhealthy life-conditions for human existence. The theme of World Environment Day in 2010, speaks volumes to us: "Many species, one planet, one future" has opened up umpteen questions and has urged us to search for steps leading to sustainable development. In our search for environmental justice, we need to initiate scientific search for ecological truths about life.

Larry L. Rasmussen remarks: "*Environmental justice is also social justice and all efforts to save the planet begin with the cry of the people and the cry of the earth together.*" The message of Pope Francis in *Laudato Si* is worth recalling: "Protect creation, confront climate change and care for the poor". In the Bible, particularly in Lev. 19:9-10, environmental justice is integrally related to the care of the marginalized. "When you reap the harvest of your land, do not reap to the very edges of your field or gather the gleanings of your harvest. Do not go over your vineyard a second time or pick up the grapes that have fallen. Leave them for the poor and the alien".

The implications of the earth ethics and the marginalized groups (subaltern) must be brought to the forefront of the mission concerns of the Church. The most suppressed and depressed groups of people who dwell on earth belong to the earth. The kinship between subaltern groups and the earth is bright as day light: the dalits to the earth, the adivasis to the forests and the fisher folks to the sea. It is also imperative to affirm the rights of all beings on this planet earth to exist and to flourish as envisioned in the wider spectrum of Deep Ecology.

In Deep Ecology, the accent falls on Gestalt (*wholeness*). All the living creatures-birds and animals too have hunger and thirst. This aspect is very often ignored in an anthropocentric attitude to life. The so called project proposal for the inter-linking of Rivers is an unjust philosophy. *The living beings other than human beings are denied of their existence in such an initiative*. The hills and the wetlands, even small lakes are also for the survival of micro-organisms, birds and animals. As an Asian contribution to the Christian liturgy, prayer for plants and animals be included. What is required is to affirm the holistic vision of the Psalmist in liturgical prayers (See Ps. 104).

In a prayer of thanksgiving, we affirm our faith in the God of all grace. The prayer of the Harare (Brazil) assembly of the WCC (9th) is worth recalling in this context. "*God, hear the cries of all creation, the cries of water, the air, the land and all living beings, the cries of those who are exploited, marginalized, abused and victimized*". This is a prayer to grant us wisdom and understanding in solving the problem at large. The theme chosen for the 11th assembly of the WCC to be held in Germany in the year 2022: "Christ's love moves the world to reconciliation and unity" is indeed an affirmation of life for the whole humanity.

The prophetic call of Vandana Siva for *an earth democracy* makes sense in our search for eco-justice. The "Earth democracy is a movement which allows us to move from the dominant and pervasive culture of violence, destruction and death to a culture of non-violence, creative peace and life. It is the democracy of all life..... It is an alternative to the life affecting tendencies of Globalization". Again she says, "Globalization, at the most fundamental level, is rewriting our relationship with the earth and her species, alienating land, water and biodiversity from local communities, transforming commons into commodities. It is a break from all earlier stages of human relationships with the earth and her resources." *How can we maintain and support globalization without marginalization?*

Environmental Rights - A Justice Issue

In his encyclical, *Laudato Si,* as mentioned earlier "On care for our common home", Pope Francis has reaffirmed the need for a common culture of care. To quote, "The earth is essentially a shared inheritance where fruits are meant to benefit everyone." He also adds that "access to safe drinkable water is a basic and universal human right". In the UN Charter of Human Rights, *the environmental rights are not clearly spelt out.* The marginalized sections of the community (dalits, tribals, fisher folks etc.) are very often denied of their basic rights to drink unpolluted water.

Water and air are gifts of the Creator to all living beings. As water and oxygen are the gifts of the Creator, they are meant to be shared by all. There is a necessity that is laid upon us across religious or cultural divide to protect the earth from deforestation. Environmental rights in all their aspects will have to be recognized, respected and enforced. The Holy Books treasured by the religions of Asia make it clear that there existed *a symbiotic relationship between man and nature* in all the religious traditions of Asia.

The Ancients even uttered a prayer of forgiveness before the cutting of a tree and even the killing of an animal. Reverence for life is the basic pillar for the corporate survival of the created order. Water and air on sale is simply the denial of *creational rights* of all living beings. The right to breathe fresh air has become an ecological right in the Covid 19 scenario.

An Eco- vision of the Earth Community

The moment we look for eco-spirituality that sustains us, we are asked to look beyond and to regard the Church as a fellowship of seekers after the truth. Church as the Eucharistic presence of the Kingdom does not negate truth in all religions and cultures. It carries God's call in Christ to build a fraternal community. This attitude is relevant today as it speaks about the dialogical existence of the earth community. The continuous activity of God through the Spirit to mend the brokenness of creation is the basic philosophy for the integrity of creation. In our search for an Asian oikoumene, the Asian Reality provides a connecting thread along with a challenge.

One cannot deny the fact that the world today is seeking new forms of spirituality that are less dogmatic. The Post-C scenario of the world has made a new impact on the Church for a search in the New Normal. One should know that irrelevance is sin we are called to interpret "the signs of the times" in fulfilling mission concern. It is an attempt to seek for life-enhancing potentialities in the plural world. Eco-spirituality- an effort to grasp and to realize the Ultimate Truth- affirms the sacramentality of creation and ecological sensitivity. In affirming the Ultimate Truth in the order of creation, the eco-sins committed by the humans, are to be noted with grave concern for which we need to ask God's forgiveness.

"O Creator God, How Great Thou Art!"

The doyen of Theology, Thomas Aquinas, has rightly said, "any misunderstanding about Nature leads to a misunderstanding of God". In 'God-talk', we search for the reverence of life and interrelatedness between humans and other living beings. As appreciation leads to adoration, we look for the buckle that binds all human beings with the flora and fauna on this planet. *This is in tune with the compassion of the Lord*. The cultural slogans of India such as *vasudaivakudumbakam* (the whole world is one family) and *Loka samastha sukhino bhavantu* (Let the whole world be happy and prosperous) find a fitting place in the affirmation of one Creator God. The wonder of creation as exclaimed by the Psalmist in 104:24, "0 Lord, how manifold are thy works; In wisdom has thou made them all" is a golden thread that runs through all the religious Scriptures of the world.

Let me illustrate the above point with excerpts from a song of Jim Reeves:

> "*We thank Thee each morning for a new born day; We thank Thee for the sunshine and the air that we breathe; We thank thee for the river that runs all day; We thank Thee for the flower, that blooms, birds that sing; fish that swim; We thank Thee for the pastures where the cattle may mow; We thank thee for the love so pure and free, 0 Lord*".

The lessons that we learn from the order of creation is that life is meant for giving and that Nature is the best gift of God to all across any religious or cultural divide. So Jesus said, "for he (the heavenly Father) makes his Sun rise on the evil and on the good, and sends rains on the just and the unjust"(Matt. 5:45). The Psalmist adds a note of exclamation, as "the heavens are telling of the glory of God; and the firmament proclaims his hand work" (19:1). The above words of wonder could be summed up in the famous hymn, "All things bright and beautiful: All creatures great and small; All things wise and wonderful; The Lord God made them all".

The veil of Nature is rendered transparent and helps us to breathe afresh in a world choked by the noxious gases of greed, lust and profit making. In our understanding of flora and fauna, there are quite a few *unraveled mysteries.* We could count the number of seeds in an apple. But none is able to say with absolute certainty the number of apples could one harvest from a sapling of the seed. So also God's rose bud. None is able to open the petals of a rose bud by hand without crushing it. So great is the unraveled mystery of creation. In the book of Job 38-41 one may find texts which throw a fled of light on the Ubris of man.

In the ecological Psalm of 104, particularly verse 24-30, we get a glimpse of God's love and care manifested in the universe "0 Lord, how manifold are thy works. In wisdom hast thou made them all." (v.24); (cf.Ps.24:1-2). According to the Psalms, God is not immanent in creation, but He is imminent in a personal way with humankind" (N.H.Snaith). Nature by itself does not reveal God, it only serves as a means of revelation". "Nature is a constant reminder of the reality of God to those who have the eyes of faith" (K.V.Mathew). In the Psalms we do not find any natural law as independent from God.

The humans are asked to learn from Nature (Pro.6:6-11). As Nature is God's peculiar language (Robinson), creation and ethics should go together. According to Ps. 147: 16, Nature is the creative word of God that is at work in the ongoing process of growth and change in Nature. This gives "order and regularity in the ecosystem". It is God's faithfulness and love that sustain the world (Ps. 139). A sacramental approach to Nature is the key to the poetic insights of the Psalmist.

The humans and other living beings come together as partners in praising God, the creator. In a theology of the Sacramentality of Creation, *creation carries the footprints of Christ.* Any disrespect to creation leads to the defacement of the image of Christ. Therefore, the pollution of any kind is to be considered as sin against the Creator and Christ. When the integrity of creation is established, "the earth shall be filled with the knowledge of the glory of the Lord as the waters cover the sea" (ls. 11:3).

The Kingdom of God - Call to Live with Ecological Sensitivity

The teaching of Jesus gives us a blue print of *vasudaivakudumbakam* with concern for all. In the parable of the Mustard Seed (Mark 4:30-32), there is a divine call to care for the least and to value the inherent potential of all that is good and noble. For Jesus, all that is seen and unseen unfold the face of true humanity in its pristine form. The reference to the Sun and the rain (Matt.5:45); the scorching heat and the south wind (Lk.12:55); the clouds and the showers (Lk.12:54); the earth and the sky (Lk12:56); the flashing of light; (Matt.24:27); the rock and the sand (Matt.7:26); the seeds and the grains (Matt.4:2-8); the lilies and the grass (Matt. 6:28-30); the thorns and the thistles (Matt.7: 16); the figs and the grapes (Matt. 7:16); the moth and the rust (Matt.6: 19, 20); the sparrows and the eagles (Matt.10:29); the dogs (Lk.16:21), the fish and the serpent as well as the scorpions (Lk. 11:11); the sheep and the goats (Matt.25 :32) etc. are imageries taken by Jesus to illustrate God's care of the universe. *A triadic relationship of God, creation, and human beings is vividly seen in the teaching of Jesus on the kingdom of God.*

As members of the Faith Community, we are challenged to pray as Jesus taught in the Lord's prayer: "Let your Kingdom come on earth as it is in heaven" (Matt.6.9,10;Lk.11.1-4). Reference to "earth" (*gen*) and "food" in the prayer makes it *ecological* as food is grown not in heaven, but on earth! The Climate crisis has a bearing on food crisis. The UN declaration of 2008 as "Year of Potatoes" and 2014 as

"The year of family farming" is meant to highlight the importance of agriculture. If the earth's topography is changed, earth will ultimately harm the food production.

The year 2010 as UN "Year of Biodiversity" speaks of the need to preserve all living species on this planet as Noah did in his ark. So the UN theme for 2011 "Forests: Nature at Your Services" is a reminder to preserve our forests. The UN theme for the environment day on June 5, 2015–"7 Billion Dreams, One Planet, Consume with Care" urgently calls forth a form of development which is economically and environmentally sustainable. The theme chosen for the XIV General Assembly of the Christian Conference of Asia (CCA) in March 2015 (Jakarta): "Living together in the household of God" has brought out the dialogical relationship of the Asian Churches offering its *ecumenical and ecological mission paradigms in their search for the New humanity in Christ.*

The Seers of the Vedas said about the secret of human bonding: "We are the birds of the same nest". A few verses from the Vedas are quoted below:

We are birds of the same nest
We may wear different skins
We may speak in different tongues
We may believe in different cultures
Yet we share the same home - Our Earth.
Born on the same planet,Covered by the same skies
Gazing at the same stars
Breathing the same air
We must learn to happily progress together
Or miserably perish together
For man can only live individually
But can only survive collectively:

'When you walk across the fields with your mind pure and holy, then from all the stones and all growing things, and all animals, the sparks of their soul come out and cling to you, and then they are purified and become a holy fire for you' (Martin Buber).

The Covid-19 Spiritual Lessons

We notice the resurrection of spiritual values in different cultures when we pass through adverse circumstances. In the Indian culture, truth, order and beauty (*sathyam, sivam sunderam)* are the noble virtues for the joy of living. The lockdown period all over the world has taught us several values for an authentic existence. Our needs are not made of greed during this period. We have learned to live with the minimum and manifested the art of simplicity. Several of us have said good-bye to our habits known as 'disposable syndrome'. Wearing mask in the public has taught us to care for other's health. The age old Vedic slogan: "**we are the birds of the same nest**" has found practical steps in our common pursuits. We have also learned the importance of peace with Nature. The amount of Co_2 in the atmosphere has come down. The sky has become clear; so also waters in the seas, the rivers and the lakes.

The lockdown period has been a period of blessings for all living organisms. We have been able to reduce all kinds of pollution around us. It is widely held that the lockdown period has turned our homes as places of worship. The online worship services and preaching have helped us to search for alternatives in our religious observances. The Webinars have become part of our interpersonal relationships and communications. The silent periods in our homes have also strengthened family bonds in different ways. It is true that youths and old people had to bear with several psychological problems. May God help them.

Let me conclude with the words of Rabindranath Tagore: "My Lord, this is my prayer: Help me to root out all pride and arrogance from my heart. Help me to continue the pilgrimage of life gladly in the midst of joy and sorrow. Give me the power from above to translate my love into fruitful service for humanity" (Gitanjali-36-a free rendering).

---

* **Revd Dr M. J. Joseph** holds a doctorate in The New Testament and he is the former Professor and Principal of the Mar Thoma Theological Seminary, Kottayam. He is the former Principal of the Indian School of Ecumenical Theology (ECC-ISET) and the former Director of the Ecumenical Christian Center, Bangalore. Dr Joseph was a member of the Faith and Order Commission of the World Council of Churches, and Secretary of the Board of Theological Education of the Serampore University, Calcutta. He is the author of several eco-poems and writings in Malayalam and English. Currently he is the convener of the Eco- commission of the Mar Thoma Church, Kerala, India. (E-mail: drmjjoseph_65@yahoo.co.in)

7

Denominations are Abominations

*Chhotebhai **

When Christians come together they talk of denominations. I find the word abominable. In an era of competition between different Churches, the term was used to distinguish between them. In today's ecumenical era of co-operation and commonality between Churches, the term becomes redundant. I prefer to refer to them as "Sister Churches". Did not St Paul write to the Churches in Corinth, Thessalonica, Ephesus etc? Does not the Book of Revelation talk of the Spirit speaking to the Churches (in plural) not in the singular? So shouldn't we too be comfortable with the plurality of Churches, rather than insisting on the singularity of one's own particular Church?

History is replete with instances of Churches being hostile to and in open competition with each other. Criticism of the "other" was rampant. If in 1302 the 189th Pope, Boniface VIII, summarily declared that there was no salvation outside the Catholic Church; there are even today, several Churches, mostly from the Evangelical stream, that are merrily sending all the unbaptised "pagans" to hell. Personally, I do not believe in a God that is hell-bent on packing "sinners" off to hell.

As a Catholic myself, I will restrict myself to the current teachings of the Catholic Church, especially in the post-Vatican II era. For those unfamiliar with the term, I am referring to the Second Vatican Council held from 1962-65, in which over 2500 bishops and theologians from across the world participated. It was a watershed moment in the life of the Catholic Church. With its changed self-understanding, it also brought about a tectonic change in its relationship to other Churches, other religions, the natural and behavioural sciences and the world at large.

This change is most evident in the events of 1054 and 1965. The first is what is described as the "Great Schism of the East", when the western Churches based in Rome and the eastern ones based in Constantinople (Istanbul today) separated and ex-communicated each other. It took 911 long years for those ex-communications to be lifted by Pope Paul VI and Patriarch Athenagorus, when they met, warmly embraced and lifted the sanctions in 1965.

The Catholic Church, in the post Vatican II era has come a long way from the sad events of 1054 and 1302. Vatican II promulgated 16 documents, collectively known as the Documents of Vatican II. Of them the most significant is the "Dogmatic Constitution of the Church" better known by its Latin opening words – Lumen Gentium (LG).

Before that the Catholic Church was like the cat's whiskers, steeped in its own pride and exclusivity, a head and shoulders above other "lesser" mortals. Now it very humbly calls itself "an initial budding forth of God's kingdom" (LG No 5), not a full bloom basking in the sun. She "embraces sinners in her bosom" (LG No 8), not a rarefied puritan, and admits that it is still "a pilgrim", not one that has arrived at its destination, or attained its goal. From absolutism it has moved to relativity. This is a crucial change reflected in its attitude or approach to others, including the Sister Churches. Of them it says, "The Church recognizes that in many ways she is linked to those who, being baptised, are honoured with the name of Christian" (LG No 15). This is the official dogmatic teaching of the Catholic Church. Unfortunately, there is a yawning gap between precept and practice.

I have no hesitation in saying that there are many Catholic priests and even bishops in India who are uncomfortable with the relativism and inclusiveness of Vatican II ecclesiology. They are often more at ease with the fundamentalist, absolute, binary pre-Vatican ecclesiology of Me or You; not Us. That black or white binary refuses to recognize the various shades of grey, or the multi-coloured coat of Joseph.

Jesus' last prayer included an impassioned one for unity. "May they all be one, just as, Father, you are in me and I am in you, so that they also may be in us, so that the world may believe it was you who sent me" (Jn 17:21). We find that Jesus is linking unity with witness value. Conversely, Christian disunity or division is the greatest stumbling block to Christian witness and evangelization. This is evident in colonial India, where each western Church came with its own ideological and theological baggage, totally confusing those who had never heard of Jesus. In contrast, the apostle Thomas in Kerala and St Francis Xavier in Goa were successful, partly because of a unified message. There was no counter witness. We will revert to the Indian Church later.

For now let us return to apostolic times. Those who oppose organized religion, derogatorily referred to as churchianity, point to the early Christian community. "The whole group of believers was united, heart and soul; no one claimed private ownership of any possessions, as everything they owned was held in common" (Acts 4:32). This was too good to last. Shortly after, there was a division among Hebrew speaking Christians and the Greek speaking ones (cf Acts 6:1). The second dispute arose between circumcised Jews and proselytes (circumcised Gentile converts to Judaism) and non-circumcised converts on the other. St Peter had to step in to breach the divide (cf Acts 11:1-18). There are several other instances of both Sts Peter and Paul admonishing the neo-converts for their ethnic divisions and personal loyalties.

If in the first flush of apostolic times, when the Holy Spirit was powerfully manifest, unity was at a premium, then how much more difficult is it for us today; bombarded as we are by multiple messages and factors in both history and the present all-pervasive media? It requires both prayer and humility.

The history of Christianity in India is different from that of the West that suffered persecution for 300 years till Emperor Constantine's Edict of Milan in 312 CE, effectively making it a State religion. It was also spared the ignominy of being subjected to Roman, Byzantine, French, German and Spanish emperors, as also the scars of the Crusades. The infamous Inquisition was limited to a section of Goa.

However, with colonialisation came missionary expansion and various white missionaries towing the line of the Churches of their native lands. It was this conflict and confusion that greatly contributed to the failure of Christianity to make its presence felt in India. When I was in Jyotiniketan Ashram, Bareilly, we had an ecumenical meeting. I recall the words of Revd Kenneth Sharp of the Brotherhood of the Ascended Christ, an Anglican order. He said that we may be divided in thought or belief, but we can always be united in service where there is no room for dispute.

Some years later when I had organized an ecumenical meeting under the aegis of the Kanpur Catholic Association, the main speaker, Dr A.B.K. Sebastian of Christ Church College said that in India there was no need to perpetuate the divisions of European Christianity. Words of wisdom!

It is for this reason that I find Pope Francis refuses to get sucked into theological debates of hair splitting. He prefers to directly reach out to people, saying that we should leave the debates to the theologians. I saw him address a joint gathering of Catholics and

Lutherans. A person in the audience asked him a tricky question – "Whom do you prefer – Catholics or Lutherans?" Pat came the reply, "I equally dislike lukewarm Catholics and Lutherans". It reminds one of how the Pharisees tried to trap Jesus by asking him if it was proper to pay taxes to Caesar? (cf Mat 22:21).

Pope Francis has repeatedly adopted a pastoral, rather than a dogmatic approach to complex issues. He gave the telling example of the field hospital in battle. You don't stop to check the injured soldier's cholesterol or sugar levels. You first bandage his wounds. In his latest encyclical "Fratelli Tutti" he talks at length about the Good Samaritan, a detested "outsider". Jesus upholds him as a paragon of virtue (cf Lk 10:25 ff).

This doesn't mean that Christian Churches may just do as they please, often pulling in opposite directions. St Paul gave us two beautiful analogies of the Church as a body and as a bride (cf I Cor 12:12-30, Eph 5:23). Both indicate some kind of organic unity and bonding, if not exactly organizational.

Interestingly, Jesus himself never used the word "Church"; though some English translations use the word (cf Mat 16:18 & 18:17). The actual Hebrew word used by Jesus was "qahal" that meant a community or assembly of believers. The Greek word "ekklesia" from which the English word "Church" is derived, also has the same meaning.

However, there is an evolution discernible in the New Testament itself. In the Acts of the Apostles the word "Church" is used 23 times, and in the Pauline letters 65 times! So obviously, as the community grew, it needed to be better identified. For those critics of churchianity who say that Jesus never founded a Church; and personal discipleship would suffice, I give the example of a human embryo. It is just a few cells, with no head, hands or feet. Yet it bears all the intrinsic qualities of a baby and later an adult. So too with the Church. It grows and evolves and sometimes mutates because of external influences. This should not detract from the reality that Jesus wanted his disciples to have some form of spiritual, organic and even organizational unity.

This can never be fully achieved. If the apostles failed with small numbers and no excess baggage, then we have a slim chance of getting there. This should not deter us from moving forward as pilgrims seeking to convert the bud into a full bloom, while embracing sinners in its bosom.

Management gurus teach us about areas of concern and areas of control. I may be concerned about the world economy, over which I have little control. But I do have control over my own domestic budget. Instead of bemoaning my inability to transform the world, let me first address what is within my control. Many Christians may feel that they are facing insurmountable odds in climbing the treacherous mountain of Christian unity. They then despair. Let alone the Evil One, even sociologists, psychologists and political pundits tell us that despair is the easiest way to accept the inevitable and be resigned to one's fate. However, the Holy Spirit spurs us to action. That is why I reiterate that humility and prayer are pre-requisites for Christian unity.

Like Pope Paul VI and Patriarch Athenagorus let us begin by warmly embracing each other and stop seeing each other as antagonists. There are two small steps that we can adopt immediately. The first is to stop criticizing each other. The second is stop "sheep stealing", grabbing disgruntled or dissatisfied members from sister Churches, especially from what are described as the "mainline" Churches. They are soft targets for preying evangelical Churches. Not that they are the only culprits. Catholics do the same with their superior organization and financial resources. This has been widespread in the Punjab, Uttarakhand and North East regions. It must stop. If at all some of us are determined to increase the number of Christians through conversions, then let them go out and share the message with those who have not heard it, instead of sheep stealing.

Well-meaning non-Christians sometimes ask about the difference between Catholics and Protestants. Often they are told that Catholics give more prominence to Mother Mary, instead of to Jesus himself. While the criticism is not entirely unfounded, especially in the pre-Vatican II era, it is unfair and unwarranted, especially in India where great significance is attached to the Mata in the Bhakti tradition of Hinduism (which is also the most common). For Muslims too, Mary is not anathema. There are more references to her in the Quran than in the Bible. My point is that we achieve nothing by pointing fingers at each other. With prayer and humility we will surely find light at the end of the tunnel.

Now let us come to the pandemic. Earlier the big C was Cancer. It is now Corona. What has been its impact on Christianity in India, and more specifically Christian unity? I am reminded of Jesus' analogy of the two house builders, one on sand and the other on rock (cf Mat 7:26 ff). It was only in tribulation that its strength could be tested. I am inclined to believe that cracks appeared and we were found wanting. Despite the claims of Caritas of the Catholic Bishops' Conference of India distributing protection and relief material and getting an award from the Union Health Minister, I felt that the ground reality was different. Most Christians shied away from being frontline warriors. Some Christian hospitals shut gates and pulled strings to ensure that they were not conscripted as Covid hospitals. I did not see any evidence of a concerted ecumenical approach. Most were happy with a photo-op on their distributing dry rations to the poor and needy. It placated their conscience, without any risk factor.

I have also been disappointed with the response after the lockdown was lifted. It seemed to be business as usual, as though nothing had happened. People were meeting and greeting in churches, more relieved to get out and socialize, than sensing the need to reach out to those in need. Worse still were those who had got accustomed to the online services in the comfort of their homes. Such services were neither communitarian, congregational or challenging. Pope Francis was among the first to oppose online gimmicks.

I became starkly aware of the divisions among Christians when I visited the Holy Land in 1980. Not only were there divisions among Christians, Jews and Muslims; there were scores of them among Christians themselves. The worst example of this was the Holy Sepulchre. The six feet slab has three altars; one belonging to the Catholics and the other two to different Orthodox Churches, possibly Greek and Armenian. When celebrating the Holy Eucharist at these altars the respective priests must ensure that their hands do not extend beyond their allotted two feet. It is scandalous.

Nevertheless I would like to end on a positive note, again from Jerusalem. I had been invited there by the Anglican archbishop, at the behest of Revd Murray Rogers, the founder of our ashram in Bareilly, who had since relocated to Jerusalem. I was there during Holy Week itself. On Holy Thursday we attended a Catholic service. It was presided over by a bishop of the Melchite (Greek) Rite. The choir was led by French speaking Vietnamese nuns. Revd Rogers was an Englishman, a pastor of the Anglican Church, who wore ochre robes and lived like an Indian. He was vegetarian and regularly used Hindu texts in his own liturgy. And there I was, an English speaking Indian of the Latin Rite! Could that congregation have been more cosmopolitan or Catholic (universal)?

For the Easter vigil we again attended a Catholic service presided over by an African cardinal. Later during coffee there was a blackboard on which people from different countries wrote Easter greetings in their native languages, mostly in the Roman script. I wrote in Devanagari script in Hindi at the top of the board "Jai Sri Yesu". It caught the eye of the cardinal. He immediately asked me where I was from and was thrilled to know that I was Indian.

After coffee we proceeded to the Russian Orthodox Church. At that time Christianity was still banned in the communist Soviet

Union. A ninety-year-old retired army general was playing the organ. It was about 3.00 a.m. but the service was still warming up for the few elderly people there. I could not help but wonder at some churches' inability to adapt to the times. Many of us fossilised Christians are in urgent need of perestroika, glasnost and aggiornamento (opening up and updating to change).

In these Corona times let us prayerfully and humbly listen to what the Spirit is saying to the Churches (Rev 3:22), for denominations are an abomination for the disciples of Christ today.

---

* **Chhotebhai (Allan de Norohna)** is a well-known Author and Freelance Journalist. He is a former President of the All India Catholic Union. He was the youngest Catholic ever to hold this post. He is presently the Convener of Indian Catholic Forum.

8

Relations with People of Other Faiths

Fr Dr M. D.Thomas *

Introduction

Faith is integral to human life on earth. But, it is not the same for all individuals and groups. Therefore, there is always the 'other' in the sector of faith, as in other realms. Now, do I dare to reduce the other to a potential 'me' or do I have to consider the reality of another entity other than me and enter into friendly relations with him or her? Well, there is a call for unlearning and relearning the way we conceive human being as well as God and live our faith. It is also a call for enlarging the horizons of our lives, lest the dignity and the sacredness of the divine, along with the human, get fragmented or shrunk and lost. At the end of the day, the 'social character' in the humans demands 'friendly relations' with people of other faiths. These are some insights this article vouches to examine, explore, and explain.

1. Notional Considerations

The notions connected to relation, relations, relationship and the social character that make them possible, along with their basic or inner sense compose the base of our discussion on the main title above. Notional considerations unearth in brief and make clear the implications of the key words in question.

1.1. Relation or Relations

'Relation or relations' could be described as 'connection between two or more things'. It is the 'various connections, association, involvement, alliance or friendship in which persons are brought together'. It is 'the way people, groups, countries, etc. feel about or behave towards the other'. In other words, it is 'social, political or personal connections or dealings between or among individuals, groups, nations', and the like. As per the focus of the relation, relation could be personal relations, foreign relations, public relations, business relations, social relations, and the like.

1.2. Relation/s and Relationship

Relation/s and relationship have the following nuance between them. 'Relation' refers to the 'way to the connection or the way things are connected', while 'relationship' refers to the 'connection itself or the sense of relation'. The difference is not spacious. But, while 'relations' describe larger contexts, like countries, cities, companies and large families, 'relationship' is used for smaller groups of people, making things more personal or human. For instance, relation, in science, refers to the 'interconnections between and among the parts of a system', like neuron in the brain cells. Relationship, in databases, is a 'situation that exists between two relational database tables'.

1.3. Relations and the Social Character of Life

Relation or relations is rooted in the 'social character' of life. Manifestly, the social fiber admits degrees, dimensions and gradations. The humans stand atop in the 'collective sense', which is the core shared element in them that cannot be parted with, as 'homo sapiens', rational animals or social beings. That amounts to state that 'relation or relations' is the direct outcome of the social character. While human beings are born and they pass away as individuals, they are born from the society, live in the society and even for the society. Only together, can the humans make the best 'social sense' out of their lives.

2. The Backdrop of the Theme in Question

The theme in question has a significant backdrop that paved the way for evolving a Christian and a truly catholic thought in the Catholic tradition. This thought launched the runway for a family culture, in the larger context, for the Catholic and Christian mission to take off its course for the future. The backdrop presents the highlights of the Second World Catholic Council, along with its momentous document 'Nostra Aetate', and its radical implications, and critiques their limitless prospects, along with its unfortunate setback in the course of its journey ahead.

2.1. The Second World Catholic Council of Vatican

The sixties of the twentieth century made history anew and thus marked a new beginning, not only for the Catholic Christian community, but also for the other Christian communities and people or communities of all faiths, religious or not religious. The Catholic Church emerged then as an adult and pioneered the 'new wave of inter-faith relations or dialogue', first time in the history of the world. 'Nostra Aetate', meaning 'in our time', was the name of that significant document, which thoroughly shook the entire religious world, the secular world as well, with a distinctive 'culture of inter' among the humans. 'Interface, interaction, interchange and cross-border relations' are a few of the catchphrases of this core culture of the believers, humans as well.

2.2. Christianity Back to Its Roots

Pope Francis, the most brilliant and down-to-earth pope of the modern times, observed, 'the Second Vatican Council was a serious attempt to take the Church back to its roots'. The roots of Christianity would mean 'the human-divine person of Jesus Christ and his amazingly sublime values', which ceaselessly glow with a sense of 'good news', by way of a loving openness to and acceptance of one and all, beyond all borders. The document, along with the entire Council, was a clarion call for a 'restart' and a 'refresh' of Christianity. It could even be said as 'the second coming of Jesus' and therefore 'the second phase of Christianity'. 'A new way of being Christian' was its revitalizing maxim that emerged from the above epoch-making event. 'Being a humane and relational Christian' in the essentially plural world was the call of the hour, too.

2.3. Nostra Aetate and Its Genius

The ground-breaking and thought-provoking realization Nostra Aetate presented before Christians, all human beings as well, reads thus, "if Christians treat other individuals, groups and peoples in a manner that is not befitting sisters and brothers, they have no right to call God their Father". That makes it mandatory for Catholics to extend 'fraternal behavior' to people of all faiths and affiliations. Discriminating persons on any ground would be a major violation of the Christian faith in God the Father, whom Jesus revealed, as one who sends sunshine and rains on the good and the evil alike (Mt 5.45). The breach of the above 'ethics' would land Catholics and Christians the tragic fate of finding themselves out of the campus, as rendered faithless. That would amount to state that Christians have to necessarily engage in friendly dialogue or interaction with people of all communities, religious and not religious as well as Christian and other. Such is the revolutionary genius of the above document.

2.4. Credits in the New Dimension and Style of Mission

It is heartening to note that, taking impetus from the Council, several Councils at the Pontifical level and Commissions at the national level of the Church (CBCI in India) were launched, for promoting dialogue with people of other religions as well as Churches. Several Institutes and Commissions were established by Congregations and

Dioceses, too. Seminaries started courses on 'ecumenical and inter-religious dialogue' and hundreds of scholars emerged, who wrote several books and articles on the diverse areas of the theme. Lots of sessions of interaction were organized, involving leaders and members of all communities of faith, too. Some individuals and institutes made outstanding contribution in the area, at local, national and international levels, with a considerable impact, noticeably so. These efforts motivated lots of people in other communities to initiate similar efforts, as well, efforts that were perhaps more applied to the social context than ever before.

2.5. A Theoretical Setback in the New Mission

All the same, it has to be admitted with deep regret that on the whole the Christian community at the level of the leadership took a 'back seat' in this great mission. A bird's eye view of the reasons could be the following. The new area of the mission was to engage in 'dialogue, inter-religious dialogue or interfaith dialogue'. The word 'dialogue', used independently, sounded too classical or ambiguous.

'Inter-religious dialogue' had too much of a theological connotation and so was understood to be the business of theologians. Theologians, by way of theorizing it, seem to have complicated it more than necessary, unfortunately so. 'Inter-faith dialogue' was slightly simpler, but still was thought of as something only scholars or leaders could attempt. As a result, the above mission was not owned by most heads and members of the Catholic and even Christian community, either for not understanding it properly or for finding it difficult or not to the taste or to the ultimate advantage of doing what a 'screw driver' could do.

2.6. Practical Prospects of the Mission of Relations

The main title of this article, 'relations with people of other faiths', suggests clearly a Christian and a catholic (all-embracing) mission, human mission too, within the reach of every person. Promoting 'friendly relations' with all human beings has various degrees, grades, levels and dimensions and one of them or some of them can suit all peoples, irrespective of gender, age, education, position, class, caste, creed, and the like. 'Good human relations' is everyone's cup of tea and people of all persuasions will equally relish it, as well. 'Good relations are the outcome of faith, in the real sense of the term, too. Language is the 'door' to enter into the world of the other, and therefore, proficiency in the national and/or regional language/s of the country will go remarkably a long way in fostering relations with people of any affiliation or level who would come on one's way in life. However, it is the mindset of the believer that matters, how he or she conceives faith, God, other, life, mission, and the like. 'Travelling the path oneself' will reveal to the Christian and all believers that the lasting prospects of the mission of promoting friendly relations are highly promising and is the closest to the mind of Jesus.

3. Conceptual Motivations

The basic role of the concept is to motivate and inspire the humans in a certain direction, purposefully so. An idea can change the world. In fact, only an idea can evoke real change in human beings. Law and fear of punishment, along with goody-goody instructions, devotions and observances, can do only temporary patchworks. Only a 'motivated human being' can pursue an idea, a thought, an ideal, a vision and a mission, even single-handedly. Good sense, along with guts and calibre, keeps the mission clearly geared towards the destination, too. Achieving the objective would necessitate being informed, equipped, enlightened, energized and empowered to shoulder a mission and to translate the same in to the various routines of lives, even unsupported and un-collaborated. It is a motivated concept that facilitates the above process into fulfilling an effective mission. The current concept is socially motivated and it is strongly inclined to promoting 'good relations with people of other faiths and affiliations', irrespective of the fact there is a world of difference in the way individuals, families, institutions, communities and nations conduct themselves, religious or other.

3.1. Relations – Friendships and Partnerships

In line with the linguistic and notional implications cited above, a few of the crystal forms of relation could be 'acquaintance, friendship, partnership and fellowship' among believers of all faiths and associations. Relations branch out into 'interpersonal, inter-family, inter-institutional, inter-community, inter-national relations', along with its major and minor offshoots, like 'inter-faith, inter-religious, inter-ideological, inter-linguistic, inter-disciplinary, inter-gender, inter-age, inter-caste, inter-class, inter-tribal and inter-cultural' relations. Relation/s is an attitudinal mindset, in which sentiments of 'goodwill, respect, appreciation, esteem, understanding, love, care, help, cooperation', etc guide the destinies of friendship with other believers, thinkers and followers.

Relation or friendship can prosper only on 'equal footing', which is above considerations of superior and inferior, right and wrong, good and bad, powerful and weak and rich and poor. Good relations are 'inclusive, interactive, participatory, collaborative and harmonious' in character and they usher in friendships and partnerships in life, which can last much more than the calculable span of life. What is required is a talent for building bridges, however distant the gap of 'difference' between the pillars.

3.2. The Other – Friend, Brother/Sister, Better Half

The 'other' is he or she who exists or is present in addition to me. He or she is not the same as me, but is clearly 'different' from me. Male and female are a case in point. Male is not female and female is not male, and are not supposed to be either. Both are different from each other. Both reflect the divine image. Even as clearly defined individual human beings with different identity, dignity and role, they share the same human nature. In a similar fashion, the other individual, even in one's own tradition, has a different or different dimension of faith, experience, ideology, perception of life, and so on, along with a clear identity and dignity, but either of them shares the same human nature.

They are not enemies to each other, and not meant to be. They are intended to be friends, companions and co-pilgrims, as extension of one's own being. The difference in each other is not a negative factor, but is an element of enrichment. The 'others' together, like the colours in the rainbow, make sense collectively, true to their social quality. The reciprocal value in being brotherly-sisterly/friendly, even better half, one to another, is what defines and qualifies the other. Such a 'beauty in difference or diversity' is fundamentally intended by the Creator. It couldn't be otherwise, at any rate.

3.3. People – Family, Community, Nation, Society

Human beings exist as individuals and groups, at the same time. Groups can be family, institution, institute, organization, forum, community, nation and society, along with its sub-units. 'People' is composed of a collection of individuals, small or big. Every individual who joins the group is an 'other'. Living alone in the physical sense does not mean being cut off from the people, family, community or society. Living together in a group does not guarantee being a family, community or a society, too. 'Staying tuned to each other' with a unity of purpose and mutual bonding, leading to relation or friendship makes the difference. The dignity and merit of being a people, family, community, nation or society is inherent in balancing the equation between 'one and many', like 'one body with many parts', which is a perfect blend of rights and duties as well as the best paradigm of dimensions of difference in an effective interplay. The spirit of 'unity in diversity' and 'diversity in unity', as a collection of several 'other's, defines the moral fibre of being 'a people, a family or a community'. This is a divinely oriented 'ethics' by itself, the core ethics of being human and humane.

3.4. Faith – Inter-faith, Harmony among Faiths, the Divine in Full

More often than not, faith is understood to be the sole property of the religious sector. But, as a matter of fact, it is not so. Being a religious doesn't guarantee having a qualitative faith. Being not a religious can never rule out having a meritorious faith either. To say the least, everyone has a faith, religious or other. Faith is larger than religion. Faith is a perception, an idea, a conviction, a trust, a commitment to the power above, a devotion to one's conscience, and the like. A scientist or a thinker also is dedicated to the supreme energy or knowledge beyond him or her. Moreover, faith is plural and three-sided in its character. It has individual, social and spiritual facets, as faith in oneself, faith in the other and faith in God, all existing as one shared but single reality. It is inclusive, relational, interactive, participatory, collaborative and complementary, necessarily so. The spirit of being one, as in a musical concert, articulates what faith is all about. Therefore, faith can exist meaningfully only in unison and it is geared towards 'interfaith, multi-faith, all faiths and harmony among faiths'. 'Sharing with' the other the best of my values, along with 'sharing in' the best values of the other' is the dynamics of a living and sensible faith. Only when one is able to live the 'ethics' of such 'collective sense' in faith, one's hearts, minds and spirits will be large enough to contain God or the divine, in the real sense of the term, or in full. Well, divinity, along with humanity, is much larger than religion and even faith. That is the logic of life, human life in special, which finds its expression in friendly relations.

4. The Mission of Human Relations

The idea of the 'mission' has evolved from the Christian world, to be more exact, from Jesus Christ who, with a singular vision, performed a unique and universal mission in the world, which became a 'paradigm par excellence'. While being a Jew, he emerged beyond the Jewish religion, beyond religion itself, blending all that the human and divine realities can contain, a 'mission of human relations'. A brother and friend to one and all, even as a teacher and master beyond comparison, a man for all seasons and a singular revolutionary to that effect, he became an unparalleled epitome for the mission of making good relations with one and all, radiating the divine effectively, outstandingly so. The mission of human relations has to be applied to every person, institution, community, entity and context, in favour of strengthening the relational network of the family of God across the globe.

4.1. The Foundational Values and Directives of Jesus

Jesus articulated in a crystal clear way the 'ethics of human relations', by way of the human, relational and reciprocal 'culture of inter', 'do to the other what you would have him or her do to you' (Mt 7.12). This 'golden rule' governs the dynamics of inter-personal, inter-family and inter-community relations, irrespective of all differences the human world can gather. Further, Jesus summarized all his values of love into a paradigm of 'human-divine blend', 'whatever you did to one of the least of these sisters and brothers of mine, you did to me' (Mt 25.40). The relations with the humans, even the so called least, are balanced with the divine world, that too, on an 'equal footing' in effect. Pope John Paul illustrated the dynamics of this culture further when he addressed People of Other Religions (Madras, 1986), "By dialogue, we let God be present in our midst, for as we open ourselves to one another, we open ourselves to God". Being open to one and all, without discrimination and leading to good relations, is the Christian and human way to approach God, the God of all, positively so, and definitely not otherwise.

4.2. The Latest Papal Guidelines for the Christian Mission of Social Relations

In the recent encyclical 'Fratelli Tutti', meaning 'fraternity and social friendship', Pope Francis luminously underscores the mission of promoting relations with everyone in an outstanding way. The above words were coined by Saint Francis of Assisi to address his brothers and sisters and they intensely radiate the flavour of the 'good news' of Jesus Christ, markedly so. Further, the Joint Declaration of Pope Francis and Sheikh Ahmed el-Tayeb, Grand Imam of Al-Azhar, in

Abu Dhabi, 2019, reads "God has created all human beings equal in rights, duties and dignity, and has called them to live together as brothers and sisters". The deep commitment to the brotherly and sisterly sentiments reflected therein make a clarion call to transcend all sorts of difference, distance and otherness, religious or other, and to touch upon the realm of social friendship, beyond all human-made and silly borders. This 'maxim of relations' summarizes all that the humans can gather during their sojourn on earth as well as the sublime values Jesus lived and taught, towards launching a culture of a 'human-divine pursuit of life', even much beyond or different from the religious jargons.

4.3. 'Making the Family of God the Father on Earth' – the Umbrella Outcome of the Mission

Grounded in the filial experience of God as 'Father', Jesus became fraternally incarnate to every person, as an elder brother, a Master, a friend, a companion, a healer, a giver of new life, and the like, all these roles in the spirit of 'he does all things well' (Mk 7.37). In point of fact, the mission Jesus launched was truly catholic and all-embracing, 'making the family of God the Father on earth', the 'mission par excellence' and a 'mission with a difference', for Catholics, all Christians, for all faiths and for all humans, for all times as well. Therefore, all human beings are daughters and sons of the same Heavenly Father and are sisters, brothers and friends, one to another, beyond the human-made borders of high and low, right and wrong, first and last, and the like. That would amount to conclude that 'promoting friendly relations with people of all faiths, ideologies and cultures' is the real Christian mission, in the larger context. All other dimensions and details of the Christian mission have to be conducted in such a way that this 'larger ethics' is not violated and, at the same time, ultimately accomplish the 'paternal-filial-fraternal' style of family relations of God the Father on earth. Commitment to the larger mission of making a 'family of families', an 'institution of institutions', a 'community of communities', a 'nation of nations' and a human society that is 'charged with the divine nerve' is the call of the hour.

Conclusion

'External relations' define the larger social fibre of nations, communities, families, institutions and individuals. Establishing, maintaining and promoting friendly relations with all 'others' is the litmus test of a faith that is worth being had, too. The 'ethics' of good relations, leading to 'fraternal friendship and cooperation' with people of all communities, especially well-meaning persons, in view of making a better nation and society, is the right response to the challenging context of the bitterly viruses around as well as the rightly motivating insights and divinely charged human values of Jesus. The Christian community is called to rise above tendencies of making 'islands', 'parallel lines' and 'cobwebs' as well as of 'cutting the limbs to suit the ready-made churchy coat', in the name of the mission of Jesus. Rather, it will do well 'delving deep and large' in to the ocean of the human and environmental world of the very same Creator of all, God the Father, after the fashion of Jesus Christ. Committing oneself to opening the large umbrella of God the Father or the Creator of the entire creation for all the humans and beings to gather together in relations, I believe, will be the way of giving due credit to the dignity of being born as well as to the giver of life.

---

* **Fr Dr M. D. Thomas**, a Ph.D. in Hindi Literature, on a multi-disciplinary theme 'Kabeer and Christian Thought', is a scholar, a leader and an active promoter of 'cross-cultural perspectives, inter-faith relations and social harmony', and is a writer, speaker and a social analyst to that effect. He was the Diocesan Director of Institute of Religion and Culture, Ujjain; National Director of Commission for Religious Harmony, CBCI, New Delhi; and Editor of multi-faith journal 'Fellowship'. Currently, he is Founder Director of Institute of Harmony and Peace Studies, New Delhi. He can be contacted at 'mdthomas53@gmail.com'.

9

Ecumenical Mission in the Post-COVID World

*Revd Dr Valsan Thampu**

Ecumenism in the Indian Context

Ecumenism is native to the Indian outlook. This is implied in the vision of '*Vasudhaiva Kutumbakam*', seeing the whole of the created order as one family. Ecumenism cannot get wider than this. So, ecumenism doesn't have to be imported into India from an alien climate of opinion. The word is alien, the concept is not. In the core spiritual vision of India, the world is one family. Jesus' vision that the world is one kingdom, the Kingdom of God, is identical to this. Indeed, spiritual vision is essentially ecumenical. The fact that religions are not ecumenical proves how far from their own spiritual light they have drifted.

Ecumenism as a way of life is more natural to Hindus than to the practitioners of other religions. Hinduism disowned ecumenism when it became a religion, which it was not meant to be. As a religion, Hinduism fragmented itself into an ensemble of sects, compromising its ecumenical genius and heritage. It alienated itself also from its philosophical vision. The more religious it got, the more exclusive the sects and castes became. The more exclusive, the more zealous; the more zealous, the more hidebound and intolerant it has become. Hinduism is, therefore, an allegory on the metamorphosis of religions. All religions are alike in this respect.

This is not to discredit any religion. Religions, as religion, are the same. All religions exemplify the same pattern, though they make competing claims and do what they can to accentuate superficial differences and theological-mythological angularities. Recognizing the pattern alluded to above is essential to forming an informed consensus on the nature and scope of a new ecumenical vision for the global community, which has to transcend conventional religiosity to attain shared spirituality.

Easily, the most critical issue in this context is how we view religion itself. The key ecumenical truth is that religion is the means, not the end. Nearly all problems in the inter-religious domain have arisen from deeming religion to be, de facto, an end in itself. Of course, this is not stated as such; it is merely assumed, and everything is strategized from this standpoint. The ecumenical spiritual truth is that religion is made for human beings, not the other way around. If religion is made for human beings, how can they be used and misused for the sake of religion, and minds poisoned with religion-based hate and alienation? Today everything is planned and executed with a view to maximizing the interests and gains of religions. Human beings are mere tools in this process. This wonky priority is not native to the essence of any religion. It is an aberration imported into religions. This pernicious curse humankind has suffered for millennia. Correcting this should be the quintessential goal of any ecumenical mission worth the name.

The roots of Christian ecumenism, in the Indian context, lay in mission fields in the past. Missionaries, who served beyond in the wider context, felt hindered by Christian disunity. Christianity is universal in its vision and proclamation, but it is parochial and fragmented on the ground. Contrary to the public perception, the

Christian community is widely and deeply divided. The truth of this becomes clear and problematic in the context of mission. Christian disunity created a miasma of hypocrisy around missions. So, the cry for Christian ecumenism –in contrast to wider, inter-religious ecumenism- emerged from missionaries.

This led to the Church Union Movement of which the Church of South India (CSI) and the Church of North India (CNI) were the outcomes in 1947 and 1970 respectively. But these 'united' churches ceased to be 'uniting' churches, for reasons that need not detain us here. It only needs to be stated that there is a tension between parochialism and ecumenism, which needs to be confronted. That is because ecumenism, as embraced and practiced in the past, was merely an adjunct to parochialism. As a result, wider unity in the service of expressing God's love for the world could not be formed. Each denomination, sect or religion stayed keen to protect its own territories. If a new ecumenical vision is to come into existence in the post-COVID world, it is necessary that this stumbling-block is recognized for what it is, and attempts made to overcome it. The good thing is that the post-pandemic world affords a more conducive context for it than was ever obtained in the past.

A third thing needs to be flagged as well. Amity and meaningful cooperation among religions is no longer a luxury or optional extra. It is an imperative. It is an imperative even for religions. For one thing, the unprecedented stress and strain that the pandemic induced to the human condition has put all religions to test. The extent of their relevance to human needs now stands exposed for what it is. Habitual religiosity, which accounts for much of popular religious affinities, has been diluted under lock-down. Believers across religions have realized –they say so openly- that they don't feel deprived due to the disruption of formal religious practices. Religions need to attain a new level of vitality and relevance, if they are to stay useful and valued.

Furthermore, peace of humankind depends on peace among religions. This 'peace' is not a matter of absence of open hostilities.

Peace, in its religious connotation, is a positive concept. It denotes a positive state of total welfare. Religions need to contribute its mite to the commonweal. From this vision, they are not mutually exclusive or competing forces, but co-servants of human welfare. They need to discover, as never before, spheres of cooperation in fulfilling their spiritual mandates.

What is Mission?

Perhaps the simplest way to understand mission is as comprising everything that promotes human welfare, as understood from a spiritual perspective. The foremost priority is freedom. There can be no human welfare without freedom. Liberation is understood or interpreted varyingly in different spiritual traditions; but there is none that discounts this purpose. To be indifferent to human freedom is to be blind to the need for mission.

The cornerstone of mission is the significance of life upon the earth. Attempts to deflect this focus, by offering compensations in afterlives and afterbirths, undermines mission. Mission seeks to create conditions of life in which all human beings can attain and enjoy fullness of life, here and now. Life stands on fullness. Just as there is no half-breath, or half-leap, there is no quarter life, half-life or three-quarters-life. Life, if it is life, has to be lived in its fullness. What falls short is mere existence. Talents and aptitudes vary; but the need for exercising them to the full, does not vary. Anything short of the benchmark of fullness breeds restlessness and frustration. Living life to the full, in a meaningful way, is the secret of joy and dignity.

Festivals symbolize this joy, fleetingly. The spiritual norm is that life is itself the festival; not, that life should be sparsely dotted with festivals. What we celebrate in festivals is fullness. Ironically, the need for a series of festivals arises because life is lived short of the mark of fullness. Those who merely exist celebrate festivals by way of compensating the fullness they miss. To those who live life in its fullness, life is the festival.

The goal of spirituality is to transform life into a universal festival. This is the ideal. The reality falls far short of this. Hence, the need for missions. From a spiritual view of life, fullness of life is possible only through God-centredness. But God-centredness necessarily means life-centredness. Life is as important before death, as it would be in afterlife. Welfare in life beyond death is inseparable from welfare in life before death. To drive a wedge between the two is to be hypocritical. Mission is, therefore, a healing intervention in the human condition. Mission addresses specific symptoms of the illness of our species; but does so, from a spiritual angle of vision.

The fortunate thing is that all human beings, irrespective of their religious identities, can share this vision. In a non-religious or secular understanding, to have a sense of mission is to have a goal or purpose in life. Arguably, it is a blessed state. The choice is between being missionaries and being parasites. The former enrich life. The latter, impoverish it. Even from a secular point of view, to live is to have a worthwhile purpose to live for. Short of it, individuals drift through life. Life becomes vital because there is a mission; life becomes noble because the mission pursued is godly; and life becomes fruitful because it is pursued with passion and vigour.

The basic purpose of ecumenical mission is to imbue individual lives with meaning and purpose. One must be in mission, primarily, for one's own sake. One does justice to others as a by-product of doing justice to oneself. Being in mission is the supreme good one can do to oneself. Mission is a spiritual state in which one discovers one's universal kinship, which is suppressed in routine religious contexts. To have a purpose in life, and to pursue it vigorously, is to grow continually in stature and character. This prospect of dynamic growth is the good news for all human beings. It does not have any religious label. Indeed, it should not. What it needs to have is a universal spiritual foundation, which is integrative, not divisive.

COVID and After

What a pandemic means, or does not mean, is a matter of perspective and interpretation. From a spiritual point of view, there is nothing either meaningless or fortuitous. The altered idea of mission, in the post-pandemic scenario, will depend on how we understand its message and significance. The following aspects are obvious and relevant to our theme-

1. The universality of the human predicament stands asserted and demonstrated through the pandemic. The virus has broken through every fortress of human segregation and fragmentation. It has revealed the globe to be one domain, equally vulnerable everywhere. The virus is truly ecumenical, even if it is so tragically and ironically.

2. The pandemic has revealed the global unpreparedness to face the unpredictable. This is not a matter of resource-constraints, but of wrong priorities. The systems of the world are neither life-oriented, nor people-centred. The virus has silenced familiar oratories. It has punctured pretensions. It has also, in the process, demonstrated the need for humankind to establish itself on the foundation of cooperation, rather than competition; of caring mutuality, rather than thriving at each other's expense.

3. The pandemic has also exposed the crisis of relevance brewing behind the facade of conventional religiosity.

4. The post-COVID situation needs to put the spotlight on the human predicament and the needs thereof, with life as its shaping priority. It is no longer possible to rely entirely on rituals and priest-craft. The industry is re-calibrating itself to be relevant to the emerging context. Why not religions?

5. This means that the emphasis needs to shift from doctrines, dogmas and rituals to mission. Mission is all about responding

to realities, which are common to all people. This augurs well, because a common ground exists for cooperation. It is easier to cooperate on the basis of deeds than on the basis of words. The time has come to shift from the dialogue of words to the dialogue of deeds. Nothing helps to forge human solidarity better than shared deeds and struggles.

What Shall We Do?

1. Bring about a change in the existing religious outlook. Men of action tend to be impatient with theory; yet nothing on the ground changes, unless thinking changes. The prevailing religious outlook is unhelpful for missions of wider ecumenism. The roadblocks in this regard need to be identified and addressed. Literature conducive to the formation and propagation of the changed outlook needs to be produced and popularized.

A word of caution is in place here. This process should avoid esoteric issues that theologians are fond of hair-splitting about. All matters pertaining to religion-and-sect-specific dogmas, rituals and customs should be avoided. They are divisive in intent; certainly, in effect. The focus of the new spiritual awareness should be on life, as well as the need to empower and celebrate the goodness and innate nobility of humankind. This implies a shift from religion to spirituality. Spirituality is light. Light furthers life. Whatever hinders life is darkness. The new line of distinction should not be between religions, but between those who promote and those who hinder life; especially, though not exclusively, in religions.

2. Theory is only as good as it is acted upon. In the religious domain, the perennial problem is the gulf between theory and practice. They go in different directions. Ideals abound in all religious traditions, but the life of the communities concerned goes on as if they don't exist. The power of spiritual values and ideals is felt only when they are made to prevail in the life of a society, a nation, and the global village. As Sree Narayana Guru said, 'It does not matter which religion

you practice; what matters is if you are a good human being or not, for the religion you profess'. This should be universally acceptable.

3. Putting the post-COVID spotlight on life has a few points of emphasis. First, Work. A spiritual idea of work needs to be evolved, characterized by accountability to God and a caring concern for all forms of life. It is rarely emphasized that mission is work in its pure state. Or, it is work as it should be; free of selfish interests, and meant to benefit fellow human beings in need, so as to glorify God as the fountainhead of justice.

Second, social life needs to be emphasized in place of the exclusivity of parochial life. Opportunities to share life with all in the range of one's life must be created, in place of fellowship only with one's co-religionists. The insight in all religions that all human beings are children of God must be emphasized in order to promote this wider ecumenical sense of belonging together. Attempts to alienate human beings from the web of life in the name of God should be abjured, as this bears false witness to God.

Third, relationships should be liberated from fetters of religious narrow-mindedness. It makes no sense to assume that partnerships of wider ecumenism will emerge and flourish, even as negativity and suspicion are harboured regarding inter-religious relationships of love and marriage. Love needs to be liberated, if human beings are to be free. Promoting human solidarity, unhindered by man-made bottle-necks, must be accorded a high priority in the ecumenical vision to be pursued.

Finally, lifestyle needs to be harmonized with life, which is not the case now. The former undermines the latter; a problem of particular relevance to the life of the rich and the privileged. It also has serious implication for the health and wholeness of the environment.

4. A sense of wider responsibility needs to be fostered, especially through education. To be responsible is to be caring and responsive. It is to renounce parasitism in relating to the world. The crisis of

environment and the logic of successive disasters, have a reference to the abdication of responsibility on the part of individuals and collectivities towards Nature, its life and its resources. Instead of remaining exploiters of Nature, human beings need to be re-trained to be care-takers of it. We are meant to be gardeners in relation to Nature. We have become hunters. We need to return to the basics.

5. The resources of education must be geared to the creation of a values-enriched society. Education is the secular counterpart of religious formation. Education cannot bypass the responsibility for social engineering, in the best sense of the term. The present and increasing trend of seeing education as a handmaiden of economic and corporate interests is perilous and counterproductive. Wealth-generation cannot be, should not be strategized at the cost of social life, if wealth is to mean enrichment of life. Having everything to live with, but not a humane society to live in, is meaningless. A radical revamping of education is required. This is as much the responsibility of the spiritually sensitive, as it is of academics, policy-makers and politicians.

6. As regards religion, the emphasis needs to shift from 'afterlife' to the present life, from future births to the present birth. The dualism of the sacred and the profane must be rejected, in favour of an integrated vision of life. God is present everywhere. A piety that is not valuable and impactful in the wider world is not worth much. The priority should be to empower individuals, on the analogy that it is the individual immunity that protects human beings against infectious diseases and pandemics like COVID-19. As in the old dictum, 'sound mind in a sound body', it is true that good individuals can exist and attain fulfillment only in a good society. Abject dependence on priests and religious establishments must be balanced against empowering individuals to take care of their spiritual needs. After all, 99% of human life is lived outside the priestly tutelage. How people live should be a greater priority than how people worship; unless worship is an end in itself.

7. Politics must be humanized and rendered conducive to human welfare and social health, which is not the case today. This is possible only if it is re-established on a firm spiritual foundation. That was Gandhi's conviction. He identified 'politics without principles' as one of the seven deadly sins. The Indian model of secularism as equal treatment of religions must give way to political processes and the democratic culture being guided by spiritual values and ideals, as set out in the Preamble to the Constitution. If politics becomes demonic, no margin will exist for wider or narrower ecumenism. All will be enslaved by the monster of tyranny, and citizens will become mere tools of the State, to be used at will by the powers that be.

8. The present religiosity is hardly conducive to wider ecumenism. The general trend can be put simply as: the shell is hardening and the kernel is decaying. Shells are meant to enclose, and to exclude the outer world. It is the kernel that connects, in nourishing and meaningful ways, to what is beyond itself. The cracking of the shell is the moment of new life. When it comes to religion, it is dogmatically assumed that hardening the shell is the ultimate religious achievement! Certainly, the spiritually enlightened men and women of faith in the past did not think so. They believed that the vulnerability of a religion is the sign of its vitality. Making religious boundaries porous is a precondition for paving the way to ecumenical cooperation. How can people be shut up in religious isolation camps, indoctrinated with negativity regarding the wider world, and expect them to become ecumenical missionaries?

9. A shift in emphasis from religious loyalty to commitment to personal authenticity needs to be brought about. This is nothing new. It was the core purpose of all spiritual ferments in the past. People of every persuasion can cohere on this purpose. It is divisive religious agendas that tear them apart. The logic of what is advocated here is well illustrated by the pandemic. There can be no 'herd immunity' without individual immunity. It is in religion alone that individual empowerment is neglected, and their parasitical dependence on

religious systems deemed the ultimate good. Consider the growing popularity of yoga, as a case in point. It is gaining universal acceptance because it is relevant to the life of individuals, which is recognized as the bedrock of collective vitality.

10. The proof of vitality is the readiness to respond to the prevailing and emerging realities. Mission agendas cannot be set, once and for all. The broad format can be spelt out; but specifics have to be formulated as we move along. There are a host of issues to be addressed. It is not necessary in a prefatory essay like to itemize them. Suffice it to say that it is in making a people self-reliant, rather than maintaining them as appendages to religious and political establishments, that hope for the future rests.

Conclusion

The shift from knowing to doing is, in itself, a salutary revolution. One cannot be a doer, without also becoming a thinker; unless one works mechanically. But working mechanically is anything but doing mission. To be in ecumenical mission is also to cultivate the discipline of thinking and seeking together. The problem with organized religion is that they then claim to be closed systems, which were born full-grown and perfect. This excludes the discipline of seeking on the part of individual believers. The truth, however, is that different religious traditions came into being only because individuals thought and sought. They had the vitality to kick at fixed boundaries and enlarge human awareness and freedom. They sought the infinite within the finite. If this were not the case, there would have been either no religion, or only one religion, in the world.

So, the by-product of ecumenical mission in the post-pandemic world will be, if it is pursued in the freedom of the spirit, the emergence of a new spiritual vision for humankind. The critical importance of this cannot be exaggerated. Spiritually, humankind has lived off the past for too long. The growing signs of decay and disarray we see in the domain of religion is a positive sign. It is a call to go beyond.

It is similar to the birth-pangs induced by the maturity of the fetus. The time is come. The pandemic is like the *mahapralaya.* It signals the birth of the new. How many in the present generation are free to respond to the call of the hour and move into the future, time alone will tell. As regards the need itself, there is no doubt. The writing on the wall is bold and clear. Those who have eyes to read, let them read.

---

* **Revd Dr Valsan Thampu** is a Pastor of the Church of North India and a renowned educationist. He has authored many books. He was the Principal of the prestigious St Stephen's College, Delhi, from 2008 to 2016. He has also served as member of Delhi Minority Commission, National Commission for Minority Education, National Integration Council and National Steering Committee for Curriculum Revision. He is also a thinker, columnist and activist. He is a prophetic voice for the Christian Churches in India today.

10

The Indian Politics Guided by Prophetic and Inter-religious Spirituality

*Revd Dr Joseph Neetilal Vattakunnel, IMS (Neeti Bhai) **

In this Article, I shall try to share some of my reflections and suggestions that will be useful for the mission of Christian Churches in the post-pandemic India. I am glad that it will be presented in the ecumenical mission manual which is being published for the Christian Churches in post-pandemic India.

I shall speak from my background of more than 60 years of life and work in North India, where the life is presently very much influenced and led by a mixture of Hindutva religion and politics. Since this article is meant for the ecumenical mission manual for the use of the Christian Churches, I shall focus on Christian spirituality in following Jesus' own spirituality, which I consider profoundly prophetic and liberative. In the present-day Indian context, it can lead us to an inter-religious secular spirituality. When integrated with the practical, simple Gandhian spirituality, it can give us Indians an added sense of relevance and meaning.

The Seven Deadly Sins that Enslave Us

Mahatma Gandhi enumerated the following seven deadly sins from which one must be liberated if one is to succeed in his/her quest for Truth, which according to him is the final destiny of the humans. One needs to realize the liberation from these sins here on earth too. That can be a long struggle. The following are the seven deadly sins enumerated by Mahatma Gandhi:

a. Wealth without work

b. Pleasure without conscience

c. Knowledge without character

d. Commerce (Business) without morality (ethics)

e. Science without humanity

f. Religion without sacrifice

g. Politics without principle

Unfortunately, 'We the People of India' today seem to be enslaved by all these seven deadly sins. This is our present context. However, the two deadly sins that affect the national life of India most adversely today are 'religion without sacrifice' and 'politics without principle'. All people of good will agree that it must change. Our main concern here is how to bring about a change and free the nation from these deadly sins.

I feel that a rediscovery of the biblical Jesus' spirituality, as lived by Him, as lived by His first disciples following Him, and a shift in the present-day Christian spirituality from merely devotional and cultic religiosity to a prophetic participation in Jesus' own spirituality and mission can be very useful for us Christians in helping India liberate herself from these deadly sins.

Jesus' Spirituality

Jesus experienced God as unconditional Love. He experienced this profoundly at His baptism by John. As my professor, George Soares-Prabhu, the internationally renowned biblical theologian of happy memory hinted, this profound experience erupted into His life, shattering the ordinary patterns of existence, as all such call experiences do (think of Saul/Paul too). This God-experience allowed Jesus to address God as "abba", a name which is an invocation, not a description. "Abba" is the normal invocation Jesus henceforth used to address God and to speak about God (Lk 10: 21; Mk 14: 36; Jn 11: 41). It is this 'Abba' experience that impelled Him to adopt the life of an itinerant charismatic preacher and teacher who announced in word and deed (through miracles and parables and through deeds of table-fellowship with the outcastes) the imminent coming of the 'Kingdom of God'.

In the Jewish religious tradition, which stressed the transcendence of God to such an extent that his name was never spoken, this usage of Jesus was absolutely unique. Nowhere in Jewish tradition and in the OT, is God simply addressed as "Father" without any qualification. The language of Jesus is unique and points to a unique experience of God.

The God-experience of Jesus frees Him. For deeply experienced love always leads to a freedom from inner conditioning and from all compulsions and fears that hold us in bondage. Jesus who has experienced God as love was supremely free. In a society that was politically colonized, socially patriarchal and religiously conservative, He moved around with absolute freedom and authority. His freedom was all the more remarkable because he never sought position or power. This authority of Jesus enabled Him to confront the religious, social, and political establishment of his people with sovereign freedom. This sense of freedom led Him to communion and fellowship and to a deep sense of Justice. He Himself was the dawning of God's

Kingdom with its triple values of freedom, fellowship (love for others) and justice (Cf.George Soares-Prabhu, Dharma of Jesus pp. 86-94).

Jesus had a spirituality of intimate relationship with His Father, Abba, and a radical and prophetic relationship with His fellow-beings, including enemies. Jesus was a prophet par excellence. His key message of the Kingdom of God was prophetic, quite contrary to the expectations of Jews and even his disciples. His message is to be understood through His life-style, options, and His prophetic & liberative mission (Lk 4: 18-19). *"Freedom, Fellowship and Justice are the parameter of the Kingdom's thrust towards the total liberation of man. Together they spell out the significance of the Kingdom and tell us, what the Kingdom, in practice, means today*"(George Soares Prabhu, ibid. pp. 64-68).

To realise His vision Jesus made an unambiguous and uncompromising option for the oppressed and stood by them, defying authorities and challenging structures that were reducing the people into poverty and misery. Jesus challenged the oppressive social structures. It is the most striking feature in the NT.

The Palestinian Society of Jesus' time was highly hierarchical and social differences were strictly observed. Jesus' life, attitude, and teaching violated this social set-up. He kept company with the people of the lower strata of the society. He freely mingled with all kinds of people, to some extent identifying Himself with the social outcastes of His time, against the norms of the society. It was a radical living by Jesus, which the Pharisees and His critics could not accept.

Jesus struggled against religious oppression. He questioned the practises, doctrines and even the motives of the religious leaders. He undoubtedly challenged their authority. His action was definitely calculated to shake and ultimately to shatter oppressive structures and narrow views. His parables were subversive stories (the parables of Good Samaritan, Prodigal son, His sermon on the mount) all going against the prevalent value system. This Spirituality of Jesus with this double dimension of being both mystic and prophetic must be the model, strength and source of the spirituality of His followers.

Christian Spirituality is Following Jesus in His Spirituality

Christian spirituality consists in following Jesus in His spirituality. It means precisely sharing in His God-experience, in His love-relationship with His 'Abba'. It means to experience God in the way that Jesus experienced God. It must be also a sharing in his experience of love-relationship with all his human fellow-beings. Our Christian spirituality in following Jesus characterizes an inner disposition and relationship with a double dimension:

(a) Our experience of filial intimacy with God our Father after the model of the mystic relationship of Jesus with His Abba and in a way participating in the Sonship of Jesus.

(b) Our brotherly/sisterly love-relationship with all human beings after the example of Jesus, who loved "the least of all human beings" including his enemies and who commissioned us to do so.

This Abba centred spirituality makes us to relate ourselves to God our Father in love and accept the love of our Father which is inclusive, generous, unlimited, non-sectarian, non-discriminatory and "perfect" (Mt. 5: 45-48). It would lead us to an experience of our participation in the "eternal son-ship" of Jesus with God our Father and His eternal brotherhood with all human beings. Experience of this generous love of the Father, impels us to love one another, every child of the Father, and his entire creation. It would definitely lead us to follow Jesus in a prophetic way in our dealings with all our fellow human beings as Jesus did.

Following Jesus, the Prophet, the Master, the Way and the Truth, and the Guru, the followers of Jesus too need to become prophets today. To be a prophet would mean, to speak out as Jesus did, to read the signs of the times and respond to them as Jesus did and to take a stand as a messenger of God on issues and events that affect His people, as Jesus did at His time. This leads inevitably to tension and conflicts between the prophet and establishment. We have very many examples of it in the life and mission of Jesus.

In the context of today's rampant corruption, oppressive social structures and discriminations of all kinds and anti-people policies to the extent of destroying the poor and common man in our country, the followers of Jesus as prophets, as messengers of God, are called upon to speak out and take a stand on behalf of justice, freedom and fellowship.

Shift Needed

This specific spiritual and theological perspective in the understanding of Christian spirituality would call for a change/ shift in our traditional, devotional experience, approach and practice of us Christians. Today in all our Churches we are more interested to live and promote a ritualistic devotional type of spirituality. Our concern is to worship Jesus rather than to follow Him. Jesus is the object of our devotion and worship. Our Church activities and programmes are centred on devotion and cult. Taking a prophetic stand on behalf of God and on behalf of His people as Jesus did has become secondary.

Genuine spirituality is secular in the sense that people belonging to different religions can attain it. Spirituality is something going beyond religions. Its central focus is on the one hand one's deep-rooted vertical connectivity and relatedness with the Ultimate Reality, experienced and expressed in different terms and names. On the other hand, one's horizontal connectivity with all other fellow-beings too becomes important. The experience of it differs from individual to individual. Experience of enlightened persons is shared with others. We can also find similarities in the spiritual experiences of great individuals. As explained above Jesus shared His spirituality with His followers through his life and message. Jesus' prophetic spirituality was liberative. His followers, the Christians, too are expected to follow Him in His spirituality. That is how the collective spirituality of Christians becomes Christian spirituality, which is to be primarily prophetic and liberative. It is different from ritualistic religiosity, practiced and expressed differently by followers of different religions in accordance with certain set patterns laid down by particular religions. Spirituality is not the devotional ritualistic practice of religiosity.

Spirituality, understood in this double dimension of vertical relationship with the Ultimate Reality on the one hand and the horizontal relationship with fellow beings on the other hand, as explained above, can be very well understood and accepted in the multi-religious context of India. For it is an inter-religious spirituality, applicable to people belonging to all religions. The Indian contexts of Religious Pluralism and given inequalities among people demand such a prophetic and liberative spirituality. Such a spirituality is foundational for our involvement for a change, for bringing about a society based on the Constitutional values of equality, freedom, fellowship and justice for all.

Impact of Spirituality on Public Life

Jesus has shown in his life and message, as we know from the New Testament, that His spirituality is very practical and also very demanding and challenging. His followers are expected to follow Him and live this spirituality. It must make its impact on society. Then only Jesus' vision of society, "the Kingdom of God" can be realized.

Practical application of this prophetic and liberative spirituality in the national life of India can transform India. Mahatma Gandhi, though formally not a Christian, followed it and applied it to a great extent to the Indian situation. His mission included not only liberating himself from the deadly social sins mentioned above, but also helping India to liberate herself from them. At a deeper sense, 'freedom' for India meant for Gandhiji also a freedom from these deadly sins.

A value-based and principled transformation of India into a land of justice, liberty, equality, and fraternity was envisioned in the Preamble of our Constitution. Definitely enthused with such a grand vision, the young free India after Independence made a good start to liberate herself from the deadly sins of "religion without sacrifice and politics without principle". But unfortunately, at the present time we are deeply drowned in these sins. A prophetic spirituality, as explained above, is capable of transforming both our religions and politics and freeing the country from the seven sins mentioned by Gandhiji.

Gandhiji was a man of deep spirituality, not very much busy with ritualistic religiosity. As Jesus' spirituality, Gandhiji's spirituality too was prophetic and liberative, besides being personal. Both the personal as well as the prophetic and liberative spirituality are important. The prophetic, liberative spirituality springs from the deep-rooted personal spiritual relationship of a person with the Absolute he/she believes in. Here below we shall briefly deal with the prophetic and liberative spirituality of Gandhiji with its impact on public life, as it could be more contextual and more acceptable to the Indian situation.

For a societal transformation of Indian society, for a qualitative change of Indian society and for its liberation from the social sins, I find three principles of Mahatma Gandhi as foundational. They are: (1) his constant search for Truth, *Satyagrah* (2) his principle of *Sarvodaya* (welfare of all) through *antyodaya* (option for the poor) and (3) his vision of *swaraj* (self-governance). All these are to be gradually realized in society democratically through non-violent action and struggle. A principled process of community building at the grassroots and its networking leading to nation-building with a focus on defence of human rights and promotion of social justice is the way visualized for the realization of his vision. This very same vision is found in the Constitution of India with its clear goal setting in its Preamble.

Good governance, carried out following the goal and procedures set in the Constitution, is expected to initiate a process for realizing this vision. But the seven social sins enunciated by Mahatma Gandhi, especially the sins of "Religions without sacrifice" and "Politics without principles" turn out to be the greatest obstacles for the realization of the expected liberation of the people and societal transformation as visualized by Jesus and Mahatma Gandhi. Those responsible for good and principled governance are the representatives of the people in a genuine democracy. If they are not doing their job well on behalf and for the sake of the people whom they represent, they must be called back. This was the demand made by Jai Prakash Narayan, a follower of Mahatma Gandhi in the 70s, just before the declaration of national emergency in the country by Indira Gandhi in 1975. It is not possible today as our Indian democracy is not grown to that maturity. But it still remains as an ideal, since in a genuine democracy, the people's welfare, their rights and their decisions take priority and predominance.

Politics guided by prophetic and inter-religious spirituality can bring about change in this situation, although it can be a long and tedious process, full of struggles. This is what I believe; this is what I struggle for. This may take years; we may not see it realized in our life time. But it is an ideal that I cannot throw away. Jesus' love-command, more than two thousand years old, is not yet realized. It still remains an ideal that cannot be thrown away. The age-old "*vasudaivakudumbakam*" of Indian heritage is not realized. But it is not thrown away as utopia.

I know, all what is said under this section, 'Impact of Spirituality on Public Life' stands in need of explanation. Time does not allow me to elaborate it presently. Here I shall limit myself to the question of a real practical action or involvement for the realization of liberation from the sin of "politics without principle". A community building process for the realization of Gandhiji's *'swaraj'* in working with the grassroots democracy of the present-day panchayatiraj system can be one of the best opportunities today to begin with for its realization.

The Process of Community-building

I believe, all of us humans have only one mission here on earth. No one is an island. We are social beings. As such we need to care for one another. The blessings of the creation are to be enjoyed by all. No one is so privileged extra-ordinarily that he or she can appropriate the riches of this world to oneself at the expense and exclusion of others. We need a just world order, where all enjoy their rights, freedom, equality and fellowship. It is the responsibility and mission of each one of us to ensure such a situation to be available for everyone else. This is what we have learnt from Jesus Christ, from Gandhiji, from great men and women of the past from different times, nations and backgrounds.

In what way we need to exercise this mission and make a contribution is determined by the context in which we live. In the present-day context, we experience in India, as already mentioned right in the beginning of this article, politics without principles is one of the prominent social evils that go against this vision and mission. A change needs to be worked out. No change will come from heavens without the co-operation of the humans. A process of community building can bring about a qualitative change in the present-day 'politics without principles'. Through networking it must make a contribution to the nation. Finally, it must lead to nation-building and emergence of a global new just world order.

Panchayatiraj: A Step towards Change for Principled Politics in India

With the 73rd and 74th Constitutional amendments of 1992 a new system of decentralized self-governance was introduced in our country in the form of Panchayati Raj in the rural areas and municipalities in the urban areas. With it the political power in the country is very much decentralized. It brought about a new opportunity and possibility for the citizens of India to play an active role in the affairs of the nation and its governance. It gives an opportunity to the citizens to participate in the decision-making process of their communities at the grassroots level. After the central government and the state government, the panchayat is considered to be the 3rd government in the country. It offers its citizens an excellent opportunity to experience and express their participation to develop their own panchayat communities. People are not merely beneficiaries of various schemes offered by the central and state governments. They are the decision makers. With the provisions of reservation, the poor and marginalized people too are given representations. Very many constitutional provisions are given for the realization of our constitutional goals of fraternity, equality and justice as well as for the realization of Gandhiji's *swaraj.*

Although in theory immense possibilities are open, in practice here too the above-mentioned social evils are at work blocking any change. A consistent and ongoing program of community building, making use of the Constitutional provisions of Panchayati Raj can be of immense help for realizing the desired socio-political transformation and the emergence of principled politics.

I suggest the following action plan for its realization:

1) Initiation of a Process of Community-building

In this direction activities and programs are to be carried out at the panchayat level in and through the new panchayatiraj system, aiming at the following:

a. People's Awakening: conscientization on the issues and affairs that affect them.

b. People's Education: what is meant is not formal school education but mass education based on the issues and problems faced by the people at a particular time and in relation to the constitutional values of the country and their application to the particular time and situation of the place. Mass education on farm laws taking place in the country among the farmers, is a significant example to this approach.

c. People's Organization: organized people's movements, away from the interests of party politics, keenly working for the promotion of social justice, defense of human rights and the actualization of the civil rights, guaranteed by the Constitution, which are active in different parts of the country demonstrate the inner strength of democracy in a country.

d. People's Power: what is meant is not unprincipled and violent power meant for the realization of vested interests of particular groups. People's power visualized here is the moral collective power of common people, based on our constitutional values and deeply rooted in a liberative, inclusive and inter-religious spirituality as mentioned above.

e. People's Action: In a genuine democratic set up, common people need to be involved both in the planning and execution of plans.

These are the five stages of a democratic process of community building. Ultimately the elected Panchayat representatives must be responsible for carrying out this process of community building. Panchayats must function as the medium of human development. The constitutional values are to be cherished and the prescribed democratic process is to be followed. This process is to be carried out, keeping in mind the welfare of all. Presently Panchayats do not function this way. Therefore, there arises the need of supervisory bodies emerging from the panchayat communities. In very many panchayats in some States, where the elected representatives are not sufficiently educated and the literacy of common people too is poor, there may be need for enlightened activists from outside the panchayat communities. In any case, the above-mentioned five-fold activities of community building are to be democratically and simultaneously managed by enlightened activists who function as charismatic leaders and change agents. It must begin at the lowest democratic set up of the panchayats. This community building process must become part and parcel of panchayat's functioning. People's participation and local leadership must be the two main concerns that are to be realized at the initiatives of the change agents or leaders.

2) Networking

The process of building communities is a work that is to be begun at the lowest basic civil communities of wards of panchayats. These ward-communities make some impact on the decision-making process in the village panchayats. No communities formed and developed in isolation can make any impact for a societal transformation in the country. Networking among communities is very important. Mahatma Gandhi had advocated that India be transformed into a network of thousands of *gramswarajs* (village republics) to form a *mahagantantra, (*republic) of India. Every village in this Republic is visualized as a *swaraj,* self-contained and self-supporting for meeting the basic needs of its people. Kishan Patnaik, a great follower of Gandhiji and the founder of *Samajvadi Parishad* had proposed that one must "act locally and think globally".

Through networking we visualise a gradual emergence of our country into a grand republic of very many smaller republics, free from the present-day evils. There are thousands of small non-governmental organizations of people in the country, working in isolation for realizing our constitutional vision. Their networking for realizing the common goal is the need of the time. National Alliance of People's Movements is a networking association based on Gandhian principles and ideals working for the realization of our constitutional vision. There is a National Panchayatraj Campaign going on for getting the panchayatraj system properly and effectively implemented in the country. But there are very many non-governmental organizations very much involved with charitable and developmental work in the service of the people and the nation. They do not see any value in networking for realizing the Constitutional rights of the people.

3) The Leading Role of the Churches

The personnel from different Churches and all Christians can and must play a leading key role for building inclusive civil communities and for realizing the Constitutional vision and values of our country. It must spring from their prophetic and liberative spirituality in following Jesus, their master.

At the grassroots level they must move out of their exclusive ghetto communities. Taking inspiration from the mystery of incarnation, they must have participation, involvement, immersion, identification and contribution as members of the panchayat communities in which they live, to which they belong and for which they work.

I visualize the Church personnel as builders of communities. They need to encourage and motivate other Christians to participate in their own panchayat affairs. The poor among them must consider themselves not merely as beneficiaries of welfare schemes but as decision-makers in their *gramsabha* as to decide who has to get what benefit.

The Church personnel and enlightened Christians can function in the process of community building at the grassroots, mentioned above, as enlightened activists, charismatic leaders and change agents, if not elected representatives in their panchayats.

For greater impact at the national level the Churches must take a prophetic stand on common affairs of the nation. They must have networking with associations and people's movements, sharing the same Constitutional vision of the country. Unfortunately the Churches show very little interest for networking for a common cause of the people among the Churches themselves, much less with civil societies. This situation must change, if they have to be relevant.

Many more suggestions could be made regarding an effective role of the Churches for making their contribution to realize the Constitutional vision of India. What is suggested above is not any involvement in party politics. But definitely it means active participation of people as dutiful citizens in the common affairs of the country. Such an involvement is genuinely political. And as Pope Francis said such an involvement in politics can be the highest form of charity.

What is suggested above results from a prophetic liberative spirituality in following Jesus in His spirituality. A personal spirituality is a pre-requisite. Acharya Swami Sachidanda Bharathi developed five foundational principles of Gandhian spirituality recently in his latest book 'A New Creation in Christ' (pages 284-287). They are: a) Rootedness (*Sthiratha*) b) Openness (*Udarata*) c) Simplicity (*Saadagi*) 4) Prayerfulness (*Prarthanamayata*) and 5) Non-violence (*Ahimsa*). They are essential requisites expected of spiritual leaders. Their personal lives and spirituality do not remain hidden. They get expressed in action-based transformational, liberative and prophetic spirituality. Swami Sachidanada is very much interested and involved in action for realizing a change in the Indian society and in its politics. He believes that Panchayatraj system can be of great help for bringing about the Gandhian vision of *gramswaraj* and for realizing a new India free from the evil of *the* "politics without principle". I wish Swamiji and his friends success in their great mission, and offer them my prayerful support.

---

* **Revd Dr Joseph Neetilal Vattakunnel, IMS (Neeti Bhai)** is at present the President of Lok Chetana Samiti, Varanasi, an inter-faith secular civil organization for promotion of social justice and protection of human rights, which he co-founded in 1994. Since 1983 he has been active in a prophetic social action with and for the common people, living amidst them, at first in Bihar and then in Uttar Pradesh. He was ordained a Catholic priest 50 years ago in 1970. He holds a doctorate in Fundamental Theology from Leopold Franz University, Innsbruck. He has taught contextual theology in St Paul's Seminary, Trichy for more than a decade. Meanwhile

to make his social action more effective for the protection of the rights of the poor, he studied Law and practiced it for 2 years in Chatra District Court in Bihar and another 2 years in Teez Hazari Courts, Delhi, before his active involvement with people in Varanasi. He is available at <neetibhai9@gmail.com>.

11

The Need to Return to the Cross of Christ

Timotheos Mathews Metropolitan *

Introduction

The world today is going through many crises of which the prominent one is the pandemic of Covid 19. The people live in anxiety, stress and confusion with despair in their hearts. The present world also faces other problems like population explosion, environmental pollution and extinction of many species in both animal and plant kingdoms. The Christians have to face terrorism, atheism and worldliness along with degradation of moral values.

1. The Cross of Christ

The centrality of the gospel is the cross of Christ. By death on the cross and the resurrection from the dead, Jesus Christ saved the whole creation. Prophet Isaiah described it clearly in the Old Testament, "But he was wounded for our transgressions, crushed for our inequities; upon him was the punishment that made us whole. And by his bruises we are healed" (Isiah 53: 5 NRSV). The solution to the whole issues and problems the world today facing, we find on the cross of Christ, whether the problem is social, cultural, economic or ethical. That is why, St Paul, the apostle, affirmed very boldly that, "For I decided to know nothing among you, except Jesus Christ and him crucified" (1 Cor 2:2). St Paul was firm in his faith in the Risen Lord, for he knew that the love of Christ, which is found on the cross, is sufficient for any hardships we face in the world. For St Paul, the message of Christ is the power of God. "But we proclaim the Christ crucified" (1 Cor 1:23). Upon the cross of Christ the social and personal sins are sanctified. In that case, we need to return to the cross of Christ in order to find solutions to our problems.

2. The Cross of Christ as the Bridge

The relationship between God and humans are depicted on the Cross of Christ. In other words, God the Father, the Creator of the universe, is reconciled to his creation, the human beings, through the Cross of Christ. Thus, cross becomes the bridge to connect the humanity to its Creator. "But now in Christ Jesus, you who once were far off have been brought near by the blood of Christ" (Ephesians 2:13). The blood of Christ shed on the cross bridges the gap between the Holy God and the unholy humanity. "For he (Jesus Christ) is our peace; in his flesh he has made both groups into one and has broken down the dividing wall, that is, the hostility between us" (Ephesians 2:14). It means the sinful humanity is reconciled to God only through the cross of Christ.

3. The Need to Return to the Cross

Our sufferings are the byproduct of the fall of humankind from grace into sin. The Cross of Christ was that of an innocent lamb, as an atonement which is central to the mission of Christ. An innocent lamb is slaughtered for the sins of the whole world! There, and only there, on the cross of Christ, we find the fullness of grace. The grace of God is found in the weakness of the cross! "God's power is made perfect in weakness" (2 Corinthians 12: 9).

Christ identified himself with every dimension of human experience including sufferings and weaknesses. That is why orthodox theology emphasizes the imitation (following) of Christ, especially the kenotic Christ. Kenosis is the self - emptying of one's will and becoming entirely receptive to God and the Divine Will (St John of the cross). "He (Jesus Christ) humbled himself and became obedient to the pain of death even death on a cross" (Philippians 2: 8). In his book "The Dark Night of the Soul", John of the Cross explains God's process of transforming the believer into the likeness of Christ (kenotic Christ). Humanity at large needs to follow the kenotic Christ on the cross in order to be liberated from all ecological, social, ethical and economic issues today.

If Jesus Christ emptied himself, we, as Christians, need to empty ourselves. If our Lord humbled himself, we also must humble ourselves. This is a challenge faced by present day Christianity. We are unable to bear witness to the cross of Christ by emptying and humbling ourselves – as individuals and as social beings. The society at large needs a model at this Corona time and the coming Post-Corona time. If the cross of Christ is central to the Christian faith, emptying and humbling ourselves is central to the Christian praxis.

The cross of Christ is the ultimate model of humility. It is the cross that confronts the most prevalent and the gravest sin, namely, pride. Just after the foot-washing, Jesus Christ exhorted to his disciples, "So, if I, your Lord and the Teacher, have washed your feet, you also ought to wash the feet each other. For I have set you an example that you also should do as I have done to you" (John 13:14 - 15). He further humbled himself upon the cross by obeying God, the Father, and shed his blood for the atonement of the sins of the whole creation.

Human pride was in its utmost height in recent years. God sent a small virus, Covid -19, to humble the whole world. God is giving a message to humanity through this virus that human pride cannot and will not achieve anything and it is unable to triumph at all.

4. The Reasons to Return to the Cross of Christ

As we have seen earlier, the cross of the Crucified God is the point of reconciliation, where the dark and cruel arrows of the Evil One were defeated. Thus, the cross bridged the gap between the evil world and the Holy God. The blood of the Innocent Lamb shed on the cross reconciled the whole humanity to the Creator of the Universe. God forgave the sins through the cross of Christ. And God the Son showed the true forgiving love on the cross by praying for the whole world, 'Father, forgive them for they do not know what they are doing" (Luke 23:34). The peak of the forgiving love of God was shown by Jesus on the cross.

When St Paul said, "Bear with one another, and if anyone has a complaint against another, forgive each other: just as the Lord has forgiven you, so you also must forgive" (Colossians 3:13); he had certainly in mind the prayer of our Lord on the cross. St Paul emphasizes on imitating Christ, the forgiving love of our Lord. It means, as a Christian, you and I have the responsibility to imitate the forgiving love of the cross of Christ in today's world. "May I never boast of anything else except the cross of Our Lord Jesus Christ, by which the world has been crucified to me and I to the world" (Galatians 6:14). St Paul has been crucified to the world, its desires, its passions and its evils. With firm conviction he declared, "I have been crucified with Christ; and it is no longer I who live, but it is Christ who lives in me" (Galatians 2:20). What the pandemic stricken, economically degraded world needs today is the grace of God, which is to be found only on the cross of Christ.

Unfortunately, for many preachers, the cross of Christ is a mere lip-service today. They pretend they believe in the cross of Christ, but what we need today is the practice of it. As Christians, we have to take seriously the cross of Christ, live as Jesus lived on earth, and have to die bearing witness to the cross of Christ. Otherwise, the whole Christian life becomes meaningless and we may display the opposite of the true message of the cross of Christ.

Conclusion

Coming back to the cross of Christ is the foremost message of the gospel. The double-minded Christians only preach the cross; the serious Christians live it. In a pandemic stricken society to solve our problems, (both individual and social), we need to return to the humility of Christ on the cross by renouncing the selfishness and pride inherent in our weak human nature. For that, we need to imitate Christ on the cross and become Christ-like by unconditionally forgiving our enemies and emptying ourselves in every walk of life in the society.

The cross of Christ is also a symbol of hope. Human pain and suffering will certainly find peace in the Cross of Christ and the Risen Lord. Thus, let us return to the cross of Christ, which is the victory and power of God.

H.E Mor Timotheos Mathews Metropolitan

DOB: 31/05/1973

Priest: 03/07/2000 (by the hands of H.E Mor Themotheos Thomas Metropolitan of Kottayam Diocese and Secretary of Holy Synod)

Theological Qualification: BD from Serampore University,

M.Th from Paurasthya Vidyapeeth, Vadavathur (Role of Monastic Movement in the Renewal of Syrian Orthodox Church)

2010 – 2014: Patriarchal Secretary of H H Moran Mor Ignatius Zakka II, Patriarch of Antioch and all the East

2014 - 2019: Patriarchal Secretary of H.H Moran Mor Ignatius Aprem II, Patriarch of Antioch and all the East

2019: Patriarchal Vicar of Midiyan and Jerusalem,

H.E Mor Timotheos Mathews is a Member of Mor Anthonios Syriac Orthodox Monastery, Kerala.

12

Military Christian Fellowship: A Leader in Ecumenical Mission in India

"ALL ONE IN CHRIST JESUS"

*Lt. Gen. Ashok Vasudeva, PVSM, AVSM, VSM (Retd)**

INTRODUCTION

1. Ecumenism as described by Encyclopedia Britannica is a movement or tendency towards worldwide Christian unity or cooperation. The term of recent origin, emphasizes what is viewed as the universality of the Christian faith and unity among Churches. The ecumenical movement seeks to recover the apostolic sense of the early Church for unity in diversity, while confronting the frustrations and difficulties of the pluralistic world. It is a lively reassessment of the historical sources and destiny of what followers perceive to be the one, holy, catholic, and apostolic Church of Jesus Christ.

THE INDIAN PARADOX

2. Christianity came to India in 52 AD when St Thomas the Apostle reached Malabar Coast and Christian faith was introduced as *'Christu Marga'* (the Way of Christ). While

another view is that Bartholomew the Apostle is credited with simultaneously introducing Christianity along the Kankan Coast. However, there is a general scholarly consensus that Christian communities were well established in the Malabar Coast (Kerala) of India by 6th Century AD. And starting from European colonization from 15th Century several Western Christian Communities like Latin Rite Catholics and Protestants were created in different parts of the country.

3. The State of Kerala is home to the Saint Thomas Christian Community, an ancient body of Christians who take their inspiration from St Thomas the Apostle in the 1st Century AD. However, they are now divided into several different denominations and Churches and traditions. The divide is so strong that many do not see eye to eye.

4. Today most believers are segregated and isolated in their Church or in their home. If believers accept St Paul's directive to seek other believers and greet them, the Lord will have a way to build up the assembly, 'His Body'. Although there are so many Churches and Christian groups today, believers can still heed St Paul's command to go and greet fellow believers in other groups. In God's eye all of His children are in one family, in the one body of Christ (John 17:23-"I am in them and you are in me, may they be made completely one. So the world may know you have sent me and have loved them as you have loved me."). As such, believers should not acknowledge any division or at least be tolerant of other denominations.

5. The clergy must set needs to change or impacted. One knows that Christians of different denominations do not agree but they can at least agree to disagree and that is what is most required in the Church of today for us to show the unbelieving world that we love one another.

6. We need to break barriers within Churches and Evangelists need to bring those barriers down, to find ways in which Christian people can show the love of God in working together. If the world could see that we love each other and work together because we believe in Christ that would be one of the greatest things that could happen. Churches' true mission is to be dynamic and tangible where God makes visible His ongoing reconciliation of the world. Churches' true life lies in coming together rather than being together. This places ecumenism at the heart of Church life and witness.

MILITARY CHRISTIAN FELLOWSHIP- A MODEL OF ECUMENISM:

7. **Brief History**: The Association of Military Christian Fellowship (AMCF) is the result of God's working at different times and in various places in the lives of His children serving in the Defence Forces of their respective countries. Most of the national Military Christian Fellowships (MCFs) associated with the AMCF trace their beginning to 1851 when Captain Trotter a British cavalry officer serving in India, felt the need for Christian fellowship. As a result of that burden, he laid the foundation of what became the Officer's Christian Union (OCU) in Britain. That organization began as a prayer fellowship. Similarly in different countries like Chile, Singapore, Dominican Republic started among the Defence Forces 'Worshipping and Fellowship Organizations' which later joined AMCF.

8. Fellowship among Military Christians on an international basis began in the 1920s. A Dutch officer Major (Late Lieut General) Author Smith became the leading force in establishing an international fellowship in 1930. It was called Fellowship of National Officers Christian Unions (FNOCU).

It was FNOCU which finally was called AMCF in 1980. This was set up as a fellowship which would be non-political, without ties to any particular denomination or Church with no central organization, budget or staff except for the President who operates from his home. Similarly each national MCF that joined the fellowship would be self-governing, self-supporting financially and emerged to develop along national lines.

FUNDAMENTALS

9. With the motto "All one in Christ" (Gal 3:27-28) AMCF is open to all traditions of Christian confession of Faith. Each country MCF should strive for unity among the Christian brothers and sisters in Defence Forces along with veterans of their respective Armed Forces. Since the MCF of each country is independent but striving for the same goal, each country's MCF has its own nuances. Each country MCF must integrate and encourage non-denominational gatherings and fellowship. Each of the 156 MCFs are inclusive and exclusive in their outreach. Inclusive of all Armed Forces personnel (Christians in Indian Armed Forces) both present and past that profess Jesus Christ as their Lord and Savior and exclusive of heretical or non - Christian religions.

MISSION AND GOAL

10. The Mission of MCF is to bring the Good News (Gospel) of Christ to Military men and women.

    The MCF believes in simple tenets of membership seeking to be inclusive without compromising essential beliefs. For example the Apostles Creed is widely used as an inclusive statement of faith which is

- Profess a personal faith and loyalty to Jesus Christ as Savior and Lord.

- Endeavour to achieve daily Bible reading and prayer in which they remember each other.
- Maintain fellowship with other Christians in seeking to extend the Kingdom of Jesus Christ through consistent Christian conduct, conscientious application to duty and personal witness to His Power.

Based on the above, the AMCF Prayer is

"Heavenly Father,

We thank you that the Blood of Jesus Christ cleanses from all sin

Bless the service men and women of all nations

And grant that we who know the joy of being

All one in Christ Jesus may be filled with your love and pass it on to others

Through the power of the Holy Spirit

Until his coming again.

Amen"

UNDERSTANDING MCF

11. The mission of MCF is to bring the Good News of Jesus Christ to Military men and women of the Christian faith irrespective of their denomination.

The message is very simple. It is Jesus Christ : who He is, what He did, what He taught and what He asks of us.

MCF's aim is not to establish great organizations or religious systems, to support a certain Church or mode of worship, or to win political or economic power. Our mission rather is to tell people about Jesus Christ so that each person may have the hope of eternal life, so that each person may be free from guilt and the penalty of sin, so that each person may have the priceless privilege of walking with God. God is not the captive servant of any denomination or race, or mode of dress, or culture, or religious creed or seminary or language or economic system, or political system or form of worship.

12. God is not impressed with military power, rank, economic wealth, or ecclesiastical position. What God desires are men and women whose hearts are warm and responsive towards Him, and whose lives are living demonstrations of His respect for the value and dignity of every human life.

ACTIVITES OF MCF

13. MCF begins when two or three or more military Christians from the same nation meet for fellowship, prayer, Bible study, and witness. Every national MCF is a place where military Christians can have fellowship with each other and with the Father and with His son(I John 1:3).

14. Any activity which pleases God and honours His Son Jesus Christ is appropriate. The activities are generally based on a Passion for God – "Love the Lord your God with all your heart and with all your soul and with all your mind" (Mathew 22:37) and 'A Passion for Men "Love your neighbor as yourself"(Mathew 22:39). It is worth noting that the principal objectives of MCF usually include:

   a) Carrying out the Great Commission within the Armed Forces and

   b) Helping members reach spiritual maturity.

15. The typical activities to achieve these objectives are briefly discussed below:

   a) **Bible Study**: Study of the Bible is essential since God's Word is the primary source of revelation to His followers today. There are different ways of Bible study. They can be ranging from formal to private study. Principal objective being carrying out the Great Commission within the Armed Forces and helping members reach spiritual maturity. Inductive Bible study has been found to be most effective in this regard.

b) **Nurture New Believers**: New believers need someone to help them learn the basics of Christianity from God's Word. They need a spiritual parent to help them get started in spiritual life. They need someone who can help them get up when they fall and share God's promises with them.

c) **Discipleship Training**: This is the type of training encouraged by Paul when he wrote to Timothy "—the things you have heard me say in the presence of many witnesses entrust to reliable men who will also be qualified to teach others" (2 Timothy 2:2). This is based on the multiplication principle.

d) **Fellowship**: This simply involves being together with each other and with God. Usually Military Christians get together to be together with spiritual dimensions.

e) **Retreats**: Members sometimes go away together to some place, where they be uninterrupted to follow MCF activities while they accomplish some particular purpose.

f) **Prayer**: Jesus taught his disciples to pray. The scriptures teach us that all believers should "Pray without ceasing". Prayer is simply talking with God and involves the elements of adoration, confession, thanksgiving and supplication or petition. We find conversational prayer is a good way to get the new members involved. Other activities in Prayer activity followed are:

   (i) Published Prayer Request

   (ii) Prayer Chains

   (iii) Prayer Meetings

(iv) Intercessory Prayer Group Ministry

(v) Pray and Plan

g) **Social Activities**: There are times when members get together simply for the joy of being together for fellowship, getting to know each other and drawing closer to each other and the Lord.

16. Some of the activities have been listed above. There are no hard and fast rules and MCF can organize any activity which would bring them closer to the Lord.

RESOURCES

17. Any organization must utilize all its resources in order to achieve its objectives. Likewise, in MCF we utilize some of the easily overlooked resources which are:

a) **Other Supporting Organizations**: Any task is more difficult when done alone than when others are involved. There are many agencies and organizations, which help MCF from time to time.

b) **Veterans**: They have more time to dedicate to the Ministry. In addition, they bring years of experience and maturity to the MCF.

c) **Spouses**: The spouse's support is essential to the service members. Their involvement in the Ministry is imperative and their involvement in MCF activities enhances the MCF functioning.

SUMMARY

18. The activities discussed above are often combined. The most common and the most important activity of MCF is the frequent regular gatherings of members in small groups for prayer, Bible reading, fellowship and witness. It bears repeating

that whatever is pleasing to God and honours His Son Jesus Christ is appropriate. MCF is His and for His Glory.

CONCLUSION

19. A very effective and workable example of ecumenism has been given above as adopted by MCF. One is not suggesting for a moment to break away from Christian denominations but to remain within the existing framework. Ecumenism should be at the heart of Church life and witness. We need to

- Change one's mind
- Modify one's doctrinal convictions.
- Broaden one's outlook to Christianity.

20. India as a country believes in *'Vasudhaiva Kutumbakam'*, all-encompassing and tolerant. Therefore, we need to consider a league of Churches like legion of Nations and form Indian Council of Churches to work for the cause of Christian Unity to include major Denominations. One does not imply re-uniting of the historically established denominations but recommends a unity of local congregation of Churches in a National Communion.

21. We, therefore, pray to the Holy Spirit for the grace, to be genuine, humble, gentle and self-denying in the service of others and to have an attitude of mutual generosity towards each other. Ecumenism must be based on conversion of hearts and upon prayer which will lead us to the purification of Hearts. We need to move away from fraternal rivalry to a deeper understanding of the unfathomable vibes of Lord Jesus Christ.

"ALL ONE IN CHRIST JESUS"

---

* **Lt. Gen. Ashok Vasudeva,** PVSM, AVSM, VSM (Rtd) is a highly decorated General of the Indian Army. He was commissioned in June 1967. After glorious

service of 40 years he retired in December 2006. Thereafter in 2010 he joined Commonwealth Games as Additional Director General, where he served till February 2012. In December 2014 with the help of a few Defense Christian Veterans he started the Military Christian Fellowship (MCF) - India, as suggested by the International President of the Association of Military Christian Fellowship with the motto: 'ALL ONE IN CHRIST JESUS'. MCF-India under his leadership has already become pan India with a number of Chapters all over India, keeping the love for Lord Jesus Christ foremost.

13

Inter-religious Cooperation for a Culture of Peace in Post-Pandemic India

Revd Dr Subhash Anand *

We need two hands to clap! So too, if international peace is to become a reality, all who aspire for it need to work together. Some individual or a particular community may take the lead, but without the cooperation of the others, the desired goal will continue to elude us. We all need to accept a common minimum agenda. The present article is an attempt to spell out some attitudes that all the participants need to have for collaboration to be possible.

1. Respect for Religion

The living organisms have a survival instinct. Food takes care of our individual survival, while sexuality ensures the survival of the species. Humans have the ability to find newer and newer ways to make survival easier and more comfortable. All the discoveries of science have enhanced our capacity to survive. We now have a longer life span. We have also formulated newer ways of social organization, so that even the weakest has the chance of survival. All this progress is supported by our capacity to reflect on our experience, an experience that is also shared by others. This is the realm of empirical knowledge (*darśana* followed by *manana*). Survival is linked with an environment, shaped by space and time, by land and season and, therefore, an experience of boundaries.

But human fulfillment is much more than survival. It entails the experience of truth, beauty and goodness. We have the ability to ask questions, and the answer to one question leads to the next question. The point of arrival becomes the point of departure. To be human is to be on an unending journey. We slowly discover that sometimes the answer to our question is the result of grace, of a free disclosure by another. Often the depth of our own existence is better discovered within a frame of grace (śravana followed by *manana*). This, I believe, is the realm of religion. In other words, religion helps us in our journey unto transcendence, a journey beyond ourselves, a journey towards others and with others. Religion takes us beyond boundaries. We become fellow-pilgrims on the way of peace.

Religion becomes problematic precisely when some of its followers lose sight of this specific characteristic, and use it to gain economic, social and political advantage. Then religion begins to create boundaries and build vote-banks. Then it promotes competition and generates conflicts. Since social security depends on numbers, the followers of one religion try to 'convert' others. They legitimize their undertaking by generating a suitable but self-defeating discourse: "You will be free of all boundaries if you accept our boundaries! You will attain the infinite only if you accept our presentation of the infinite!" In their zeal for the salvation of others, these missionaries do not see their own bondage.

2. Respect for History

Most religions have a long history. When individuals and communities exercise their freedom, they act within a frame of presuppositions and convictions. They are not omniscient; nor are they all-loving. They are bound to make mistakes; even indulge in dehumanizing tactics. Often we are guided more by the survival instinct that we inherit from our pre-human ancestors than by our specifically human qualities. In this process the followers of one religion may even resort to violence not only towards the followers of other religions but also towards their co-religionists. As we look at our past we may feel very humiliated. We may be tempted to whitewash our past and to project it as the Golden Age, as the Paradise Lost. Then we too will be lost. Only when we honestly accept our past, will we have an honest future. *Historia magistra vitae*. History should become our teacher. Then, and only then, we will not repeat the mistakes of our ancestors and commit the crimes they are guilty of.

We not only have a history, but we are in history. History, as different from evolution, is the specifically human mode of self-expression and development. It is shaped by the interaction of the freedom of many. Hence we cannot control it fully, but neither can it control us fully. Given the advanced technology at our disposal today, ours is a fast-moving world. All this can give us the 'future shock': "too much change in too short a period of time."[1] Every community needs to respond to changing situations in order to survive. To legitimize the changes, the leaders retroflex them into the life of the founder, or trace their origin in their scriptures. In course of time these changes do not serve any purpose. Some would want them to be put aside. Others would insist that their retention is a sign of orthodoxy. Only honest and critical historical research can clear the confusion. Hence all religions must promote such studies. That will also help us avoid repeating our mistakes. A critical approach to our history will help us to see that many of the accretions of the past are more of block in our journey towards a more meaningful future that will involve collaboration with all people of good will.

We have a responsibility towards the younger members of our community: we owe the truth to them. We may think that by filtering the information we pass on to them, we will protect their religious loyalty. Today, thanks to internet, we cannot control the sources of information available to young people. When they are imparted the painful truth with commitment and maturity they will become more authentic in their own commitment. Otherwise they may remain with their infantile beliefs and become fundamentalists or they may abandon their religious affiliation. When we have the courage to accept the dark side of our history, we will be more tolerant towards the dark spots in the histories of other communities. We will also appreciate the beautiful chapters in the history of others and they will surely reciprocate our kindness.

3. Respect for Science

Ancient communities did not make a clear distinction between the religious and secular realms. When empirical science was not as advanced as it is today, religion provided the explanation for many mysteries we experienced; it provided the answer to many questions that troubled our minds. Similarly in the realm of food, whatever was good for humans was ordained by the gods, and whatever was harmful was forbidden by them. There were auspicious days and months, healthy foods and drinks. In course of time empirical science not only found the explanations and answers we needed, but also enabled us to manipulate our surroundings. Food that was once considered impure can today be purified and made fit for human consumption. Diseases that were once attributed to the working of malignant spirits are now traced to different forms of infection.

If religion has to be meaningful for humans and a source of wellbeing for them, it has to enter into dialogues with physical, biological, psychological and social sciences. All these base themselves on a lot of empirical data and professional surveys. They come to conclusions that evoke disturbing questions for the followers of traditional religions and of the ethical norms proposed by these religions. For instance, traditional myths about the origins of the universe and of the human race can no longer maintain their position. So also, long-standing patriarchal constructions of the human society are not able to respond to the data provided by cultural anthropology and ethnology, not to mention history.

4. Respect for Philosophy

I see philosophy as the struggle of the human mind to understand human existence independently of all authority. Philosophy is not a .... (*bhāya*?) on some ancient text composed in a language accessible only to a few scholars. It is a commentary on experience that is within the reach of every honest human, using those skills that are available and acceptable to every honest human. In this process, it is critical of itself. Hence an authentic philosophical undertaking by its very nature can draw together people of different religious backgrounds, provided they are prepared to take a critical distance from the dogmas proposed to them by their religious authorities, be their texts or teachers.

In recent philosophical discussion the two most significant topics are related to epistemology and hermeneutics. The big question is how do we know what is true. Closely related to this is how humans construct meaning. We are becoming painfully aware that our societies can control the way knowledge is generated and disseminated. We are humiliated to learn that in all our reflection, we as individuals and as communities are guided by prejudgments and prejudices. Every text, however holy we may claim it to be, comes from within a context and is shaped by that context. It seeks to perpetuate that context. Texts are often the discourse generated by the group in power to legitimize and perpetuate their being in power. Hence we need a hermeneutics of suspicion.

Contemporary philosophy is engaged in the postmodern project. Postmodernism is affecting all of us. Postmodernism

> is a story about stories, a belief about beliefs, and in time—probably a very short time—it will become a central part of the worldview of most people... It fills our daily lives with uncertainty and anxiety, renders us vulnerable to tyrants and cults, shakes religious faith, and divides societies into groups contending with one another in a strange and unfamiliar kind of ideological conflicts not merely conflict *between* beliefs, but conflict *about* belief itself.[2]

In postmodernism there is a shift from reason to intuition, from objective to subjective, and from universal narrative to individual experience. As a result we face even radical pluralism and relativism. Postmodernism questions the reality of foundational events and the normative character of overarching and universal narratives.

> In the present cultural scenario of pluralism, liminality and mobility, common people out of socio-cultural compulsions construct a faith which does not make them belong to any religion per se... People are quite imaginative and intelligent in this regard and take profound freedom to interpret their faith in context. People increasingly say that they believe in 'spirituality' rather than 'religion'.[3]

This phenomenon generates a lot of insecurity especially among traditional 'priests' of all religions. Not only their religion—and for many of them this may be a greater concern—but also their livelihood is threatened. They may pretend that nothing is happening and try to keep their flock in the dark. Then those 'priests' and people will enclose themselves in a fundamentalist ghetto. That is dangerous for us all, because ghettoes generate violence.

5. Respect for Human Rights

Some beings appear to be totally without life. Others have life, but this life is of different degrees. The plants and trees are rooted in the earth. If there is a forest fire, they just cannot run away. On the other hand, the birds and animals in the forest can get away and find another habitat. Their potential for survival, however, is limited. In contrast to these living creatures, there are others who have consciousness. They can be present to themselves, recognize themselves: "I am so and so." They are reflexively in possession of themselves. They are persons who are in possession of themselves. They are not totally governed by the laws of Nature. To a certain degree they are free. They can shape their today and tomorrow. This is specifically the human mode of existence.

Any religion that tends to deny in some way or the other this freedom, violates the human dignity. I am not saying that a religious tradition or community cannot have a set of laws. These can be proposed to people, who are then free to decide for themselves. No community can use any kind of force to compel somebody to follow its rules and regulations. For the same reason, no community can use any kind of force to compel somebody to remain in the religious affiliation given to him or her by birth. Even when a person continues to profess a particular religion, he retains his freedom to think and even think critically. This critical thinking may well be a real service to his community. Since humans are persons, they cannot be subservient to non-persons. The life of persons is more sacred than the life of non-persons. Hence any violence to humans in favour of non-humans is not religious.

6. Respect for Human Values

Peace can only come when all feel safe and secure. This will be possible if religions give priority to human values. Right now the impression is that the 'priests' of traditional religions emphasize ritual practices: going to places of worship, visiting pilgrim centres, honouring statues, reciting some prayers, wearing some special marks on their body, using specific styles of dressing, marking some time as particularly sacred, following some peculiar norms governing food and drink, reading some holy books, etc. All these practices have one feature in common: they imply a boundary. There are those who are authorized to perform these practices, while others may not. There are some people who are holy, while the others are not. All these pious practices are human creations, and hence are bound to reflect the limitations inherent in human existence.

All rituals and cults are human creations—the reflection of our own being-in-flesh. Cult necessarily implies boundaries; it separates us from others. On the other hand, the human ability to love is innate to us. It is also recognized by almost all religions as a foundational human characteristic. If we reflect a little, we will see that the most important moral values are an expression of our ability to love and be concerned for others. It is the sincere practice of these values that make us truly human and humane. Moral values cut across all boundaries; they bring us in communion with others. Cult belongs to the realm of religion, while moral values make the secular sacred. The more we make moral values the focus of our concern, the more we become fellow-pilgrims with other people of good will, whatever be their religion or culture.

7. Respect for Human Limitations

Can any human possess the absolute religious truth?

Does not the claim to possess the absolute religious truth constitute the prejudice—popularly and hermeneutically—that distorts our perception of others and their claims?

8. Respect for Civic Space

In the past our villages and cities were more homogenous. The inhabitants had a common ethnic origin; they spoke the same language and followed the same religion. Hence any cultural or religious function was also the function of the whole village or city. However noisy it might be, it did not create any problem. Today things are very different. Sometimes even in the same building we have people of different ethnic origins; they speak different languages and follow different religions. Hence the celebration of one is not the celebration of all. This calls for the creation and acceptance of civic space. Civic space is not merely a spatial concept. It includes time, culture, and religion.

Our cultural and religious functions may not encroach on this civic space, even if we are the majority. For instance, our processions should not create traffic problems for others. Our use of public sound system must not disturb others, especially when they have a right to have a good sleep after a day of hard work. There are also others who are bed-ridden due to sickness or age. Similarly, fireworks and pyrotechnics not only create noise pollution, but also pollute our atmosphere. More and more people are having hearing problems. Little children who are woken up by loud noise of fireworks may not only have ear damage but also a psychological trauma. We cannot expect shops to close down because of our religious observances. Nor can we decide what other people should eat or not to eat. Our religious symbols are part of our religious space and they should not trespass the civic space.

9. Respect for the Secular State

As we are moving towards greater and greater multi-cultural and multi-religious societies, we can no longer entertain the legitimacy of a theocratic state: a state with a particular religion as the official religion, with its legal code as the law of the state. People who harbour such aspirations should not move out of their native states. If we are to live in peace and work together to build up the nation, the only option open to us is to create a secular state. This means that before the state all religions are equal. No religion is given a privileged standing. The laws that govern this state are not taken from any book or tradition but reflect a genuine concern for common good. They result from an honest discussion among the citizens of the state. Only those things are required of the citizens that promote the welfare of all and respect the fundamental rights of all. Similarly only those things are forbidden that would create law and order problems and impinge on the rights of others.

In a secular state there are no minority groups as such. Hence the concept of reservation for a particular group as such makes no sense. There are individuals and families that for different reasons and through no fault of their own are economically and educationally backward. These definitely deserve special attention from the state. Similarly there are no minority rights just as there are no majority privileges. So too, no group can expect the secular state to accept its personal law. That expectation would be legitimate where the state is theocratic. In the secular state there is one law for all, a law that is based on fundamental rights and universal human values.

Peace in society will be a reality if we all give primacy to fundamental rights and universal human values.

10. The Fundamental Duties as a Common Minimum Agenda

The 11 Fundamental Duties of Indian citizens given under Article: 51-A of the Constitution of India contain within them a common moral regeneration programme for all religious communities in India. These Fundamental Duties are included below for easy reference.

"It shall be the duty of every citizen of India

a. to abide by the Constitution and respect its ideals and institutions, the National Flag and National Anthem;

b. to cherish and follow the noble ideals which inspired our national struggle for freedom;

c. to uphold and protect the sovereignty, unity and integrity of India;

d. to defend the country and render national service when called upon to do so;

e. to promote harmony and the spirit of common brotherhood amongst all people of India transcending religious, linguistic and regional or sectional diversities; to renounce practices derogatory to the dignity of women;

f. to value and preserve the rich heritage of our composite culture;

g. to protect and improve the natural environment including forests, lakes, rivers and wild life, and to have compassion for living creatures;

h. to develop scientific temper, humanism and the spirit of enquiry and reform;

i. to safeguard public property and to abjure violence;

j. to strive towards excellence in all spheres of individual and collective activity so that the nation constantly rises to higher levels of endeavour and achievement;

k. who is a parent or guardian to provide opportunities for education of his child or, as the case may be, ward between the age of six and fourteen years."

The above Fundamental Duties of Indian citizens can constitute a Common Minimum Agenda for religions in India for rebuilding the post-pandemic India on a peace and sustainable development paradigm through interreligious dialogue and cooperation. They can unite all Indian citizens irrespective of the religious, linguistic, cultural or political affiliations on a nation-building mission.

Conclusion

The present mode of development pursued by India and many other countries, especially the 'advanced' countries in the world is not sustainable. Exploitation of fellow human beings and exploitation of Mother Earth are embedded in their development discourse.

Peace in the world is impossible without peace among religions in the world. Without peace, there cannot be sustainable development. Religion plays a very important role in the lives of most of our fellow Indian citizens. Hence, without interreligious dialogue and cooperation, we cannot hope to rebuild the pandemic devastated India on the strong foundation of a peace and stainable development paradigm. The mission ahead of Christian Churches in post-pandemic India is to be 'the salt of the earth and light of the world' in rebuilding the post-pandemic nation on a strong peace and sustainable development paradigm.

I hope and pray that this Article will be useful in the historic mission ahead of Christian Churches in post-pandemic India.

---

* **Revd Dr Subhash Anand** is a Catholic Priest from Udaipur Diocese. He has been a Professor of Philosophy in leading Seminaries. He is also an Author and spiritual guide.

14

Political Perspectives of the Mission of Christian Churches in Post-Pandemic India

*M P Joseph IAS (Fmr) **

In Mark 12:17, Jesus says to those who try and test him and thereby to all of us, 'Render unto Caesar the things that are Caesar's, and unto God the things that are God's.'

And like those to whom He spoke this two thousand years ago, we marvel at that clear distinction that He made between the Church and the State.

Yet, throughout the ages, the Church has not held back from intervening in the affairs of Caesar's realm. There have been times, no doubt, when the intervention has crossed that magic Lakshman Rekha, for managed by us mortals, it is often difficult for the Church to determine where that Lakshman Rekha lies.

It is not as though that magical line is one etched on stone. On the contrary, the Lakshman Rekha that divides the affairs of the State from the affairs of God and Church is constantly in a state of flux.

That Lakshman Rekha is not a static line. It is a line that is being continuously drawn and redrawn in time and place. It changes with time and from place to place.

But the fundamental principle of giving to the State what is in the realm of the State, and to God and Church, what belongs to the kingdom of God and Church has not changed from what Christ postulated, including His repeated assertions that His Kingdom was not of this world. That fundamental, simply stated asserts then as now, that the Church should keep out of politics. That is a fundamental that does not change with time or place.

Christ's Exhortation to the Nations

There is however an essential difference between the Church interfering or even merely intervening in politics and the Church carrying out the mission that Christ entrusted to it. That mission is abundantly clear in the Gospels, with Christ reiterating it in many places, but nowhere more strongly than in Mathew's Gospel when He describes the Day of the Last Judgment, when Christ tells us that He would come in glory on clouds and will gather all the '*nations*' of the world before him.

'And before him shall be gathered all nations: and he shall separate them one from another, as a shepherd divideth his sheep from the goats. And he shall set the sheep on his right hand, but the goats on the left.

Then shall the King say unto them on his right hand, Come, ye blessed of my Father, inherit the kingdom prepared for you from the foundation of the world:

For I was an hungered, and ye gave me to eat, I was thirsty, and ye gave me drink: I was a stranger, and ye took me in: Naked, and ye clothed me: I was sick, and ye visited me: I was in prison, and ye came unto me.

Then shall the righteous answer him, saying, Lord, when saw we thee an hungered, and fed thee? Or thirsty, and gave thee drink? When saw we thee a stranger, and took thee in? Or naked, and clothed thee? Or when saw we thee sick, or in prison, and came unto thee?

And the King shall answer and say unto them, Verily I say unto you, in as much as ye have done it unto one of the least of these my brethren, ye have done it unto me.

Then shall he say also unto them on the left hand, Depart from me, ye cursed, into everlasting fire, prepared for the devil and his angels: For I was an hungered, and ye gave me nothing to eat: I was thirsty, and ye gave me no drink: I was a stranger, and ye took me not in: naked, and ye clothed me not: sick, and in prison, and ye visited me not.

Then shall they also answer him, saying, Lord, when saw we thee an hungered, or a thirst, or a stranger, or naked, or sick, or in prison, and did not minister unto thee?

Then shall he answer them, saying, Verily I say unto you, in as much as ye did it not to one of the least of these, ye did it not to me. And these shall go away into everlasting punishment: but the righteous into life eternal.'

When Christ speaks of *nations* who will be gathered in front of Him on the Day of the Last Judgment, He speaks as much to the Caesars of those nations as to the Church. And what Christ says to the Caesars and the Church across nations is very simply that it is *service to man that is service to God*, that there can be no love of God, if there is no love of man, of neighbour, indeed if you do not love even your enemy.

This injunction to the nations of the world, is therefore not only an injunction to all of us as individuals, and to the Caesars of the world, but is an injunction to the Church as well. The message of Christ to the Church is that while the Church must not interfere in what belongs to the realm of the State, that yet the Church has an inherent Christian duty to feed the hungry, give water to the thirsty, care for the sick, take care of the stranger, the migrant, the refugee, the prisoner, the injured and the dying.

That exhortation is a pronounced directive of Christian faith to all Churches that they must not stand aside and merely watch when there is hunger and poverty, when there is thirst and pain, when there are refugees and outsiders, when there are prisoners and when there is injury, sickness, death and pandemic.

The Karma of the Church

Krishna's advice to Arjuna in the Bhagavat Gita, is on the same lines. Krishna exhorts Arjuna and thereby exhorts the Arjunas in all of us, that we have an inherent duty to do what is right, to fight evil. Evil can come in many forms. It can come as hunger and poverty and thirst and pain and as those thrown out of jobs and without incomes, those who are sick and marginalized, those that suffer from Covid or those who have recovered from it or those left penniless and orphaned by a Covid death in the family.

That is also Christ's exhortation to the Church that the Church has an inherent Karma, a duty to man. The Karma of the Church is to have in place clear perspectives – indeed political perspectives - to respond to and mitigate the loss and pain of a post - pandemic people.

Keeping in mind the secular nature of our country and the clear demarcation that the Constitution has put in place between the Church and the State, the Church in India has yet a duty to provide a social and political response in support of those who have been left behind by Covid.

Christ's Personal Example

When money changers, traders and businesses desecrated the Temple by converting His house of prayer into a commercial Mall, Christ did not demur from driving out from the Temple all those who thus dared to desecrate His Temple. The Gospels tell us that he used a whip to drive out those desecrators, overturning tables where the money changers had stacked up their coins, freeing doves that had been caged for selling, and disrupting the commercialism that had crept into the House of God.

That personal example of Christ is a continuing message to us today.

A Time for Silence and a Time to Speak

As Ecclesiastes 3:8 says, there is a time to keep silence, and a time to speak.

Post-Pandemic is the time for the Church to speak, a time to speak for those who cannot speak. To provide a voice for those voiceless who have been left behind. A time to place clear politico-social perspectives before the governments at the Centre and the State and before administrative bodies and administrators at all levels from the Village to the Tehsil and most certainly at the District and the State level.

Placing such perspectives before different levels of governance and administration should involve bringing strong pressure upon policy and decision makers and before and upon the implementers of such policies and programmes at all levels from the bottom-most to the highest to respond genuinely and generously in favour of those who have been most affected by the pandemic.

And Who Are These that Have Been Left behind by the Pandemic?

Those who have been affected by the pandemic are not merely those who have had to suffer from Covid. The lockdown, the loss of jobs, the closure of tiny, micro, small and medium businesses, the consequent loss of employment and loss of incomes, those who have had overnight to migrate from cities leaving everything behind and their many millions of dependents are all those who have been left behind by the Pandemic. They are those who do not know how they will feed their children, how they will be able to send their children to school, how they will buy books and clothes for their children etc.

And who are they? They are the poor and the downtrodden in the country, the marginalized and the vulnerable whose numbers have increased tremendously because of the pandemic.

Now is the time for the Church to make its political and social voice heard in favour of those poor and vulnerable who have had to suffer most because of Covid and who today continue to suffer greatly.

The mission of the Church post-pandemic in India today is to be the voice of the voiceless, the voice of the poor and the marginalized, the voice of the vulnerable, the voice of farmers and marginal and small agriculturists, of those who are fighting unjust laws, of the landless and the deprived.

That is as much a political mission as a social one, the twain being intertwined inextricably.

The Church must embolden itself to take a stand for the poor. Come out of its cloisters and Houses and sit in meetings and across desks in government offices and before Ministers and Chief Ministers and all other policy making and implementing authorities advocating for the poor and those who have been most hit by the pandemic.

The Church must Promote Pro-Poor Persons to Occupy Political Space

The Church needs to promote people with calibre to occupy the political space, to take to elected offices, to represent the poor in Gram, Block and Zilla Panchayats, in Legislative Assemblies and in Parliament.

It needs to promote and support persons with calibre and profile and with a track record of having done good, of those who are proven to be pro-poor, to contest and win elections to all elected Local Bodies, State Assemblies and the Parliament, so that the voice of the poor is heard loud and clear in these bodies and then is echoed across the village, district, state and country.

This is the mission of the Church in India today: *to take an open and uncompromising stand for the poor, those that have been most affected by the Pandemic; to Speak Up for them; to push forward and support pro-poor persons to represent the poor and the pro-poor in elected bodies from the top to the bottom.*

Not the Time to Vacillate

As Shakespeare put it so succinctly in Hamlet, now is not the time to vacillate and consider 'to be or not to be'. Now is not the time 'to suffer the slings and sorrows of an outrageous' pandemic fortune. But now is the time 'to take up arms against a sea of troubles *and by opposing them, end them*'.

The time for Silence is over. The time to speak and speak loud and clear is upon the Church.

As Christ himself set a personal example to rid the Temple of exploitative systems and businesses, as Arjuna did in obeying Lord Krishna's exhortation, so today is the time for the Church to step up and speak up on behalf of the dispossessed, openly, bravely and in public.

---

* **M P Joseph IAS (Fmr)** is a former District Collector of Ernakulam; Mayor of Cochin; Labour Commissioner Kerala; Founder Executive Vice Chairman of Bhavanam Foundation Kerala; Cashew Special Officer, Kerala State; Chief Executive of the Kerala State Headload Workers Welfare Fund Board; General Manager District Industries Centre, Kollam etc. Later he joined the ILO and worked on the children's education and the elimination of child labour in India and abroad for 20 years. His last posting was as Advisor to the Government of Kerala in the rank of Additional Chief Secretary.

The author is a writer, speaker, and TV anchor. His Chapter on the Syrian Christians of Kerala in Rutledge Publications tome, Eastern Christianity and Politics in the Twentieth Century is a much valued analysis of the past, present and future of Syrian Christians of Kerala.)

15

The Mission of Christian Churches in Post-Pandemic India: Economic Perspectives

Josil Mathai *

Economic perspectives for the Mission of Christian Churches are very imminent and essential for a thought process, before pursuing any projects. This simply empowers the community which eventually moves towards an economic freedom of the individuals and families. Covid Pandemic has affected the sociological and economical balance of the families and communities as a whole.

Many Companies were brought down "next to nothing" resulting in a greater toll on employment. Economic stability of the people has been blighted with no scope of recovery. The mere existence and sustainability was at stake. Many families were forced to face hunger, malnutrition, health crisis, unemployment, financial crunch etc. in this pandemic time. Church, which was the so called community of families, faced a sharp and profound decline in the revenue. This was the crude reality of the Pandemic. Without a financially secured position, no one will be able enough to spare a portion of money for the church. This deepened the economic deficit of the community or the church. To pursue on the solutions for the above problems, honest efforts must have to be envisaged to improve conditions of the affected people.

Mahatma Gandhi's economic views were humanitarian in nature, stemming from the concern for toiling peasants, factory workers and jobless people. These are some of his beliefs, which are holding greater values till today. He believed that ***"Nature produces enough to meet the needs of all the people, but not enough to satisfy the greed of any man".*** First, that everyone should get sufficient work to make the ends meet and second, means of production of necessities should be under the control of the masses. In 1944, '**Gandhian Plan**', which emphasized the decentralization of power, agricultural development, and cottage industries etc. was put across by Shriman Narayan Agarwal. He also wrote the famous book called *"Aap bhale to jag bhala"* meaning- If you are good, then the world will also be good. According to Gandhiji, *Khadi* means the decentralization of production as against monopoly of companies and distribution of the essential commodities to the common people.

The United Nations Economic and Social Council (ECOSOC) works on the principles of sustainability. Sustainability is made up of three pillars: the *economy, society, and the environment.* These principles are also informally termed as profit, people, and planet.

1. Co-operative Sustainability

Co-operatives have always endeavoured to enable people to have access to goods and services without exploitation – to realise their needs and aspirations. This has led them to pursue a convergence among the economic, social, and environmental interests – building triple bottom line sustainability. The basic principle of sustainability is defined as by investing in communities and investing in people. *Philippe Cousteau*, an environmentalist, perceived co-operators at the International Co-operative Alliance's General Assembly in Cancun, Mexico in 2011, *"We cannot have environmental sustainability without social sustainability.*" Hence social sustainability becomes the ground for any greater achievement for sustainability.

The difference between *corporation* and *co-operation* is that a *Corporation* is an organisation—usually a group of people or a company—authorized by the State to act as a single entity (a legal entity recognized by private and public law 'born out of statute'; a legal person in legal context) and recognized as such in law for certain purposes. On the other hand,*Co-operation*, however, is an association of individuals voluntarily co-operating for the promotion of mutual, social, cultural, and economic benefits.

2. ILO (*International Labour Organisation)* COOP now turns 100 years (Co-operating for social justice since 1920)

The driving forces for the ILO's creation arose from security concerns, humanitarian, political and economic considerations. The founders of the ILO recognized the importance of social justice in securing peace, against a background of the exploitation of workers in the industrializing nations of that time. There was also an increased understanding of the world's economic interdependence and the need for co-operation to obtain similarity of working conditions in countries competing for markets. Reflecting these ideas, the Preamble of the ILO Constitution states:

- Whereas universal and lasting peace can be established only if it is based upon social justice;
- And whereas conditions of labour exist involving such injustice, hardship and privation to large numbers of people as to produce unrest so great that the peace and harmony of the world are imperiled; and an improvement of those conditions is urgently required;
- Whereas also the failure of any nation to adopt humane conditions of labour is an obstacle in the way of other nations which desire to improve the conditions in their own countries.

The ILO views co-operatives as important in improving the living and working conditions of women and men globally as well as making essential infrastructure and services available even in areas neglected by the state and investor-driven enterprises. Co-operatives have a proven record of creating and sustaining employment and continue to contribute by promoting decent work conditions and advancing sustainable development goals.

The International Co-Operative Alliance (ICA) says, "Around one billion co-operative memberships exist across the world today, which is about three times the number of individual shareholders in share market-traded companies and from the 1. 4 million co-operatives in operation across the world, more than 3 billion jobs are created."

The highest score was found in Brazil, which achieved a CVS (Co-operative Values Score) of 2.19. Norway followed (2.06), then Uruguay (2.02) and Canada (1.93). Spain, Finland, Argentina, Iceland, France and Great Britain are among the top ten.

3. The Necessity of Co-Operative Systems

The socio-economic, political, psychological and gender impacts can be devastating when crisis and disaster strikes. Unfortunately such events seem to be becoming more widespread in many parts of world today. The first reaction in such situation is to call upon external expertise and frequently in many countries this is the only feasible immediate response. However, in most situations, the local population, particularly those at the lower end of the socio-economic scale, are left to cope with tremendous problems evolved. It is often only when self-help and mutual aid approaches are adopted, sustainable solutions for recovery can be found. In these circumstances it is important to properly identify where, when and how Co-operations could be most usefully encouraged and supported to contribute to the crisis management and recovery process.

4. Trusteeship (example: ABC Church Co-operative Trust)

Trusteeship is a socio-economic philosophy that was propounded by Mahatma Gandhi. It provides a means by which the wealthy people would be the trustees of trusts that looked after the welfare of the people in general. This concept was condemned by socialists as being in favour of the landlords, feudal princes and the capitalists, opposed to socialist theories. Gandhi believed that the wealthy people could be persuaded to part with their wealth to help the poor. Putting it in Gandhiji's words "Supposing I have come by a fair amount of wealth – either by way of legacy, or by means of trade and industry – I must know that all that wealth does not belong to me; what belongs to me is the right to an honourable livelihood enjoyed by millions of others".

5. Initiating "*Trusts*", which are under the church, stake holding and beneficiary of the parish members

This explains that the benefits are directly paid to the stakeholders, which are the parish members / church community. The church can have "*Trusts*" formulated by its members as stakeholders and beneficiaries maintaining transparent transactions.

The result of this exercise will be financial improvement or empowerment of the community and promoting overall quality of living.

Production units, Service units, Education and Health care systems are some of the projects which can have under these "*Trusts*".

Principles of any co-operative trust are the following

- Open and Voluntary Membership
- Democratic Member Control
- Member's Economic Participation
- Autonomy and Independence
- Education, Training, and Information

- Co-operation Among Co-operatives
- Concern for Community

Its aim is to serve the interest of the poorer sections of society through the principle of self-help and mutual help. The main objective is to provide support to its members. The intention of joining a co-operative society is not to earn profit. However, on an economic level, co-operatives foster regional economic self-reliance and independence from outside control, empowering local people. They create employment, circulate money within the community, and offer a wide range of goods and services.

Some of the examples of the co-operative trusts with respect to our area of interest are elaborated below:

- Consumers Co-operative Society
- Producers Co-operative Society
- Workers Co-operative Society
- Co-operative Farming Society
- Shared Services Co-operative Society

1. Consumers Co-operative Society

These societies are formed by ordinary people for obtaining their day-to-day requirements of goods at cheaper rates. Consumers' co-operative stores are organized by such societies to meet the purpose. These societies make their purchases in bulk from wholesalers at wholesale rates and sell the goods to members (sometimes also to non-members) at market prices.

The difference is represented by the surplus which is distributed among the purchasing members in the form of a bonus on purchases. This is the oldest form of co-operative organization. In India, consumers co-operatives have received impetus from the Government attempts to check price rise of consumer goods and essential commodities.

Some areas of activities are shown below:

- Stores / Outlets
- Remote Distribution
- Home Delivery

2. Producers Co-operative Society

Also called industrial co-operatives, these societies are voluntary associations of small producers formed with the object of eliminating the capitalist class from the system of industrial production. Sometimes consumers' societies may join hands with the associations of producers.

The term ***"co-partnership societies"*** is used for such societies. These societies produce goods for meeting the requirements of consumers. Sometimes their production may be disposed of to outsiders at a profit and can be distributed among the producers after earmarking agreed percentages for welfare and general purposes.

Some areas of activities are:

- Renewable Energy Production
- Micro Solar Power Plants

3. Workers Co-operative Society

Workers co-operative is a co-operative that is owned and self-managed by its workers, a registered *society* within the significance of Co-operative Society. For example, **Indian Coffee House** is a restaurant chain in India, run by a series of workers co-operative societies. It has strong presence across India with nearly 400 coffee houses.

Some areas of activities are:

- Workers Welfare, Health & Safety
- Skill Training

5. Co-operative Farming Society

The co-operative farming societies are basically agricultural co-operatives formed with the object of achieving the benefits of large-scale farming and maximizing agricultural produce. Such societies are advocated for countries like India, where excessive fragmentation and sub-division of agricultural and farming land has happened. Societies are expected to prioritize the necessity between the food crops and cash crops. Food crops are essential for the very existence. Unfortunately in Kerala, we fail to organize such farming communities. We tend to depend on other people to cultivate the food crop and feed us. The crop choices of farmers in Kerala nowadays are mainly focused on Cash Crops – primarily Rubber Plantation. Considering the present day reality of Kerala State, once produced coconut, banana, rice, vegetables, cashew nut and spices for own use and to export, today not producing same but rather depends on the truck loads arriving from other states, which are not entirely safe for consumption. How did we arrive to this situation? Self-centred and less organized cultivation, resulting in the diminution of the wellbeing of humans, animals and the natural ecosystem inherited over the centuries. Initiatives should be enforced to reconstruct a well-balanced natural environment. Farming groups have to be organized to practice disciplined methods adopted to address this issue.

Some areas of activities are:

- Fish farms – aqua-phonics, hydro-phonics
- Poultry farms
- Dairy farms
- Vegetable garden for every household
- Coconut Plantation Restoration

5. Shared Services Co-operative Society

These societies are meant to provide services from outside to the communities which are deprived of modern technical know-how. Well organized professional teams can be very useful for building up service units for the maintenance of equipment within the community level.

Some areas of activities are:

- Technical support & maintenance - IT based instruments, mechanical, plumbing & electrical, automotive, construction.
- Health Care support system - child care, health care clinics, and funeral services
- Recycling Units

Amul (India), is an Indian dairy co-operative society, based at Anand in the Indian State of Gujarat. Formed in 1946, it is a co-operative brand managed by a co-operative body, the *Gujarat Co-operative Milk Marketing Federation Ltd.* (GCMMF), which today is jointly owned by 36 lakh (3.6 million) milk producers in Gujarat. Amul spurred India's White Revolution, which made the country the world's largest producer of milk and milk products. Amul co-operative was registered on 19 December 1946 as a response to the exploitation of marginal milk producers by traders and agents in small cities.

Angered by the unfair trade practices of those days, the farmers approached Sardar Vallabhbhai Patel under the leadership of local farmer leader Tribhuvandas K. Patel. He advised them to form a co-operative (Kaira District Co-operative Milk Producers' Union) and supply milk directly to the Bombay Milk Scheme instead of Polson brand (who did the same but gave them low prices). He sent Morarji Desai to organize the farmers. In 1946, the milk farmers of the area went on a strike which led to the setting up of the co-operative to collect and process milk. Milk collection was decentralized, as most producers were marginal farmers who could deliver, at most, 1–2 litres of milk per day. Co-operatives were formed for each village, too. By June 1948, the DCMPUL had started pasteurizing milk for the 'Bombay Milk Scheme'. The co-operative was further developed and managed by Dr Varghese Kurian with H.M. Dalaya. Dalaya's innovation of making kim milk powder from buffalo milk (for the first time in the world) and a little later, with Kurian's help, making it on a commercial scale, led to the first modern dairy of the co-operative at Anand, which would compete against established players in the market.

The GCMMF is the largest organization of food products marketing of India. It is the apex organization of the dairy co-operatives of Gujarat. It is the exclusive marketing organization for products under the brand name of Amul and Sagar. Over the last five and a half decades, dairy co-operatives in Gujarat have created an economic network that links more than 31 lakh (3.1 million) village milk products with crores of consumers in India.

Example of Shared Services Co-operative Societies

SEWA (India) – The "Shri Gitanjali Mahila SEWA Industrial Stationary Producers Co-operatives Ltd" is an Indian co-operative established in 1995 and involved in the manufacturing of various paper products made from recycled waste paper. The objectives of the co-operative are to reduce and recycle waste, to provide an alternate livelihood and to teach new skills to waste pickers who are members. The waste pickers are mostly women, who pick out recyclable materials from mixed waste to create hand crafted products. Among the products of the co-operative there is a wide range of paper products made from the waste materials such as notebooks, diaries, pens, paper bags and innovative jewelry. Workers not only play a vital role in the society by keeping the surroundings clean and tidy, but they also earn an income for their families. The co-operative is promoted by SEWA, Self-Employment Women's Association, also a co-operative group, involved in the organization of waste-pickers' work since its creation in 1972.

Examples of Producers Co-operative Societies

Ecopower cvba (Belgium): As peak, oil becomes a favourite topic and energy prices continue to rise, renewable energy is on the minds of governments, businesses and citizens. The Ecopower co-operative has brought back co-operative values into Belgium and is a blueprint for new co-operative development. Ecopower functions by collecting funds from members which are used to develop renewable energy sources. The key to this co-operative is giving members both a personal stake and a share in sustainable energy sources.

Ecopower cvba was founded in 1992 as a co-operative under Belgian law. The organization has three main goals:

(1) To invest in renewable energy

(2) To supply 100% green electricity to co-operative members

(3) To promote a rational use of energy, renewable energy and the co-operative business model in general.

By the end of 2013, Ecopower was a co-operative with 48004 co-operative members, 197017 shares and 40818 customers. Ecopower has private equity (capital) of 48.5 million euro and a balance total (assets) of 66.8 million euro. The annual turnover in 2014 was 31 million euro which resulted in a net profit of 1.7 million euro.

Coconut Producers Society, CPS(India)

The Coconut Development Board initiated the formation of Coconut Producer Organizations with an objective of uplifting the socio economic status of the coconut farmers. These organizations have a three-tier structure and comprises of Coconut Producer Societies (CPS), Coconut Producer Federations (CPF) and Coconut Producer Companies (CPC) and it ensures maximum participation from coconut cultivators.

Coconut Producer Societies are a non-subsidized knowledge based, farmer centred approach of organizing farmers which aims in socio-economic upliftment through productivity improvement, cost reduction, efficient collective marketing and processing, and product diversification.

The largest group of cultivators in Indian agriculture are small and marginal farmers and 85% of operated holdings are smaller than or about two hectares and amongst these holdings, 66% are less than one hectare. The small farmers' organizations such as co-operatives are expected to enhance incomes, reduce costs of input purchases along with transaction costs, create opportunities for involvement in value addition including processing, distribution and marketing, enhance bargaining power and provide an access to formal credit. Thus organizing farmers is the key to overcome so many challenges that farmers are going through.

Working Model of a Co-operative Farming Society

Aquaponics Farming

Kerala is known for its abundant natural resources, especially water. The State has 44 rivers, 27 backwaters (mostly in the form of lakes and ocean inlets), 7 lagoons, 18681 ponds and over 30 lakh wells. From an area of 38,863sq. km an approximately 10% (3610 sq. km) is low land area which is only up to 7m elevation from MSL (mean sea level). This region is characterized by marine landforms consisting of beach ridges and beaches with swamps and lagoons. The low land region is well known for its backwaters with extensive rice fields and coconut plantations.

From the above facts, it is clear that Kerala State has favourable condition to choose aquaponics as the best model for Co-operative Farming Society.

Aquaponics is a form of agriculture that combines raising fish in tanks (recirculating aquaculture) with soil-less plant culture (hydroponics). In aquaponics, the nutrient-rich water from raising fish provides a natural fertilizer for the plants and in return, the plants help to purify the water for the fish.

Aquaponics uses 90% less water than traditional farming. With this system, we can grow any time of year, in any weather, anywhere on the planet. Because aquaponics recycles the water in the system, we can grow in droughts and areas with little water. Less pests to deal with and being a closed system it does not pollute any river water. This is more environment-friendly than organic farming as it does not allow us to practice any harmful farming.

Conclusion

To sum up and to conclude the subject, a very strong recommendation to promote the "co-operation" culture amongst the community is of greatest significance. With the collective co-operation of individuals in farming creates better financial security, concern for the fellow beings & Nature, cleaner environment, etc. can be achieved upholding the values of ***tyagarchana*** spirituality.

The word *tyagarchana* is constituted by two Hindi / Sanskrit words - *tyaga* and *archana.Tyaga* means conscious and willing self-sacrifice. *Archana* means love-offering made to God with faith and devotion for the common good of humanity. Hence, the term *tyagarchana* can be defined as "*conscious and willing self-sacrifice lovingly offered to God with faith and devotion for the common good of humanity*".

Co-operative Farming Societies play their *tyaga* part by sacrificing effort, time and wealth. The *archana* part is exercised by offering the produce for the benefit of the needy. *This is the perfect guideline for any Co-operative System, where tyaga and archana are well ingrained.*

Luke 6: 38 -*"Give, and it will be given to you. A good measure, pressed down, shaken together and running over, will be poured into your lap. For with the measure you use, it will be measured to you."*

Here Sadguru Jesus Christ is informing people about the archana part of **tyagarchana.**

The foundation for any Co-operative System is the contribution which is archana in our terms. For any co-operative movement to initialize, contributions in terms of money, time, activity and thought process are very much required.

Bringing forth the pure form of food for human consumption, through compassion and affection towards Nature and other living beings is indeed true spiritual expression.

Church, playing a pivotal role in the crisis situation, can organize and initiate "***Trusts***" as the launch-pad for the co-operative societies like vegetable farming, aquaponics farming etc. The Church or its parish can take up this *Co-operative Society* scheme as a challenge, fulfilling the needs of the impoverished society. The revenue generated can be utilized for the enhancement of its co-operative movement, i.e. welfare of its stakeholders, rather than constructing extravagant building assets. The ultimate goal is to maintain sustainability for better living and to protect the Mother Nature from all exploitations through real ***"Co-Operation".***

Proverbs 11: 24 - 25 - *"One person gives freely, yet gains even more; another withholds unduly, but comes to poverty. A generous person will prosper; whoever refreshes others will be refreshed."*

---

* **Josil Mathai** is an Engineer by profession. He has voluntarily retired after serving as Offshore Survey Data Center Manager from Fugro, headquartered in The Netherlands. He has worked for and with Fugro/Reliance Industries/ONGC and Genesys International Corporation. He has been in Singapore, Malaysia, UAE, South Africa, Angola and the UK, carrying out Offshore Geological & Environmental Studies for Oil & Gas Industry, Offshore Construction & Engineering Projects. Presently he is involved in **Aquaponics farming and sustainable development initiatives in his native village near Thiruvalla.**

16

Psycho-spiritual Health Perspectives in the Post-COVID 19 Era

*Sadhak Dr A Rajkumar Bharat, MD**

As we enter the post-covid 19 era, it becomes inevitable and incumbent upon every individual to take care of one's own health and healing. There are many ways to getting and keeping a good health. Apart from scores of hundreds of scientific findings, we have thousands of ideas on the Google including Youtube. We are either skeptical, brousy or even ignorant of this. The most important fact is that nearly 75% of the diseases we see are due to our inappropriate ways in which we take our life, our mindset leading to bad eating habits, lack of minimal physical activity, sleep, rest and relaxation. From the studies in placebo effect 56% of healing comes from psychosomatic ability. Finally coming to energy, medicine, and spontaneous remission, the sky is the limit. The energy aspect is essentially spiritual one. Thousands of instances have been recorded and being studied of spontaneous remission and back from death remission. In short, I dare to say that your health can be brought back and kept well by keeping your energies resonating with the healing energies of Nature and universe.

The Paradise Lost

From time immemorial we had GPS. What I mean is not 'global positioning system' but what I call as 'God positioning system' by which human beings got the guidance from unknown essence of the universe, GOD. According to Dr Bruce Lipton there is clear evidence that there is biology, a healing biology behind a good and appropriate belief system that we carry around. The scientific and technological advancements have taken us to very great heights of material comforts but unfortunately it has broken our age-old connection to the cosmic conscience which had kept us from destroying ourselves and our environment. Science and technology in the hands of leadership and the common man who are incompetent, materialistic and selfish means disaster. And that is what we do see now. Global disaster Covid-19 has shown that with global lockdown the Nature started healing. The smoky fog formed by the smoke from automobiles and factories stopped and once again the sky cleared. People could see the Himalayas once again like it was 200 years back. The satellite studies showed that ozone holes healed. It is clearly evident that we the human beings have spoiled not only our environment but also our health.

Coming to health, let us see what is happening now. The global health care system started after the formation of UNO and consequent WHO has become nothing less than a health scare system in the hands of deep state. Though we call modern medicine evidence-based scientific medical practice, an unbiased deeper study will reveal that it has deviated away from its objectives. According to true researchers in medicine like Dr Marcia Angles, Dr Judy Micovich, Dr BM Hegde etc., medical science is in a total mess since it began piggyback on the natural sciences. It is still deep into conventional laws of deterministic predictability, even though it deals with a dynamic human system that does not follow those rules for even a second. Therefore, we have been predicting the unpredictable future of hapless patients and making life miserable for them. IOM report in the US has shown that doctors and hospitals are the third most important cause of death. This was the position in 2000. Dr BM Hegde in his book "What Doctors Don't Get to Study in Medical School" in chapter 41, brings home the fact how we are in a state of scientific superstition. He meticulously demonstrates how the scientific methods we follow like risk factor hypothesis, use of statistics, randomised controlled studies, blind extrapolation are defective added to the research fraud by the drug company sponsored research. Dr Shiva Aiyyadurai has with the help of contemporary media locked horns with what he calls "the deep state", behind the scene lobby (could be called mafia) that influence and manipulate world Governments. According to his definition **deep** state are groups that work secretly in order to protect their particular interests and to rule the country or the world without being elected. So it is very clear that our health care system is highly defective and needs a total revamping. So in public and individual health too the picture is "**paradise lost**".

A Look at the Real Solution to the Problem

Human beings are a part of the Nature and the universe itself. Our body is a self-developing, self-correcting and self- maintaining system. The lenier medical science we follow is inadequate to understand and rectify a closed – loop system that our body-mind complexis. Apart from this, it is also influenced and supported by electromagnetic fields produced within and from outside our body. Our present understanding is that the human body is a bundle of vibrating leptons, which are held in 50 to 100 trillion individual body cells. The reality is that human body is a colony of 50 to 100 trillion living cells that are descendants of individual beings which lived as independent living organisms for millions of years before coming together as a colony. Each cell has its own mind (in the cell wall) and is capable of all basic activities that the whole body is capable of.

Bio-photon camera of physicist Fritz Albert Popp can now track the photon light emission from each atom in the human cell. It can also deduct whether they are in sync. If they are in sync, then the body is healthy. If not in sync the body is heading for illness. It looks as if our cells love each other so much that they work for our common good. If for any reason we hate another person, the cells get confused with that "me-you" concept. This hatred (or greed, jealousy, anger, hyper- ego etc.) might sow the seeds of a new malady in our system. Every single disease from common cold to cancer will have its root cause here. From then on individual disease chart their own course based on environmental circumstances and/or metagenetic makeup. Dr BM Hegde calls this aetiopathogenisis as "socio-autoimmune" aetiology of many diseases we see now. From this we may come to conclusion that our bodily diseases have an origin in mind and the mind should be controlled by the spirit as our ancestors said in Ayurveda.

In the present context (quote Max Planck who wrote that the "consciousness is fundamental" - all matter is derived from consciousness), we cannot get behind consciousness. Consciousness is universal wisdom of which human mind is but a small fragment. "What we understand is that our functional conscious and subconscious mind are connected to our super conscious mind which carries metempsychotic information. This super conscience is connected to the cosmic conscience which has the metadata of all the living and non- living beings. Here comes my metaphor of GPS (God Positioning Systems). The Cosmic Conscience, which I mentioned before, is what we used to call God, the generator, operator and destroyer. To get and keep good health to ourselves and others we need to get connected to the Cosmic Conscience through our individual super-conscience. How is this possible? The way is through your own search and the support of an enlightened guide, whom we used to call "guru", a spiritual mentor, who can guide you to your self- realisation.

I found in Acharyasri (Swami Sachidananda Bharathi) such a Karana-guru, who could practically guide me to my own mission here on earth and also bring back my health.

Swmiji's guidance is complete and holistic. It covers physiological, psychological, social and spiritual aspects of health and wellbeing. It is appropriate for the current global scenario. It is simple and practical. Any changes in the world should start with individual self and the best time is now and it should be simple. I have personally reaped the fruits of inner peace meditation and Tyagarchana. My transformation from a crippled doctor of medicine who was disillusioned and physically handicapped (due to a vascular necrosis of my left hip and failed THR leading to destruction of 1/3rd of my thigh bone) to a social catalyst sitting on wheelchair most unexpectedly helping dozens of destitute mothers with female children to get their safe homes and many more to get free treatment, happened in a time span of nine years. Added to this is another miraculous event of a three-staged hip reconstruction surgery from a leading team of doctors from AJRI. In short, now I am walking without the help of crutches.

The Promise of Wellbeing and Reversing Your Disease: "New Creation Movement"

It is when I changed myself from 'run-on the mill' repetitive loyalty to medical science, to creative fidelity of the reality of health and healing (through the guidance of Swamiji) that I started becoming a different person, a paradigm shift in thinking and being. From treating people for disease to healing them and of course myself.

Now I come to understand that our body has the capacity to heal itself even from the most hopeless diseases and even death. This is based on observation and recordings from thousands of cases in what we call as spontaneous remission and NDE(near death experience), provided that we give the right input to our body – mind complex. Let us look at these inputs:

Mind: Mind needs to be kept in appropriate way that it is not having hostile feelings towards others or engaged in emotions that lead to illness. It is also important that it should be directed towards your super conscience which means positive thinking, acceptance of others' limitations, 'I am ok - you are ok' attitude, developing higher emotional competence, assertive behavior, and finally meditation and devotion to the higher being.

Food: Food and nutrition is found to be very important factor in healing disease and keeping good health. There are scores of hundreds of research papers to support this. There are many doctors, who are treating diabetes and heart diseases by food alone. Plant-based diet is seen to be the best in healing and keeping good health.

Minimal Physical Activity: Our body is a dynamic machinery of nature and it has to be worked upon on a regular basis. If any of its myriads of working parts are kept idle for sufficiently long time, it leads to illness. Mayo Clinic recommends a minimum of 5 days in a week, 30 minutes a day, aerobic activity like brisk walk or running with 5 minutes of flexibility warm ups before and 5 minutes of relaxation after the exercises as minimal physical activities to keep our body in good condition.

Rest and Relaxation: Like any other machines, our body too needs overhauling and repairing. The only difference is that it is done on a regular basis. Sleep is number one. We need to sleep at least 4 to 6 hours in the night for proper repair of our body. Relaxing oneself in-between continuous physical as well as mental activities is also needed to support wellness.

Putting all the above factors into proper practice will help to keep away the doctor and huge medical bill which is imperative and difficult in the coming months of Post-COVID era.

We are planning to bring out a guiding manual for healing and health for the Post-COVID 19 period, and also an action plan to keep people hale and healthy. This will be a more detailed guide book supported by direct training programmes.

Let us join hands to bring up healthy, responsible citizens and committed leaders.

NB: My paper is based on scientific scholarly works of sincere doctors and researchers in the field of medicine and psychology of which some are contemporary.

---

* **Sadhak Dr A Rajkumar Bharat, MD,** is a medical doctor, psychologist, hypnotherapist, & counselor. Worked with WHO through its Charter FAMS India. Campus Doctor, HCE- Chennai. M O for Tsunami Bheema Yojana-Chennai. Fellowship: Kerala Hypnotists' Association, Life time Member : Kerala Counselors Forum & Foundation for Applied Medical Sciences India; FAMS Award winner for his work in Alternative Medicine; Winner of many Commendation Letters from Government as well as NGOs for services to humanity.

17

Rethinking the 'Way of Being the Church' in the Post-COVID 19 Times

Revd Dr Prem Antony, IMS *

Introduction

Covid-19 has unmistakably taught us that the entire world is one little place, and that what affects one somehow necessarily affects everyone else, too. Being the great leveller that it has turned out to be, it has simply shown us that none of us is invulnerable. Positively, it has taught us that our being is actually inter-being and the fundamental dynamics of our existence is our in-depth interrelatedness.

The one Bible verse that comes to my mind when I think of the current pandemic is Lk. 17.27 that says, "They ate, they drank, they married, they were given in marriage, until the day when Noah entered the ark, and the flood came and destroyed them all." A scriptural reflection is never complete without taking care to understand the social meaning of the scriptures or what is traditionally termed 'the world in front' of the gospel. The world in front of this particular gospel passage is the way we have lived so far, unmindful of our required spiritual orientation and our fundamental interconnectedness as human beings, created in the image and likeness of God. Life seemed so normal and regular to most of us until the tsunami of this virus hit us all out of the blue, and so hard. No one seemed prepared and powerful governments were thrown off their guard, not knowing what to do and how to protect "their" citizens.

1. The Old Normal

The "old normal" had its own characteristics. When life becomes a routine, everything gets taken for granted. Nearly all of us lived our lives, thinking mostly about ourselves and our needs. We defined our happiness merely in terms of ourselves. It was a make-believe world. All that came crushing down with the arrival of Corona Virus Disease - 2019. Let's have a brief look at what we have been through and what we are facing now.

The latest reports from the United Nations Development Programme ranks India 131 in global standards of living (HDI). This should first make us sit up and think if we can together rise up as a political nation from parochialism of every kind to a true universalist thinking and the resultant focused action that should be otherwise typical of the Indian polity, '*sarvebhavantusukhinah, sarvesantuniramaayah*' (may all be happy (&) may all be healthy). The foundation of this aspiration is linked to the real identity of Indian consciousness, which is defined by our time-tested philosophy of '*Vasudhaivakutumbakam*' as found in the earliest of our Vedas. The much talked about composite culture of India, epitomised for the modern Indians in the phrase, *Ganga-Jamuni Tehzeeb*, encapsulates that distinctive culture which is open, syncretic and deeply spiritual.[1]

One very important reason why we have failed to develop as a nation and continue to remain so is the division based on our different religious experiences. This magnificent land holds a variety of rich religious experiences close to its chest. These were meant to help us become aware of our final destiny, and in a way, our in-depth interrelatedness. However, these experiences have become a cause of disharmony, and I am afraid to say that perhaps we have also contributed our mite towards the current situation of religious hate and the related socio-political turbulences that continue to create fear, isolation and even, terror. Christians in this context are called to be the salt of the earth, the light of the world and agents of Christ's peace. How do we become that we are called to become? Primarily, we need to become aware of how we have become part of the problem and then, how we can become a solution!

2. Christ, Our Common Ground

My focus in this short paper is to understand what Christians as a committed group of citizens could contribute to the building of the nation in the Post-COVID era and how we can grow up together as a body of faithful. Any decent proposal has to be placed within a theoretical framework and Post-COVID, it has to be based also on the experiential knowledge of having lived through the Covid era. Since we live in a multi-religious environment, I would advocate a Christocentric framework, rather than an ecclesio-centric one, within which we could set the context of our life and ministry. If Christocentric, it has to be open and inclusive because Christ is not the patrimony of Christians alone; he belongs to all.

The Christ of my faith is the Christ of my personal experience. One of the important issues connected to our "proclamation" of Christ is our sense of triumphalism. It is true with the members of mainline Churches, and especially with some others as well, the idea that my God or my God experience is superior to that of the others. It is this sort of arrogance of the superiority of religion that works as the stumbling block to the others from coming to acknowledge the Christ. None of us has the right to own God. God just belongs to everyone. What is unique to us is the *experience* that we have of Godhood in Christ, an experience that humbles and transforms us from inside out. It is this experience that humbled Saul, bringing him down from the seat of authority and blinding him to gradually experience the real light of Christ upon being prayed over by someone he would not have otherwise accepted. This experience of Saul made Paul truly humble in every way. And he began not to proclaim it, but lovingly and ardently share about it. It is this experience, if at all one has it, that needs to be lived, and thus shared, and not 'proclaimed'.

What therefore makes our proclamation jarring, unpleasant and even disagreeable, is our inflated religious ego with its colonial mindset of looking at everything local as base and unacceptable. What rather needs be done is a non-judgmental appreciation of other experiences while having the inner freedom to share the riches of our experience of Christ, *if at all we have one*. It is after having met, stayed and experienced Jesus from close quarters that Andrew went to Peter and 'shared' his experience with him, saying "we have found the Messiah" (Jn. 1.41). Sharing of experience is something friendly and fraternal, bereft of any one-upmanship, and therefore acceptable to everyone. Such a sharing can be more concretely expressed in a lived-dialogue with those of other faith traditions by active civil society engagements, specifically as Christian citizens. What would then qualify our engagement is not the desire for numbers or inflating our religious ego, but positive engagement with the wider sections of the society as a concerned citizen, and more specifically as a Christian. It is then that we will be found "blameless and innocent, children of God without blemish in the midst of a crooked and perverse generation," so that we "shine like stars in the world" (Phil. 2. 15).

As Christians, therefore, the categorical imperative that should rule our moral and ethical realms must be to share the message of Christ by just living it in a country like ours where there are several faith traditions within which many have lived saintly lives to the joy of many. The most important of all the experiences that we have had in the Covid era is that of global vulnerability. Rich or poor, American or Uruguayan, Christian or Hindu, we are all susceptible to sickness and death. We did also learn that we are closely interconnected and that this interconnectedness is more important than any personal identities that separate and divide us as belonging to a specific race, religion or *rashtra*. I believe this is the concept that should emerge as our solid conviction, and which we should hand over to the growing up generation as the basis for the creation of a 'new normal'. All our further activities and programmes need to reaffirm this recognition that Covid-19 has unmistakably taught us. And learning from our experiences, we need to intelligently respond and adapt to the emergent situation, which alone will ensure a local and global transformation. In fact, it is this hard learnt lesson that Pope Francis has so beautifully visualized in his latest work, *Let Us Dream*.

3. The Question of the Existence of God

One of the important issues that religious heads had to deal with was 'the distantness of God'. The one question that many atheists hurled at the believers is, 'Where is your God,' especially when you needed him the most? Why has your God allowed this to happen to you? The question may sound funny or silly, but it is of great import to both the believer and the unbeliever alike, especially since religion has a strong influence on our perspectives and behavioural patterns. Where is God and why is he so distant? Why does God allow such things?

For us Christians, God is not an absentee landlord but a personal God who listens and responds to our prayers. And yet, often we are not able to understand the ways of God. This does not mean that God does not exist. Just because the sun does not shine always, it cannot be said that it does not exist! God can use everything for purposes difficult for us mortals to comprehend. This pandemic has in fact increased faith in God for many, and has increased the quality of family life according to researches. So, it depends what we want to make out of situations such as this. And the best thing is not to blame God!

One of the things believers will do well to avoid is to think that God is punishing everyone through this pandemic. God cannot be seen through such 'human prisms'. Our God is a loving Father, and not a punishing God though he might chasten. In the context of this pandemic, what we can best do as part of our very private spiritual response is to go through a personal process of purification and get ourselves more attuned to God according to the beliefs of our faith practices and become more helpful to those in need of our assistance. Yet another very important thing to be taken care of is to become more sensitive to Nature that does not need us, whereas we need it to survive.

What we as Christians, therefore, need to do is to rise beyond any religion-enthused feeling of 'being better' and to shed any direct or indirect desire for any increase in numbers as a reason for our active involvement with the civil society and share our faith by life witness in collaboration with others. Below given are certain possible practical ways by which we can contribute to the regeneration of our society and the Church.

4. Strengthening the Idea of Our Ecclesial and Social Co-responsibility

As individual Churches we have done and shone a lot during these difficult times, but probably as a Christian community we have failed equally. Help to those in need is not an act of charity, but a serious and unavoidable responsibility for us Christians. There are two issues involved here. The first is that we have tried doing many things, and successfully so, as individual Churches. But we have been lacking despondently in common, focused action, especially in matters vis-à-vis social responsibility. This is a matter of serious concern that the Christian Churches should take note of and immediately work towards a solution as well. As a matter of immediate priority, we need to learn to collaborate and team up with one another for positive social involvement because that is the call of the hour.

Secondly, it might be easier to work during a time of emergency as many well-meaning people would join us for a 'relief mode' of action. Church groups did a marvellous job in reaching out to the needy in numerous ways and to thousands of people. We could mobilise resources and personnel for a very commendable relief work. But such interventions can only be short lived as most people get tired of giving voluntary services, which are quick responses to urgent situations. But this needs to be made a regular way of life. Our country needs a Christian ethics of caring for the least today more than ever.

The one thing that has been brought home in a very realistic manner is the way the poor suffer and the way they are taken for granted by our governments and other institutions. The necessary response is not merely to reach out to them in charity but help create systems that will educate the people and challenge unjust structures. In this context, it is an imperative that we think of institutional ways, novel and purposeful, and beyond the relief mode, in constant collaboration and dialogue with various stakeholders, to help those sections of the society to stay afloat.

5. Strengthening Neighbourhood Communities

One takeaway from our Covid experience is 'missing our neighbours and visits by friends'. In the light of our renewed understanding of our being as inter-being and our lives as deeply interdependent, we need to institutionalise informal regular gathering of neighbours so that we remain connected and available to one another. We could think of having informal 'neighbourhood communes' and regular gatherings on various socio-religious occasions and birthdays. It can also be for very focused actions like 'blood donors' group, etc. Such communes could take care of the elderly and the disadvantaged or/ and even adopt disadvantaged groups and communities. If these groups are strong, such concerned groups can ensure the better functioning of public facilities like PDS, PHCs, etc. as well.

Certain gated communities during the pandemic helped themselves by sourcing quality food items like vegetables directly from farmers, thus doing away with middle men and helping farmers greatly. These are mere tips of ways we can strengthen neighbourhood communities.

6. Care for the Others, Especially the Elderly and Those in Need

One of the things that we learnt and practised during this pandemic was caring for others. When we decided about measures of social distancing, or when we thought of washing our hands or leaving our cloths outside before entering home, we were all moved by the desire to protect others; it was a societal gesture of owning up responsibility towards one another. This gesture, and more so, the moving spirit behind it, needs to be strengthened and reinforced. We cannot any more afford to be Cains. It has dawned on us that we need to be each other's caretakers. This is also part of the practical interpretation of the Pauline description, Rom. 12.5, wherein he says that"we, though many, are one body in Christ, and individually members one of another".

7. Caring for Those who Cared and Continue to Care for Us

There are persons we remember only when we come to need them. The service personnel of the society like the police, the health workers, those in uniform, etc. do need to be shown respect for what they have been doing for us. We know how, for example, how the Americans treat their men in uniform. The respect shown to them in public spaces is worth emulating. One way to do it is to ensure them decent payment. Reserving them seats in public places, giving them preference wherever possible and ensuring that they are respected and cared for in turn are ways to show them the gratitude of the society. In fact, respect for every profession is something we need to inculcate in ourselves and in our younger generation as an outstanding value.

8. Care for Nature

Care for Nature has almost become a jargon, and therefore, even jarring. However, this point can never be over-emphasized because our very life depends on it. Although the Paris Agreement talked about limiting global warming to 1.5 degree Celsius compared to pre-industrial levels, scientists now say it will have risen to at least 3 degree Celsius by the end of the century. Although many countries have set carbon neutrality targets, not much seems to be happening. As a faith body, we cannot afford to look the other side but help find scientific and other creative ways to give back to Nature from which we kept taking to satiate our greed. I think we need to proclaim a Jubilee Period or a Sabbath period for Mother Nature. We have overused and abused Nature for long in various ways. Turning vegetarian will be one important way of respecting Nature and let things live. It may sound utopian a value, and yet many are progressively recognizing the value of going green.

9. The Necessity to Contribute

One realisation that has dawned on us during this time is also concerning financial interdependence in the Church. The widow's mite makes a lot of sense now than ever. The little offerings of the not-so-well-to-do and the generous offerings of those who can afford, matter a lot for everyone within the Church. As someone said, when God blesses us financially, what we need to do is not to raise our standard of living, but our standard of giving. That will be the real gift of gratitude to God, the giver of all blessings. We will need to give back by different ways, by adopting individuals or families or communities to systematically help them and join us on our journey.

10. Developing a Different Style of Leadership

One of the areas where we seem to have definitely failed is in taking leadership when required. Although various organisations of the Church have done commendable services during the pandemic, the vast majority of the priests and religious of at least the Catholic Church stayed indoors, cutting themselves off in a cocoon from the people who needed them then the most. This was in complete contravention to the principles of self-sacrifice and service we so proudly and publicly profess. If the men and women in uniform deployed on the borders could risk their lives in very adverse circumstances for our protection, if the health workers could jeopardise their lives for our wellbeing, then how much more are we supposed to gladly put ourselves in service of the needy in times such as this? The way we behave and the way our leadership shines in times of actual need tests our mettle and our proclaimed 'commitment' to our mission.

One of the important characteristics the Post-COVID Church should experience is humility of leadership, a leadership that trusts more in the power and strength of the Lord and less on herself/himself, coming once again from an in-depth awareness of the momentariness and fragility of life and also becoming aware of the helplessness we faced together. This awareness should lead us to harness the power of decision making in communities, whenever possible by consensus, by thrashing out issues together in 'the spirit of give and take,' with the spiritual capacity to let go and let God.

11. Living a Life of Dialogue in Action

One of the things we are noticing increasingly is the tendency in many to become easily disappointed with life and become negative towards everything. Many even end up on the verge of suicide. In the context of all these, it is all the more necessary that we teach the younger generation more purposefully about the imperative to believe in God, irrespective of which religion we belong to. Those with a deeper spiritual grounding are better equipped, psychologically and otherwise, to deal with negative situations like the one we are yet going through. While many have a tendency to be negative and therefore could be more given to despair, most religiously oriented persons rather tend to pray and hope for the better. Although religion cannot be encouraged only for pragmatic reasons, pragmatism simply becomes an added reason for one to believe in a supernatural power that we call, 'God'.

Alongside, it has become more and more necessary to work together with members of different religions to make 'social work' not a paid job, but a way of life. The current pandemic has seen several instances that have increased the faith of the people in humanity. The Church needs to work to increase it. One solid way to do it is to make our social work the coordinated activity of all faith-based communities in our neighbourhood in different ways like by involving their religious leaders, having a mixed community of staff, getting donations from various faith-based groups, etc.

Conclusion

Covid-19 has been an eye-opener in so many ways, but it has taught us that we need to stay together. It has taught us that nobody is dispensable. Let us learn it well and begin our life ahead on a clean slate with a transformed attitude and approach.

---

* **Revd Dr Prem Antony,** IMS is a Catholic priest and a member of the Indian Missionary Society. He has a Doctorate from the Department of Public Administration, University of Madras, in Political Philosophy. He is presently teaching in Viswa Jyothi Gurukul, Varanasi.

Endnote

[1] Several concerned members of the Hindu community express reservations about this concept that is touted as expressive of true Indian syncretic culture, saying that it has always worked to the disadvantage of Hindus as the others have taken this as weakness of Hindus and have made inroads into their community to poach and convert people. This, whether true or not, needs to be looked and dialogued about as it remains a festering issue in the minds of many.

18

The Mission Ahead of the Christian Churches in Post-Pandemic India: A Gandhian Perspective

Bishop Lawrence Pius Dorairaj *

The COVID-19 pandemic has shattered the whole globe abruptly and unbelievably. Now a variant of the same has begun to shake the reviving spirit of humankind. The year 2020 was perhaps the worst-hit with lakhs and lakhs of COVID-19 deaths, lockdowns, economic recession, job losses, mental depression, migration of labourers, their starvation, many run over by trains, trucks and other vehicles. All these catastrophes have taught us many types of lessons. People are making attempts to reflect upon the lessons they can learn from the pandemic, each from one's own perspective, and for one's own betterment. Thus, for example, psychologists have come out with a variety of programmes for coping with stress, trauma and so on. The economists are busy with new methods of increasing GDP. The businessmen are anxious of learning new ways to increase their wealth despite the lockdown. The medical scientists are worried about finding out an efficient vaccine, and government authorities fretful on choosing the right types of vaccine, procuring them and distributing them. So far so good.

However, if one thinks that thereby one can get back to the pre-pandemic scenario, one is far from reality. Or, if one thinks that by learning the lesson to refine our approaches to immunity and improving the existing health care systems, we should be able to come out of the ill-effects of the pandemic, nothing will be more disastrous than that. It is impossible to deny that the pandemic has shaken the very foundations of modern life. It is of paramount importance, therefore, to review those false securities of modernity the pandemic exposed. Thus one needs to learn some fundamental lessons for human existence.

Against that backdrop, then, there is an imperative for the Christian Churches to redesign their mission in the post pandemic scenario, rather than repeating the same good old methods of mission, which was devised during the surge of modernity. It is indeed promising that Pope Francis has made a note of these foundational aspects of the global tragedy and has formulated them for the benefit of humanity. In his recent Encyclical letter *Fratelli Tutti,*[1] while depicting the dismal picture of the present day humanity, he also digs out the foundational jolts and shocks that the pandemic has given to humanity. This article deems it worthwhile to glean from this historic document those portions which are related to the pandemic and investigate the possible lessons Christianity may draw re-visioning its mission in the changed post-pandemic scenario.

The purview of our consideration in this article is the Indian context. As such then, it is heartening to see that Mahatma Gandhi had articulated the very same points that Pope Francis has drawn from the pandemic as the fundamental lessons to guide humanity. The points of critique that Gandhi made of modernity in general, and of the Christian mission in particular run almost parallel to the fundamental principles that Pope Francis has enunciated in this post-pandemic context. This only shows the perennial value of Gandhi's thoughts.

Perhaps Gandhi was too ahead of his times. People did not understand the importance of his profound thoughts, stated in simple words. Now that the supreme head of the Church has driven home the same truths, but as drawn from today's context of the pandemic, we are in a better position to appreciate the significance of Gandhi's perspective.

Here is a modest attempt to unravel the parallel concerns of the two great leaders for the relevance of Christian mission and draw from them some suggestions for re-considering the mission ahead of the Christian Churches in post-pandemic India. The first part of this article elicits the fundamental lessons that Pope Francis draws out in his historic document from the pandemic. The second part attempts to cull out the views of Mahatma Gandhi that run parallel to those lessons stated by Francis. The third and concluding part elucidates the applicability of each of those six lessons to the missionary context of post pandemic India in and through Gandhian insights. My fond hope is that they could be viewed as guidelines for the mission ahead of the Churches in the post pandemic scenario.

Part I
Fundamental Lessons from the Pandemic

Already in the third month of the pandemic, Pope Francis remarked in his prayer service that "the storm has exposed our vulnerability and uncovered those false and superfluous certainties ... Amid this storm, the façade of those stereotypes with which we camouflaged our egos, always worrying about appearances, has fallen away."[2] In the same vein, and elaborating this idea further, Francis draws out certain lessons to be learnt by humanity from the pandemic in his encyclical. While depicting the 'Dark Clouds' that hinder the development of universal fraternity of humankind, Francis considers also the Covid-19 pandemic, and identifies some six lessons that are fundamental to the sustenance of humanity. They are contained in five numbered paragraphs (FT 32-37). In them one may identify six specific ideas. They are spelt out in the form of six principle-like formulations here below.

1.1. One's Own Good Is Contained in the Common Good

The Covid-19 pandemic "has momentarily revived the sense that we are a global community, all in the same boat, where one person's problems are the problems of all" and hence "no one is saved alone; we can only be saved together.... Amid this storm, the façade of those stereotypes with which we camouflaged our egos has fallen away, revealing once more the ineluctable and blessed awareness that we are part of one another, that we are brothers and sisters of one another." (FT32)

1.2. Concern for Everyone Rather than the Benefit of a Few

The world was relentlessly moving towards an economy that, thanks to technological progress, sought to reduce "human costs"; there were those who would have had us believe that freedom of the market was sufficient to keep everything secure. Yet the brutal and unforeseen blow of this uncontrolled pandemic forced us to recover our concern for human beings, for everyone, rather than for the benefit of a few. (FT 33 a)

1.3. Rethink the Virtual Lifestyle and Plunge into the Real

Today we can recognize that "we fed ourselves on dreams of splendour and grandeur, and ended up consuming distraction, insularity and solitude. We gorged ourselves on networking, and lost the taste of fraternity. We looked for quick and safe results, only to find ourselves overwhelmed by impatience and anxiety. Prisoners of a virtual reality, we lost the taste and flavour of the truly real. The pain, uncertainty and fear, and the realization of our own limitations, brought on by the pandemic have only made it all the more urgent that we rethink our styles of life, our relationships, the organization of our societies and, above all, the meaning of our existence.(FT 33 b)

1.4. Recognize the Cosmic Unity

If everything is connected, it is hard to imagine that this global disaster is unrelated to our way of approaching reality, our claim to be absolute masters of our own lives and of all that exists. I do not want to speak of divine retribution, nor would it be sufficient to say that the harm we do to nature is itself the punishment for our offences. The world is itself crying out in rebellion. (FT 34)

1.5. Re-discover Interdependence of Human Society

Once this health crisis passes, our worst response would be to plunge even more deeply into feverish consumerism and new forms of egotistic self-preservation. God willing, after all this, we will think no longer in terms of "them" and "those", but only "us".... If only we might keep in mind all those elderly persons who died for lack of respirators, ... If only this immense sorrow may not prove useless, ... If only we might rediscover once for all that we need one another, and that in this way our human family can experience a rebirth, with all its faces, all its hands and all its voices, beyond the walls that we have erected. (FT 35)

1.6. Recover a Passion for Upholding Human Solidarity/ Fraternity

Unless we recover the shared passion to create a community of belonging and solidarity worthy of our time, our energy and our resources, the global illusion that misled us will collapse and leave many in the grip of anguish and emptiness. Nor should we naively refuse to recognize that "obsession with a consumerist lifestyle, above all when few people are capable of maintaining it, can only lead to violence and mutual destruction. The notion of "every man for himself" will rapidly degenerate into a free-for-all that would prove worse than any pandemic. (FT 36)

A perceptive reading of the above mentioned principles reveal that the first is nothing but enunciation of a most basic axiom of human life. The second and third are diagnostic in nature: the former indicating the ills of the economic development in general and the latter pointing to today's malaise of the virtual world, in particular. The next two principles are prognostic in approach: the third principle helps us to recognize the cosmic unity in general, the fourth urges us to rediscover interdependence of human society in particular. The final principle may be taken to be the overall concluding principle that we ought to put into practice in the post pandemic world: "Recover the shared passion to create a community of belonging and solidarity."

Part II

Gandhian Perspective Parallel to Francis'

It is amazing to observe that Mahatma Gandhi has voiced the same kind of concerns that run almost parallel to the six points of lessons that we have drawn from Pope Francis' historic document. So, in reference to each of the points mentioned above, we would like to cite the viewpoint of Gandhi in this section.

2.1. Gandhi's Doctrine of *Sarvodaya* (the welfare of all) runs in close parallel to the first point, mentioned in Part 1 above. After reading John Ruskin's book *Unto This Last,* Gandhi was so captivated by its "magical spell" that he translated it into Gujarati, entitling it *Sarvodaya.*[3] He gives a summary of the book in the form of three principles.[4]

1. That the good of the individual is contained in the good of all.
2. That a lawyer's work has the same value as the barber's in as much as all have the same right of earning their livelihood from their work.
3. That a life of labour, i.e., the life of the tiller of the soil and the handicraftsman is the life worth living.

Of these three principles, the first in Gandhi's estimate is the most important because the other two are implied in the first. To understand it better, one may think of an organic metaphor: circulation of blood in the body. Just as concentration of blood at any one spot of the body is harmful to the whole body, so the whole body must evenly be transmitting the circulation of blood. Thus the good (health) of any part of the body is contained in the good (health) of the whole body. Likewise, Gandhi conceives the good of an individual only in the context of the collective welfare of the society. There was a time when a microscopic minority enjoyed at the cost of a greater majority. Contrastingly the majority may want to be happy at the cost of the minority. The utilitarian principle supported the 'greatest good of the greatest number'. As against all these trends Gandhi argued that the suffering of the least and the lowest inevitably interacts with the alleged wellbeing of the most prosperous. So he held that the contributions of individuals to collective social welfare is not restricted to move beyond greed, but has to be engaged in service to universal welfare, nothing less. In other words, transformation of the whole society has to be realized such that it becomes possible for everyone to be happy in the happiness of all. The basis of sarvodaya is all-embracing love. A sarvodayist mind is trained to love all and aim at the welfare of all, though he may be able to serve but a few. The sarvodaya principle as envisioned by Gandhi was not restricted to economic, social or political realms alone. It is applicable to religious context too. How? We will try to spell it out in section 3 of this article.

2.2. In parallel to the second lesson above, Gandhi criticized modern market economy on the ground that it was not concerned about the whole humankind but only favours the welfare of few. The main plank of his attack was that it anchored on mass production, for, mass production not only takes no note of the real requirements of the consumer, but also it carries within it its own limitation. If all countries adopted the system of mass production, there would not be a big enough market for their products. Mass production must then come to a stop.[5]Another important defect of the market economy, according to Gandhi, was the exploitation of the sister nations by sister nations."[6] Hence he objected to it as immoral and sinful:

> I must confess that I do not draw a sharp line or any distinction between economics and ethics. Economics that hurt the moral wellbeing of an individual or a nation are immoral and, therefore sinful. Thus the economics that permits one country to prey upon another are immoral.[7]

As against mass production, therefore, Gandhi advocated 'production by masses' because it would never give scope for starvation among the masses as "we have to provide them with work which they can easily do in their desolate homes and which would give them at least the barest living". And they would have become self-reliant and be able to support themselves. Gandhi emphasised the rise of the least and the last (Antiyodaya). He was so concerned about feeding the hungry masses that he exclaimed:

> In India we have got millions of people having to be satisfied with one meal a day, and that meal consisting of a chapatti containing no fat in it, and a pinch of salt. You and I have no right to anything that we really have until these millions are clothed and fed better. You and I, who ought to know better, must adjust our wants and even undergo voluntary starvation in order that they may be nursed, fed and clothed.[8]

It is remarkable that Gandhi also upheld that the sufferings of the poor could not fully be alleviated by doling out charity to the poor, but only by providing them with employment.

> I must refuse to insult the naked by giving them clothes they do not need, instead of giving them work which they sorely need. I will not commit the sin of becoming their patron, but on learning that I had assisted in impoverishing them, I would give them neither crumbs nor cast-off clothing, but the best of my food and clothes and associate myself with them in work.[9]

Gandhi's concern for the *antyodaya* was so intense that all his actions were guided by the talisman which he gave through a letter to a friend who was tormented by doubts. The following is the text of the letter:

> I will give you a talisman. Whenever you are in doubt, or when the self becomes too much with you, try the following expedient: Recall the face of the poorest and the most helpless man whom you may have seen and ask yourself, if the step you contemplate is going to be of any use to *him*. Will he be able to gain anything by it? Will it restore him to a control over his

> own life and destiny? In other words, will it lead to Swaraj or self-rule for the hungry and also spiritually starved millions of our countrymen? Then you will find your doubts and yourself melting away.[10]

2.3. About the need to rethink the virtual living of contemporary times, Gandhi's insights on modern lifestyle are very profound and pertinent. Of course he could not have expressed his views directly on the virtual world, as there was no computer, internet etc., in his times. However, the strong criticism he made of technologism in general is applicable to the virtual world in particular. What is important to observe here is that Gandhi is challenging us to rethink our illusory lifestyle and thus stimulating us to plunge into 'the real' world. For him, "the supreme consideration was man. The machine (computer) should not tend to make atrophied the limbs of man."[11]

> What I object to, is the '**craze**' for machinery, not machinery as such. The craze is for what they call labour-saving machinery. Men go on 'saving labour' till thousands are without work and thrown on the open streets to die of starvation. I want to save time and labour, not for a fraction of mankind, but for all; I want the concentration of wealth, not in the hands of a few, but in the hands of all. Today machinery merely helps a few to ride on the back of millions. The impetus behind it all is not the philanthropy to save labour, but greed. It is against this constitution of things that I am fighting with all my might.[12]

Gandhi's preoccupation was how to make people grasp the fact that 'the West had a surfeit of industrialism and exploitation'. Hence he gave this timely warning:

> Let us not be deceived by catchwords and phrases. I have no quarrel with steamships or telegraphs. They may stay, if they can, without the support of industrialism and all it connotes. They are not an end.... They are in no way indispensable for the permanent welfare of the human race. Now that we know the use of steam and electricity, we should be able to use them on due occasion and after we have learnt to avoid industrialism.... Our concern is therefore to destroy industrialism.[13]

It is with that concern that Gandhi was asking people like Nehru who were keen on industrializing India to look at the real situation. He pointed out that industrialism depends entirely on three factors:

your capacity to exploit, foreign markets being open to you, and the absence of competitors. "It is because these factors are getting less and less every day for England that its number of unemployed is mounting up daily. And if that is the state of England, a vast country like India cannot expect to benefit by industrialization." In fact, Gandhi expressed his concerns thus:

> ....when India becomes industrialised it is bound to exploit other nations, and thus be a curse for other nations and a menace to the world., ...Don't you see the tragedy of the situation, viz., that we can find work for our 300 millions unemployed, but England can find none for its three millions. In the process they had begun to exploit South Africa as it provided them with its vastly richer resources, natural, mineral and human. But in due course it would be a dumping ground for their wares. Thus the resources of the earth are limited and so the exploitative process of industrialism will have to come to a halt. And if the future of industrialism is dark for the West, would it not be darker still for India?"[14]

Thus Gandhi clearly exposed the illusory nature of the technologist/ industrialist approaches towards development. The same points of criticism are applicable to the Information Technology and the virtual world it has brought about. So, Gandhi's ultimate plea was 'to look at the real, and re-trace one's steps of 'development' rather than remain in the illusory pinnacle of virtual world.

2.4. As regards the lesson of Cosmic Unity, indubitably Gandhi proved to be a living illustration already during his life time, when ecological concerns were not much in vogue. Despite his hectic tours, campaigns, and political activism, Gandhi was really keen on establishing unity with the beauty of nature, whenever he got an occasion. Once when he went to Haridwar, he made it a point to go to Rishikesh. The way he describes the scenic beauty betrays not merely his aesthetic sensitivity but also his profound religiosity:

> I had heard much in praise of the Lakshman Jhula (a hanging bridge over the Ganges) some distance from Hrishikesh, and many friends pressed me not to leave Hardvar without having gone as far as the bridge. I wanted to do this pilgrimage on foot and so I did it in two stages.... I was charmed with the natural scenery about Hrishikesh and the Lakshman Jhula, and bowed my head in reverence to our ancestors for their sense of the beautiful in Nature,

> and for their foresight in investing beautiful manifestations of Nature with a religious significance. But the way in which men were using these beauty spots was far from giving me peace. As at Hardvar, so at Hrishikesh, people dirtied the roads and the fair banks of the Ganges. They did not even hesitate to desecrate the sacred water of the Ganges. It filled me with agony to see people performing natural functions on the thoroughfares and river banks, when they could easily have gone a little farther away from public haunts.[15]

Not only the scenic beauty of the living nature attracted Gandhi's sensitivity, but the inanimate cosmic beauties too! Once somebody asked Gandhi: "Is there Truth in a sun-set or a crescent moon that shines amid the starts at night?" The reply to him by Gandhi was instant:

> Indeed. These beauties are truthful, in as much as they make me think of the Creator at the back of them. How also could these be beautiful, but for the Truth that is in the centre of creation? When I admire the wonder of a sunset or the beauty of the moon my soul expands in worship of the Creator. I try to see Him and His mercies in all these creations.[16]

Gandhi did not even exclude the poisonous creatures from his cosmic love, as it is clear from the following:

> I do not want to live at the cost of the life even of a snake. I should let him bite me to death rather than kill him. But it is likely that if God puts me to that cruel test and permits a snake to assault me, I may not have the courage to die, but that the beast in me may assert itself and I may seek to kill the snake in defending this perishable body, I admit that my belief has not become so incarnate in me as to warrant my stating emphatically that I have shed all fear of snakes so as to befriend them as I would like to be able to.[17]

Gandhi even thought that snakes, tigers etc., are God's answer to the poisonous, wicked, evil thoughts we harbour in us. He believed that all life is one. He said:

> Thoughts take definite forms. Tigers and snakes have kinship with us. They are warning to us to avoid harbouring evil, wicked, lustful thoughts. If one wants to rid the earth of venomous beasts and reptiles, one must rid oneself of all venomous thoughts. One may not do so if in one's impatient ignorance and in one's desire to prolong the existence of the body one seeks to kill the so called venomous beasts and reptiles. If in not seeking to defend oneself against such noxious animals, one dies, one should rise again a better and fuller man. With that faith in me how should I seek to kill a fellow being in a snake? [18]

At the same time Gandhi was realistic enough. He did agree that no one can live without injuring other living beings. "All life in the flesh exists by some *himsa* and that *himsa* is inherent necessity for life in the body. For instance the act of respiration destroys innumerable invisible germs floating in the air. The consumption of vegetables involves *himsa*. Again there is *himsa* in the use of antiseptics". He also conceded to killing snakes in his ashram when it was impossible to catch them and put them out of harm's way. That does not mean that there is a license for us to indulge in *himsa*. 'All we need to do is that we ceaselessly try to understand the implications of great ideals like ahimsa and to practice them in thought, word and deed'.[19] That is how, Gandhi felt, the cosmic unity can be sustained.

2.5. Corresponding to the fifth lesson of interdependence of peoples, Gandhi was emphatic enough to speak about a close interrelationship among the different races and nations. Once a question was put to him: "What sort of relations would you favour between two races?" To this the reply by Gandhi was as follows:

> The closest possible. But while I have abolished all distinction between an African and an Indian that does not mean that I do not recognize the difference between them. The different races of mankind are like different branches of a tree – once we recognize the common parent stock from which we are sprung, we realize the basic unity of the human family, and there is no room left for enmities and unhealthy competition.[20]

On an earlier occasion, Gandhi remarked:

> In spite of the differences of races and religions, we shall learn to tolerate and respect one another and consider all human beings as children of one God and, therefore brothers and sisters of one another. God is the Creator of all life; all His creatures are, therefore, equal in His eyes. Humanity is a gigantic tree having innumerable branches and leaves, and the same life throbs through them all. The realization of unity in diversity is implied in the removal of untouchability. [21]

Just as the cult of patriotism teaches us today that the individual has to die for the family, the family has to die for the village, the village for the district, the district for the province, and the province for the country, even so a country has to be free in order that it may die, if necessary, for the benefit of the world... There is no room for race hatred there. Let that be our nationalism. [22]

2.6. To the final lesson of creating a community of belonging and solidarity, Gandhi has quite a lot to contribute. The very idea of 'society' that Gandhi enunciated implied a sense of belonging, equality, and solidarity. To put it in his words:

> My idea of society is that while we are born equal, meaning that we have a right to equal opportunity, all have not the same capacity. It is, in the nature of things, impossible. For instance, all cannot have the same height, or colour or degree of intelligence, etc.; therefore in the nature of things, some will have ability to earn more and others less. People with talents will have more, and they will utilize their talents for this purpose. If they utilize kindly, they will be performing the work of the State. Such people exist as trustees, on no other terms. I would allow a man of intellect to earn more, I would not cramp his talent. But the bulk of his greater earnings must be used for the good of the State, just as the income of all earning sons of the father go to the common family fund. They would have their earnings only as trustees. It may be that I would fail miserably in this. But that is what I am sailing for.[23]

Part III

Possible Directives for a Relevant Christian Mission

The main purpose of the considerations in the foregoing sections is to study the two great leaders regarding lessons from the pandemic with a view to applying them to our missionary context of India. Therefore, after elucidating their parallel concerns, now it is incumbent upon us to apply their insights to investigating a relevant Christian mission in India. This is precisely what we intend to do in this final section of the paper. In correspondence to each of the six fundamental lessons that we have drawn above, here we will try to find a relevant application to the Christian mission, mainly in and through the words of the Mahatma.

3.1. Firstly the sarvodayist lesson, when applied in a multi-religious context, would read that 'the good of a religion is contained in the good of all religions'. In other words, a harmonious interreligious relationship is an utter necessity for any one religion to survive and flourish. To put it differently, it would mean 'No religion can claim monopoly of Revelation to itself alone'. Gandhi gives a simple, but convincing argument thus: Limited as we are in our very nature, we are bound to give a variety of interpretations to the term 'God', leave alone the revelations of his. Hence, he asserts, no religion can never claim uniqueness to oneself, condemning others, much less harming or persecuting others for their different interpretation of God. To cite his own words:

> I claim to be a man of faith and prayer and even if I was cut to pieces, God would give me the strength not to deny Him, and to assert that He is. The Muslim says: He is and there is no one else. The Christian says the same thing and so the Hindu, and if I may say so, even the Buddhist says the same thing, if in different words. We may each of us be putting our own interpretations on the word God -- God who embraces not only this tiny globe of ours but the millions and billions of such globes. How can we, little crawling creatures, so utterly helpless as He has made us, how could we possibly measure His greatness, His boundless love, His infinite compassion, such that He allows man insolently to deny Him, wrangle about Him, and cut the throat of his fellow-man? [24]

Moreover, Gandhi argued out the untenability of a religion's claim to monopoly of revelation on the ground of the inevitability of human differences thus:

> Differences in the world there have been, and will be. God is All-powerful. He appears in many shapes and forms. If we search, we may find as many religions as there are men. Hundreds of men are merely striving to know the Truth. They will put the Truth in their own way. No two men will put it in identical terms. Though I know that God -- the All-powerful-- resides in every one of us, we are imperfect media. We are all different. No two bodies are identically the same. No two leaves of the tree are identically the same; there is bound to be some difference. Each one prays to God according to his own light. Who am I to judge and say that I pray better than you do? I don't judge the Muslims, Parsis, Christians and Jews. If I am a seeker of Truth, it is quite sufficient for me. I cannot say that because I have seen God in this way, the whole world must see him in that way. All religions are true

> and equal. That, however, is not to say that they are equally true in religious terms or are absolutely true. Another man's religion is true for him, as mine is for me. I cannot be the judge of his religion.[25]

As a corollary from the above, Gandhi derives this conclusion: 'no religion can involve itself in proselytization whether it was carried out by Christian missionaries as conversion, by Muslims as Tabligh or by Hindus as Shuddhi'. It is, according to him, an impediment to interreligious harmony. Such a practice would aggrandize the number of one's own fold, and thus may impair the good of other religions, which in turn would damage the common welfare of harmonious existence of religions. Hence, Gandhi once told the YMCA gathering in 1927:

> And hence I say that we do not need to proselytise or do Shuddhi or Tabligh through our speech or writing. We can only do it really with our lives. Let them be open books for all to study. Would that I could persuade the missionary friends to take this view of their mission. Then there will be no distrust, no suspicion, no jealously and no dissentions. [26]

On many occasions Gandhi disagreed with the views infused by missionaries with regard to religious conversion and proselytizing and also the norms used by the ill-motivated missionaries who themselves were not following/ advocating the real Gospel values. He commented:

> I hold that proselytizing under the cloak of humanitarian work is, to say the least unhealthy. It is most certainly resented by the people here... In my opinion these practices offering medical relief with an expectation or suggestion of a change of religion by the patient, thrusting upon non-Christians a Christian teaching in a missionary education institution, etc. are not uplifting and give rise to suspicion if not even secret hostility. The methods of conversion must be like Caesar's wife, above suspicion. Faith is not imparted like secular subjects. It is given through the language of the heart. If a man has a living faith in him, it spreads its aroma like the rose its scent. Because of its invisibility, the extent of its influence is far wider than that of the visible beauty of the color of the petals.[27]

One should clearly learn from his writings that Gandhi was not at all hostile towards missionaries. In addition, he often appreciated and accepted their selfless services, their sacrifices for the poor, the marginalized, the oppressed and the downtrodden.

He also regarded highly the missionaries who worked among the lepers and asylum seekers. He said that they deserved great respect and support in society.

Despite the fact that missionaries did good deeds for the society Gandhi questioned the motive behind their social work which was to convert. He remarked:

> If instead of confining themselves purely to humanitarian work, such as education, medical services to the poor and the like, they would use these activities of theirs for the purpose of proselytizing, I would certainly like them to withdraw...why should I change my religion because a doctor who professes Christianity as his religion has cured me of some disease or why should the doctor expect or suggest such a change whilst I am under his influence? Is not medical relief its own regard or satisfaction? Or why should I whilst I am in a missionary educational Institute, have Christian teachings thrust upon me? In my opinion these practices are not uplifting and give rise to suspicion if not even secret hostility.[28]

Was Gandhi against conversion?

Gandhi was of the opinion that all religions were true and all had the same ultimate goal of realizing the supreme power of God as most of the rivers drain into seas and oceans. He did not have repugnance towards conversion. He only took exception to the controversial ways and means applied in the process of conversion in India. To quote in his words:

> I am then not against conversion. But I am against the modern method of it. Conversion nowadays has become a matter of business, like any other. I remember having read a missionary reports saying how much it cost per head to convert and then presenting a budget for the next harvest ... it follows from what I have said about that India is not in any need of conversion of the kind I have in mind. Conversion in the sense of self verification, self -realization is the crying need of the times. That however is not what is ever meant by proselytizing. To those who would convert India, might it not be said: "Physicians heal thyself?"[29]

Conversion or changing one's religion, called for a purification, a catharsis, of the self. It demanded a transformation of one's being, a "circumcision of the heart" as Paul wrote in Romans 2:29.

However, some Christian missionaries frankly told Gandhi that but for evangelism they would not have taken up mission work. They also grounded their active evangelism upon this experience of theirs thus: 'we got the driving power from communion with Jesus, because Jesus himself was always in communion with God'. Gandhi's retort to such missionaries was this: "The greatest trouble with us is not that a Christian missionary should rely on his own experience, but that he should dispute the evidence of a Hindu devotee's life. Just as he has his spiritual experience, the joy of communion, even so has a Hindu."[30]

There were other foreign missionaries who believed that their religion was the best and they had not the slightest idea of what other religions had revealed to their adherents. To them Gandhi gave this admonition:

> Just to forget that you have come to a country of heathens, and to think that they are as much in search of God as you are. ...You have not examined all religious beliefs. But even if you had, you may not claim infallibility. You assume knowledge of all people, which you can do only if you were God. I want you to understand that you are labouring under a double fallacy: that what you think is best for you is really so; and that why you regard as the best for you is the best for the whole world. It is an assumption of omniscience and infallibility. I plead for a little humility. [31]

In sum, the sarvodayist principle, as applied to the mission in a multi-religious context would challenge the Churches to understand, accept, and appreciate other religions and promote interreligious harmony rather than claim religious superiority to one's own religion, and disturb the faith of others and thereby spoil the collective wellbeing of all religions.

The significant thoughts as envisaged by Gandhi on mission invariably resemble the view as proposed by Pope Francis in his notable Apostolic Exhortation *Evangelium Gaudium* (EG). It will be advantageous to carry out the comparative views on mission proposed by the two eminent personalities.

In his Apostolic Exhortation, Pope Francis enlightens everyone to take stock of the spirit of joy of the Gospel in preference to the methods involved in evangelization. In a similar way, Gandhi also encouraged the missionaries to practice the Gospel message and share their happiness with the local people. The parallelism flowing from the sequence of thoughts of these two personalities portray that both of them draw similar views on the problem of mission purely from a spiritual stand-point.

It is to be noted that one who whole heartedly delves deeply into his/her religion possibly can meet another who is also well-rooted in his/her religion and understand each other at a profound level. For human hearts are essentially similar in their understanding of faith or understanding of one's own religion.

During the *Ad Limina* visit of the Indian bishops in Rome, on 17th September, 2019, Pope Francis explicitly mentioned that there should not be proselytism in India. He was also precise in referring to the statement of his predecessor Pope Benedict XVI, that if at all conversion happens, it should be mainly through attraction and not by force. This theme could be visibly seen in most of his talks, sermons and interviews. Pope Francis is very much in tune with the ideals proposed by Gandhi on mission. He proposes the practical sharing of one's faith with others. Even in sharing of one's faith, he cautions us not to impose our views on others particularly by not using the old approach of proselytism.

It is clear that Pope Francis is very much conscious and aware of proselytism which caused serious criticism and confusion in the past and exhorts the church to find out suitable relevant methods of evangelization.

Both Pope Francis and Gandhi proceed in the same direction while understanding and responding to the true need for the revival of the methods involved in the process of evangelization. It is in this view point that Pope Francis clearly visualizes the nature of the present state of the Church. Based on this perception, he tries to move towards a remedial situation through which the present Church requires transformation and a proper renewal. Much before the idea put forward by Pope Francis as needing a new strategy in mission proclamation, it is evident that Gandhi had already recommended a change in the methods of missionary endeavours.

Thus we see that the proposals advocated by Pope Francis and the diagnosis provided by Gandhi are the same. It indicates that the Church has been somewhat backward in its attitude for nearly two centuries.

Eli Stanley Jones an American Missionary, who once asked Gandhi: "Mr Gandhi, though you quote the words of Christ often, why is that you appear so adamant and reject to become his follower?" To which Gandhi replied simply: "Oh, I don't reject Christ. I love Christ. It is just that so many of you Christians are so unlike Christ. If Christians would really live according to the teaching of Christ, as found in the Bible, all of India would be Christian today"[32].

3.2. The lesson regarding promotion of the 'welfare of all, not the benefit of a few' in a religious context would mean that religions should never focus on the benefit of a few religions but should rather try to promote the welfare of all religions. This can be understood by Christians only when one understands Christian mission in a broader perspective.

It is heartening to observe that Pope Francis insists upon working for the integral uplift of the human, and not of the few but of all. It is precisely in the same vein that Gandhi spelt out the immoral implications of the market economics which promotes benefit of a few. Taking inspiration from these insights then, the Christian Churches today must re-vision their mission broadly.

As opposed to the former perspective of restricting Christian mission purely to the 'salvation of souls,' it is imperative that the Churches should be able to define their mission so as to orient their believers to perceive the 'sinfulness' of the market economy, to prevent them from succumbing to temptations of consumerism, and above all help them to value frugality, adopt simplicity of lifestyle, and reduce their wants, with a view to promoting the welfare of all.

Even within the interreligious context, a broader view of mission would be to make the followers of each religion to be well-rooted in their own spiritual pursuits and help them get vertically converted from imperfection to perfection, from less perfections to greater perfection rather than encourage them to indulge in conversions in the sense of merely crossing the boundaries of their native religions. In this connection, these words of Gandhi seem to be very relevant:

> The aim of Fellowship should be to help a Hindu to become a better Hindu, a Mussalman to become a better Mussalman, and a Christian a better Christian.... If I have a suspicion in my mind that my religion is more or less true, and that others' are more or less false, instead of being more or less true, then, though I may have some sort of fellowship with them, it is of an entirely different kind from the one we need in International Fellowship. Our prayer for the other must be **NOT** 'God, give him the light that Thou has given me, **'BUT'** Give him all the light and truth he needs for his highest development.' Pray merely that your friends may become better men, whatever their form of religion.[33]

In a word, if the Christian churches were to focus on the 'kingdom concerns' in all their missionary activities, rather than indulging in proselytization then the second lesson of the post pandemic would be taken care of.

3.3. In parallel to the need of experiencing 'the real', as against people's addiction to virtual world, Gandhi was constantly appealing to the missionaries of his time to come to grips with the real faith of people's religious experience, wherever it might be found, and not to shut themselves in the pinnacle of pure theology. Gandhi was pained at the fact that those missionaries were approaching the other religions with the theological bias in favour of proving the uniqueness of one's faith, and degrading other faiths and condemning them. To such people Gandhi said: "There should be less of theology and more of truth in all that you say and do". When asked to explain, he said:

> How can I explain the obvious? Amongst agents of the many untruths that are propounded in the world, one of the foremost is theology. There is a demand in the world for many a questionable thing. But even those who have to do with theology as part of their work, have to survive their theology. I do not say that there is no demand for it. .. Great result has come through the study of Jesus not through theology or through the ordinary interpretation of theologists. For many of them contend that the *Sermon on the Mount* does not apply to mundane things, and that it was only meant for the twelve disciples. Well I do not believe this. I think the *Sermon on the Mount* has no meaning if it is not of vital use in everyday life to everyone.[34]

Thus, Gandhi was making a plea with the missionaries of his time not to indulge in theological jargon in condemning the popular expressions of faith, rather, he was pleading with them to experience **the real faith** of the local people in India:

> You, the missionaries, come to India thinking that you come to a land of heathens, of idolaters, of men who do not know God....My own experience, in my travels throughout India, has been to the contrary. ... I tell you **there are many such huts** belonging to the untouchables where you will certainly find God. They do not reason, but they persist in their belief that God is. They depend upon God for His assistance and find it, too....But does my experience exhaust itself merely with the untouchables? No, I am here to tell you that there are non-*Brahmins*, **there are *Brahmins*** who are as fine specimens of humanity as you will find in any place on the earth. There are *Brahmins* today in India who are embodiments of self-sacrifice, godliness and humility. There are *Brahmins* who are devoting themselves body and soul to the service of untouchables, with no expectation of reward from the untouchables, but with execration from orthodoxy. They do not mind it, because in serving *Paraiahs* they are serving God....I place **these facts** before you in all humility for the simple reason that you may know this land better, the land to which you have come to serve. [35]

Hence, Gandhi's clear admonition to the Christian Western missionaries:

> Do not flatter yourselves with the belief that a mere recital of that celebrated verse in St John makes a man a Christian. If I have read the Bible correctly, I know many men who have never heard the name of Jesus Christ or who have even rejected the official interpretation of Christianity will, probably, if Jesus came in our midst today in the flesh be owned by him more than many of us. I therefore ask you to approach the problem before you with open-mindedness and humility.[36]

If the Churches were really open-minded to know *the real religiosity*, of the people then their mission would be first and foremost to strengthen their faith rather than undermine it, a faith however crude it may be is yet valuable to them. Secondly, it would be necessary to re-read the message of the Bible in the light of the discoveries, not of the modern science, but in the spiritual world in the shape of direct experiences common to all faiths. This in turn would mean that religions would be involved more and more in giving and taking the rich treasures of spiritual experiences of people, so as to complement one another with the patrimony of the one Father spread out among the various traditions of humankind.

In fine, then, the proclamation of the Christian message should never be restricted to merely repeating the story of event/person of the past, but rather it should be in terms of transmitting a lived experience, addressing a life-problem here and now. The message should point to a living Christ, as He re-lives in us today, rather than re-tell a Christ of history. How pregnant in meaning are the words of Gandhi:

> God did not bear the cross only 1900 years ago, but He bears it today. It would be poor comfort to the world if it had to depend upon a historical God who died 2,000 years ago. Do not then preach the God of history, but show Him as he lives today through you.[37]

3.4. As regards the Cosmic Unity, evidently Saint Francis of Assisi stands as the best illustration in the Christian tradition. He saw the whole of creation not merely as the visible manifestation of divine life, but also as a communication of the divine life to the human soul. His outburst after contemplation in admiration of creation was so spontaneous that he personified each creature on earth. He loved even the smallest, lowliest and the most insignificant worm because it was said of the Saviour: "I am a worm and no man."[38] Francis realized that the Father in Heaven is not only the Father of human beings but also of all other creatures. Therefore he could see all creatures as his 'brothers and sisters'. The mystical vision of the Saint Assisi is very evident in 'The Canticle of Brother Sun'. Fire and light seemed to him beautiful. In winter, he used to put honey into the beehives for the bees to feed on. It all sprang from the depths of his soul to provide us with many insights into the profundity of his life of faith in the Triune God, who so deeply enters into His creation.

In pursuance of the spirit of St Francis, Pope Francis also has enjoined us to have an appreciative attitude and even a reverential approach towards the whole creation. He even devoted a whole Encyclical letter[39] to initiate Christians to ecological spirituality. In his follow-up Encyclical,[40] Francis has reiterated the same theme as one of the lessons we should draw from the pandemic.

It is noteworthy that, Gandhi manifested the same kind of approach towards nature already during his time. He expressed not merely admiration for but complete union with the whole of creation, as springing from his religious sentiment:

> My religion and my patriotism derived from my religion embrace all life. I want to realize brotherhood or identity not merely with the beings called human, but I want to realize identity with all life, even with such beings as crawl on earth. I want, if I don't give you a shock, to realize identity with even the crawling things upon earth, because we claim common descent from the same God, and that being so, all life in whatever form it appears must be essentially one. [41]

Gandhi's union with the animate beings was also substantiated with moral considerations, too:

> My ethics not only permit me to claim but require me to own kinship with not merely the ape but the horse and the sheep, the lion and the leopard, the snake and the scorpion. This hard ethic sought to govern every man and woman, because man alone is made in the image of God. That some of us do not recognize that status of ours, makes no difference, except that then we do not get the benefit of the status, even as a lion brought up in the

> company of sheep may not know his own status and, therefore, does not receive its benefits; but it belongs to him nevertheless, and, the moment he realizes it, he begins to exercise his dominion over the sheep. But no sheep masquerading as a lion can ever attain the leonine status. ...And, will it be denied that the great religious teachers of mankind have exhibited the image of God in their own persons? [42]

Thanks to the reverential approach towards Nature, he could understand and even appreciate the popular tree worship of the villagers in India.

> I find in it a thing instinct with a deep pathos and poetic beauty. It symbolizes true reverence for the entire vegetable kingdom which, with its endless panorama of beautiful shapes and forms declares to us as it were with a million tongues the greatness and glory of God. Without vegetation, our planet would not be able to support life even for a moment. In such a country especially, therefore, in which there is a scarcity of trees, tree worship assumes a profound economic significance.[43]

All this should not mislead us to identify Gandhi as an idolater. He clearly made a distinction between idolatry and idol worship.

> I am both a supporter and opponent of image worship. When image worship degenerates into idolatry and becomes encrusted with false beliefs and doctrines, it becomes a necessity to combat it as a gross social evil. On the other hand, image worship, in the sense of investing one's ideal with a concrete shape, is inherent in man's nature and even valuable as an aid to devotion ... Even so, far from seeing anything inherently evil or harmful in tree worship, I find in it a thing instinct with a deep pathos and poetic beauty.[44]

In a word, no religion should claim superiority just because it does not use an idol. Nor can a religion condemn another which seems to advocate tree-worship or idol worship.[45]

3.5. In reiterating the need to see the 'interdependence of humankind' religions have a crucial role to play. Religions in the past have erected the major walls of separation. As such therefore they must take a leading role not only to remove such walls but also positively to come together to express their interdependence to solve some of the common problems of mankind like the ecological crisis, value-crisis, consumerism, secularism etc. In the process, we must clearly acknowledge three specific points: one is that each major religion has its own independent status. The second point is that each should tolerate every other and even respect the validity of each other. Thirdly, they should even acknowledge the need of being related with one another for their own enrichment.

(a) Now as regards the independent status of religions, Gandhi affirmed that every religion has a unique feature which its followers may rightfully be proud of. "Hinduism with its message of *ahimsa* is to me the most glorious religion in the world, -- as my wife to me the most beautiful woman in the world -- but others may feel the same about their religion."[46] The spiritual solace you get from your religion is possibly got by another in his own religion. Gandhi asks us to say to ourselves: 'I have come through this route, another may come through a different route.' In this connection, he posed this question to his missionary friends: "Why should you want him to pass through your University and no other?" To this the reply was: "Because I have my partiality for my Alma Mater." That is precisely where the difficulty lays, Gandhi said: "Because you adore your mother you cannot wish that all the rest were your mother's children". If this is physical impossibility, so too the other is a spiritual impossibility. "God has the whole humanity as his children. How can I limit God's grace by my little mind and say this is the only way?" he asked.[47]

(b) Next, Gandhi proposed that religions must contact with one another with an attitude of tolerance of one another. The reason he gave is very simple: "No one faith is perfect. All faiths are equally dear to their respective votaries. What is wanted, therefore, is living friendly contact among the followers of the great religions of the world, and not a clash among them in the fruitless attempt on the part of each community to show the superiority of its faith over the rest. Through such friendly contact, it will be possible for us all to rid our respective faiths of shortcomings and excrescences. [48]Thus for instance, the excrescences may have been so longstanding that they may have become part of the religion that people in that religion may not be conscious of it as imperfections at all. Thus, in

Hinduism untouchability, and triumphalist and exclusivist approaches towards other religions in Christianity are examples. When the Christian missionaries came into contact with Hinduism they were repulsed by the Untouchability, among other shortcomings, while they themselves were not conscious of their imperialistic approach. It was only through interreligious contact the historical accretions were seen to be an additional growth, not necessarily connected with the genuine faith of each major religion.

(c) In such a context then, religions must be open minded and humble enough to show readiness to purify themselves and march towards Perfection, each within its own framework. Their openness must be to such an extent that they must be ready to learn good things from one another and enrich themselves with the acceptable features of others. Thereby we need to realize the complementary nature of the diverse religions.

This approach is not to be dubbed as eclecticism. Gandhi's standpoint was clear: 'to call a man eclectic is to say that he had no faith' and that his attempt was simply a mere conglomeration of the good features of different religions. In his case, Gandhi clearly remained a staunch Hindu, all through his life. Yet, his faith was so broad that he found room in his faith for Christian, Islamic and Zoroastrian teaching. He took to Ahimsa, which is the core of Buddhism, and followed it so seriously and systematically that he even developed a theoretical structure for it. Likewise, he was so much influenced by the *Anekantavada* of Jainism that he applied it to his interreligious living. From the Sermon on the Mount he drew lessons for his *Satyagaraha* and held Jesus as the supreme exemplar of satyagraha. He clearly acknowledged all the different sources of spiritual influences, assimilated them all and made them all part and parcel of his spiritual pursuit, with a view to bringing about a personal transformation of self as well as society.[49] "It is that broad faith that sustains me. It is somewhat embarrassing position, I know, but to others, not to me", he said.[50]

3.6. Finally, in creating the shared passion of belonging and solidarity, the role of religions is crucial. Obviously, the religious dimension is the deepest in human consciousness. As such then, if the varied religions formed an 'united front' of religions to create a community of belonging and solidarity, it will surely have a profound impact on building up human solidarity. It is heartening to know that way back, already in the year 1928, an International Fellowship Convention was convened in Gandhi's Ashram at Sabarmathi. It was indeed a fellowship of faiths and nationalities: Christians, Hindus, a Muslim, a Parsi, Indians, American, English, Swiss, a Russian and a Sweden. Its object, unanimously agreed upon, was:"to work for the widest toleration, to combine and side with the forces of light against the forces of darkness, or with those who seek God, truth and divine light against those who blankly leave God out and become materialists."[51]

Against this backdrop, Gandhi delivered his address to the International Fellowship Convention. From it we may cull the following points as implications of the objective of the Fellowship:

1. Every act of its members must be a religious act and an act of sacrifice.
2. All its members must accept that all religions were true and also that all had some error in them.
3. Whilst I hold by my own, I should also hold others as dear as Hinduism, from which it logically follows we should hold all as dear as our nearest kith and kin. A Christian should give the same love to others as he has for his own, and thereby broaden his Christianity, as a Hindu would broaden his Hinduism by loving other religions as his own.
4. Our inmost prayer should be that a Hindu should be a better Hindu; a Muslim should be a better Muslim and a Christian a better Christian.

5. There should not be any suspicion in the minds of any of its members that only one religion can be true and others false.

6. Above all, there should be such an utter truthfulness among the members that they feel for other religions as they feel for their own. "My doctrine of toleration does not include toleration of evil, though it does the toleration of the evil-minded. It does not therefore mean that you have to invite each and every one who is evil-minded or tolerate a false faith. By a true faith I mean the sum total of whose energy is for the good of its adherents; by false I mean that which is predominantly false. If you feel, therefore, that the sum total of Hinduism has been bad for the Hindus and the world, you must reject it as a false faith". (CM 130-131).

For this, Gandhi suggested to the missionary friends that they should make a careful study of others' scriptures from the standpoint of their respective believers. When people brought to his notice a man with a doctorate, who had made a study of Hindu scriptures, Gandhi commented thus: "I say it is not enough for him to read the Song Celestial or the Koran. It is necessary for him to read the Koran with Islamic spectacles and the Gita with Hindu spectacles, just as he would expect me to read the Bible with Christian spectacles". [52]

From the above it logically follows that people of different religions should hold all the members of humanity as dear as their nearest kith and kin and that they should make no discrimination between them. So, we should pray and act that that a Hindu should be a better Hindu, a Muslim a better Muslim and a Christian a better Christian. To put it differently, we should accept that the followers of different religions must work for 'vertical' conversion within their own religious boundaries rather than for conversions by crossing the boundaries.

Conclusion

The primary purpose of this article was first to draw out the foundational lessons from the pandemic. Further, in the light of those lessons, an attempt was made to propose new guidelines for making the Christian mission meaningful in the post pandemic context.

Accordingly, the considerations made in Part 1 have hopefully indicated those points which prove to be fundamental lessons to be learnt by humanity from *Fratelli Tutti*, during this COVID-19 pandemic. Availing ourselves of Pope Francis' Encyclical, as a handy tool of reference, we elucidated six such fundamental lessons from the pandemic.

Curiously enough, we found that Gandhi had expressed parallel views on various occasions, while he made a critique of modernity in general and Christian mission in particular. So an attempt was made in the second Part to cull from the massive writings of Gandhi those thoughts validating Pope Francis' thought.

Then in Part 3, we focussed on the application of Gandhi's criticisms to Christian mission with a view to helping Christian churches re-vision their mission in the post pandemic scenario.

Thus, it may be hopefully claimed that the considerations given above have already demonstrated the possibility of application of those lessons to the missionary aspects of Christianity. If they are taken seriously, they would not only serve as fresh guidelines for the Christian churches in India in the post-pandemic era, but also will make their mission more relevant and meaningful to the changed scenario.

Bibliographical Abbreviations:

- **Auto:** M.K. Gandhi, *An Autobiography Or The Story of My Experiments with Truth***,** Td., Mahadev Desai, (Ahamedabad: Navajivan Publishing House, 1927, Reprint 1976)
- **All Men:** Ed., Krishna Kripalani**,** *All Men are Brothers***:** *Life*

and Thoughts of Mahatma Gandhi as Told in His own Words, (Ahamedabad: Navajivan Publishing House, 1960, Reprint 1971)

- **ART:** M.K. Gandhi: *All Religions are True*, Ed., Anand T. Hingorani (Bombay, BharatiyaVidya Bhavan, 1962)
- **Bapu:** R.K. Prabhu, *This Was Bapu: One Hundred and Fifty Anecdotes relating to Mahatma Gandhi,* (Ahamedabad: Navajivan Publishing House 1954, Reprint 1959)
- **CM:** M.K. Gandhi, *Christian Missions, Their Place in India*, Ed. Baratan Kumarappa, (Ahamedabad: Navajivan Publishing House, 1941, Reprint 1960)
- **NKB:** Nirmal Kumar Bose, *Selections from Gandhi,* (Ahamedabad: Navajivan Publishing House, 1948, Reprint 1972)
- **TM:** M.K. Gandhi, *The Message of Jesus Christ,* Ed., Anand T. Hingorani, (Bombay: BharatiyaVidyaBhavan, 1963)
- **TG:** M.K. Gandhi, *Truth is God*, Ed., R.K. Prabhu, (Ahamedabad:Navajivan Publishing House, 1955, Reprint 1980)
- **VT**: M.K. Gandhi, The Voice of Truth, Ed., Shriman Narayan, (Ahamedabad: Navajivan Publishing House, 1969)

---

* **Most Revd Dr Lawrence Pius Dorairaj** is the Bishop of Dharmapuri. He was ordained a priest in 1981. He holds a M A in Philosophy from Madras University and a Ph D in Gandhian Thought from University of Sorbonne, Paris. 'Gandhi's Critique of Modern Civilization' is his doctoral thesis. He is a visiting Professor at St Peter's Pontifical Seminary, Bangalore & Good Shepherd Seminary, Coimbatore. He is also the Chairman, Family Commission, CCBI & Chairman, Dialogue & Ecumenical Commission, Tamil Nadu.

Endnotes

[1] Pope Francis, *Encyclical Letter on Fraternity and Social Friendship, Fratelli Tutti,* (2020). Here afterwards it will be referred to as FT in the body of this article.

[2] Pope Francis, "Extraordinary Moment of Prayer in Time of Epidemic (27 March 2020)" in *LOsservatore Romano,*(29 March 2020)10).

[3] The same was re-translated into English by Valji Govindji, M.K. Gandhi, *Ruskin Unto This Last, A Paraphrase* (Ahmedabad: Navajivan Publishing House) 1956

[4] *An Auto,* IV: XVIII, 224

[5] *All men* 160

[6] *AT,* 377

[7] *All Men,* 160

[8] *All men,* 167-168.

[9] *All men,* 171- 172

[10] R.K. Prabhu, *This was Bapu:One Hundred and Fifty Anecdotes relating to Mahatma Gandhi*, (Ahemadabad: Navajivan Publishing House, First Edition: July 1954) No 70 https://www.mkgandhi.org/thiswasbapu/70gandhitalisman.htm

[11] *VT,*381

[12] *VT,* 380

[13] *VT*, 376-377

[14] VT, 376-378

[15] *Auto,*V:VIII, 294-&296

[16] *VT,* 110

[17] *TG*, 109

[18] *TG*, 109

[19] *TG*, 110

[20] *VT*, 249

[21] *VT,* 249

[22] *VT,* 247-48

[23] Krishna Kripalani, *All Men Are Brothers,: Life and Thoughts of Mahatma Gandhi as told in his own words,*(Ahmedabad: NavajivanMudranalaya1960, www.mkgandhi.org)161

[24] *CM*, 120

[25] *ART,* 46

[26] *CM*, 120

[27] Mohandas Karamchand Gandhi, *In Search of the Supreme, Vol. III* as quoted in Lawrence Pius Dorairaj " Gandhi and the Fragrant 'Gospel of the Rose' " in A. Kunnathetalii, *To Carry New Fire Today*, Bangalore, Theological Publication in India, 2019, p.59.

[28] *Ibid*, p.60

[29] *Ibid*, pp.60-61

[30] *CM,*138

[31] *CM*, 142-143

[32] A Pushparajan, The Mahatma and Christian Mission Today: Revisiting Pope Francis' *Evangelii Gaudium* in the light of Gandhi Insight, Bengaluru, ATC Publishers,2018.P.18-19.

[33] *NKB,* article No. 734

[34] *ART,* 124

[35] *TM,* 17-18 (emphasis added)

[36] *TM,*19

[37] *CM,* 101-103, 209- 217

[38] Ps 21:7.

[39] *Laudato Si* (May 2015)

[40] *FratelliTutti*(October 2020)

[41] *VT,*246

[42] *TG,* 108-109

[43] *ART*, 34

[44] *ART,* 34

[45] For a detailed analysis of Gandhian approach towards idol worship *vis-a-vis* idolatry, one may refer to A. Pushparajan, *From Conversion to Fellowship: The Hindu Christian Encounter in the Gandhian Perspective* (Varanasi: Maitri Bhavan, Dialogue Series No 4, 1990) Ch1.

[46] *CM* 132

[47] *CM,* 139-140

[48] *TM*, 62

[49] A. Pushparajan, "Gandhi's Contribution to Interreligious Harmony, in *Sanyasa Journal of Consecrated Life,*Vol.VI No 2 (Bengaluru: Sanyasa Institute of Consecrated Life, 2011)198-199

[50] *CM,* 126- 127

[51] *CM,* 130

[52] *CM,* 141

19

Reflections on a Reconstruction of the World in the Post-COVID 19 Era

Revd Dr Thomas Kulangara *

With Covid 19 the humanity has affronted an unprecedented situation of world-wide danger before which man with all his scientific progress stood helpless. Covid 19 made its appearance as an all-pervading, invincible, but undiscriminating enemy. The chronological unfolding of the countless evils of humankind, both of individual and collective nature, it seems, has really precipitated this critical moment of history.

For believers in God, the course of the history of man and of the cosmos at large is not a haphazard, reckless and uncanny process but with all its manifold vicissitudes, is a meaningful process directed from within by the Supreme Wisdom of the Divine Agency. Nothing escapes the all pervasive influence of the Eternal Divine Guidance.

Hence, we may discern in the Covid 19 episode, not a moment of despair and helplessness but an opportune moment (*Kairos*) for effecting a divinely inspired new direction for the course of history. It is a moment for humanity to rediscover the unity and inter connectedness of the human family, not only of the present moment but also of the past and the future.

Our True Ecological Identity

First of all, Covid 19 is a divine summons for us to rediscover our true ecological identity. In fact, our true existence is a part of the existence of the whole world, the universe as a whole which is our home (*Oikos*). The universe, and in particular the earth, is our one home, which is the habitat of all its numerous inhabitants. Our life is a co-existence with the entire life on this planet. This is certainly true not only from a biological perspective, but it is also the expression of a spiritual vision at the same time.

A deep ecological spirituality envisages a spiritual transition from a separated and alienated existence in the universe towards an experiential inter-relation with the rest of the cosmic OIKOS (home). Those who grasp this new ecological identity will find in it a motivation for social and ecological action. We may continuously search for the least exploitative mode of relation with the earth and her inhabitants.

With the scientific revolution man's ambition to manipulate and conquer all forces of the Nature through the instrumentality of his reason strode leaps and bounds. It generated in man an imperialistic desire to dominate everything and everyone in Nature. Continuous attempts were made to subjugate everything and everyone under the sway of man's egoistic use of rational instrumentality. Man took a very drastic and dangerous approach to Nature. "Learn, use and dominate" became the leitmotif. Through all scientific knowledge and tools available man sought to acquire a complete domination of Nature, human body and society. Covid 19 is a shock treatment applied by the Divine Wisdom to startle the human mind to a sense of realistic humility.

According to Martin Heidegger, the most basic trait of human existence in the world (what he calls *Da sein)* is its finitude.

Nevertheless, the humans at all times, but more pointedly during our times, are tempted to forget their finitude. The real meaning of the classical Christian concept of "original sin" is the forgetfulness of this finitude. It was this oblivion of human finitude that led the humankind to the trap or slavery of technocracy.

The Divine Moral Force Operating amidst the Forces of Evil

The sombre air of Covid 19 need not fill our minds and hearts with a sense of dismay and doom. According to the Indian vision of reality, the world is constantly upheld by a divine moral force called *dharma*. The entire world with all its social, religious and political institutions is finally upheld by dharma. *Dharma* can be easily understood and explained away in terms of the cumulative effect of all moral/ immoral activities of human beings. Dharma produces its burden of *karma* (i. e, good and bad actions) which reigns over the life of the individuals and the societies. No one can escape the law of *karma*. But for the believers in God, for the devotees of the Lord, the law of *karma* does not operate blindly, but it is under the loving and merciful law of God who is the administrator of the law of *karma*. The concept of *dharma* cannot be easily identified with the law of *karma* because *dharma* includes an over plus, a divine, a scientific dimension over against the accumulations of human karmas. The *sanadhana dharma* (eternal righteousness) is not entirely a human product but implies a human participation in the eternal salvific law of God which holds the human destiny and the destiny of the world in His merciful hands.

Dharma (the divine human power that upholds the world) has its genuine matrix in the inter-connectedness of the world and in the reciprocity of the humans as makers of one world- family (*vasudaivakudumbakom*). Covid 19 demonstrates how we are interconnected concretely in the very air we breathe in. We are responsible for one another and are dependent on one another, in every breath we take in. Anyone can breathe one neighbour out of life. Every breath we take in or give out is weighed down by moral responsibility.

This subtle sense of moral responsibility may be developed into a sense of universal moral responsibility for the sustenance of life and for the promotion of common good on a global level. Moral rights and duties, when performed in accordance with the divine law, can develop into an authentic moral authority in the world. It can render moral authority to the social, religious, legal and political institutions. People wielding authority in these institutions are actually weak and unauthentic, devoid of the real moral authority they should have developed. True authority rests not in power, but on true moral authority which is generated by abiding by true eternal moral values set up in the divine governance of the universe.

The inter connectivity among the humans is a basic truth that could be undermined only by causing irreparable damages. In fact, the destiny of every individual is intertwined with the destiny of the rest of the members of the human family. The moral authority developed by the individuals in the society exerts a power over the moral authority of the societal institutions and on the authority wielded by those who are placed on the ruling and administrative power in the society. The external authority empowering the various office holders in the society (political, departmental and other institutional authority) is analogous to the spiritual, moral authority of the people who are placed in leadership, power and authority.

An optimistic attitude to the world process based on faith in spiritual realities will instil in us a sense of courage (*nirbhaya)* as we are faced with the negative energies on the air at the moment. The manifold evil that threatens the moral order (*dharma*) that sustains and maintains the world process is, like Covid 19, only parasitical in nature. It dwells on other real entities and as such it lacks an ontological being *per se*. When humanity as a whole re-emerges to live its authentic moral values, all parasitical giants, including Covid 19, however, brutal and omnipotent they appear, will naturally vanish into the nether world of *maya*. The reason is that it does not belong to the genius of the real, authentic, moral reality characteristic of humanity. The parasitical threats are only reawakening calls for us to open up our inner eyes to rediscover and relive the eternal moral values (*sanathan dharma*).

The Need for a New All-Inclusive Identity

The humans need to discover a new all-inclusive identity. In the geological time scale the human species has ascended to the status of over lordship over all other creatures of the earth and over the planet itself only very recently. In the present era the humans seem to claim to have reached an epoch of anthropo-scene. The Covid 19 has shattered this fancy-claim of the species to some extent.

Apart from our religious, cultural, and political persuasions which are deep-rooted in us shaping our belief systems, ways of thinking and patterns of behaviours, we should dare to ask the most basic anthropological question: Who am I as a responsible member of the human species? What is my basic identity as a human existence thrown into the world? Up to now in the history of our species we have assumed and developed identities in term of clan, tribe, nationality, religion, political ideology etc. Man by nature needs a rootedness and hence a particular identity as focus of belonging to. But an exclusive adherence to such de-limiting and mutually exclusive identities is the root cause of all conflicts and destructive warfare and terrorism in the world.

Covid 19 seems to teach us a viable solution to the question of identity. Our basic identity is that we belong to the cosmic home (oikos) as members of one human family. The whole earth is one family alone! An identity based on nationality, race, tribe or religion has really a healthy role in so far as it fulfils man's legitimate aspiration and need to belong to a concrete social group and to experience a sense of security, care, and well-being.

However, there is a grave danger ensuing from these small and relative identities, namely, that these identities have an inner mechanism to lose sight of their relative nature and to absolutise them, making them exclusive to our more basic sources and frame work of identity like our belongingness to the whole world, to the human species and to biological and ecological laws governing the inhabitation of the myriad species of organic and inorganic entities that make up a whole of which we are responsible and intelligent parts. The latter is our most inclusive fundamental and ontological, i.e., realistic and not virtual, identity. If we anchor on this identity, all our small and relative identities will fall in the places of their relative importance.

In other words, this identity makes us feel belonging to the whole. We are all parts of one whole. From a theistic perspective, this whole is the Divine Totality from which all finite (limited) beings came forth, and in whom they move and have their being (see Acts 17, 28). In this sense St Paul, from a Christian perspective declares that "all are yours; and you are Christ's: and Christ is God's" (1 Cor 3, 22-23). In a theistic perspective we all belong to one another bound up in a universal fraternity. We should all increasingly transcend our small identities based on nationality, caste, race, religion etc. This does not mean a total breaking away from our small, relative identities, but it means subordinating all such identities to our basic identity of being an inhabitant of the earth, our common universal house, OIKOS.

Happiness as the Supreme Goal of Human Life

Indian Philosophy (*darsanas)* proposes wealth (*artha*), pleasure (*kama*), moral excellence or righteous living (*dharma*) and eternal salvation or liberation (*moksha*) as the supreme goals of life. However, the Upanishads indicate that the deepest level of human life, right beneath his biological (*annamaya*), vital or what concerns life (*pranamaya*), mental (*manomaya*) and noetic (*vijnanamaya*) levels is the deepest layer of our existence. This layer is called bliss or happiness (*anandamaya*) (see *Taittiriya Upanishad* III.6.1). This indicates that the most supreme goal of human life is happiness.

According to Aristotle, happiness or well-being or human flourishing is not a means for something else. Rather, it is the ultimate goal of human life itself, the supreme objective of all human striving. Happiness alone is the ultimate end and final goal of all human endeavours. The Greek term for happiness (*eu-daimonia)* indicates that happiness already involves good. '*Eu*' means "good" and *daimonia* means spirit. Hence, happiness is intrinsically connected with what is good. It is the tendency of the human heart and will towards what the intellect perceives as good that brings about happiness. According to Aristotle, the good is that which "all things desire". In fact, all things desire their own perfection which is the same as their "good". All our intellectual and moral virtues are meant to serve as a united inner force that empowers and facilitates the overall perfection of the organism both on the individual and collective or societal level. An individualistic and selfish pursuit of happiness, ignoring the needs and rights of the other people to have their basic needs fulfilled and to be happy, will end up in fiasco. Such selfish pleasure and wealth seekers will never attain true happiness, but will be frustrated. This is because their pursuit of life is in gross violation of their fundamental identity which is all-inclusive. In order to ensure common good and to promote the wellbeing and happiness of all, what is primarily required is a rediscovery of and adherence to the inherent dignity involved in being a human person. The post-Covid era offers a new opportunity to discover the universal values inscribed in the declarations of the United Nations on the universal dignity of the human person and on the fundamental duties and rights of all members of the human family. The summons of the day is to recapture the true spirit of the UNO and to work for an authentic world political authority, transcending the existing national, social and religious leadership. What I mean here is a "transcendence", without a total negation or abrogation of the existing systems. All the existing authorities in the world must be transformed and subordinated to such a world political authority which should enjoy maximum moral and political power and executive efficiency. We need to start urgently journeying towards a united world as a communion or confederation of the manifold existing societies. What we have at hand is a wonderful opportunity to explore the possibilities of a more united world, striving after the common good and happiness of all, for a global solidarity in which all are responsible for one another.

The Creation of a United World

The creation of a universal human solidarity or a united world urgently requires a re-defining of our natural, territorial and nationalistic identities. There is nothing wrong in having a sense of patriotism or national pride. The danger consists in exaggerating these concepts to the extent of developing an internal and total adherence to them in an exclusive and absolute manner. Instead, we can develop a healthy notion of patriotism and nationalism in an inclusive sense, believing that we are all primarily members of an inter-national family of countries, a united world around, solicitous of helping one another, caring for one another and at the same time devoted to the common good and to the care and protection of our common mother, the earth. What we should look forward to in the post Covid 19 era is not a return to the old normalcy but ascending or evolving towards a new normalcy, where the humans will strive in solidarity for a new world, where universal justice and peace will reign.

Need for a New Economic Order

The economy of the world at large is now controlled by the principles of capitalism, free market and maximum profit. The corporate kings who rule the economy may set apart a portion of their income for the common good by way of charity. Through Covid 19 the divine wisdom unveils the gross injustice and futility inbuilt in the present economic system. The war industry promoted by the wealthiest countries under the mask of promoting peace and stability among nations is a poignant instance warring in the conscience of any human being devoted to the cause of world-peace.

What the world requires today is an ethical economy basically oriented towards the common good. Such an ethical economy may eradicate the conditions that necessitate the dolling out small portions of the exorbitant profit made by economic emperors as charity.

The new economic order envisaged here should have as its main goal not maximum profit but maximum common good. The project of the economy of communion as practised by some of the entrepreneurs belonging to the Focolare Movement is a model for a new economic order. In the economic enterprise undertaken by the Economy of Communion, business firms are run in abeyance to the ethical principles and statutory rules prevalent in the respective countries. The total profit is divided into three parts: one third is used for helping the poor people all over the world. One third is utilized for the training of the young people so that they may be transformed into protagonists of a new united world. One third of the profit is utilized for the improvement and growth of the respective economic enterprise itself. One remarkable feature of the Economy of Communion is that it seeks to avoid all kinds of unhealthy competitions and rivalries with other entrepreneurs and economic enterprises. Rather, it seeks to work on the principle of mutual cooperation, sharing and solidarity.

Such a new economic order will take special care of the following points: 1. The products and services should be geared to satisfying the real human needs. 2. The working conditions should be human, respecting the dignity of the persons involved. 3. The production processes must be environment- friendly. 4. The sales and purchases policies of the enterprise should abide by right ethical principles. 5. The profits are to be distributed in a just manner, keeping the common good and the needs of the poor people in top priority. 6. The women should be ensured equal pay for equal work. 7. The employees should be involved in the core-strategic decision making process.

The Need for a New Ethics

For the reconstruction of the world in the post Covid 19 era, we need a new ethics based on the values of common good, unity of humanity and the protection of the most poor and vulnerable. This ethics should be more dynamic, inclusive of the ethical values of other people and ultimately oriented to the wellbeing and happiness of all peoples and all beings. *Lokasamasthasukhinobhavantu* (May the whole world be in a state of wellbeing) should be the leitmotif of such an ethics. Such a new ethic would be different from the status quo ethics which is primarily built up on conventional values like obedience to legalistic behavioural pattern and ritualistic and cultic sets of practices which are naively accepted as moral standards.

Aristotle had visualized an ethics based on the pursuit of the natural tendency of existing things towards greater and greater unity and simplicity that would promote the good and welfare of all beings. It is a virtue-centred ethics and it stands in contrast with the static-rules based ethical models which all tend to be rigid and legalistic.

At the same time it should not be miss-constructed that the new ethics proposed here is a kind of ethical relativism. Any ethical system that sanctions or tolerates an absolute and radical relativity in matters of ethical values and practices will be self-defeating because it cannot cope up with the perennial demands of the *sanathana dharma* (the eternal righteousness) which alone upholds and maintains the human society and the world at large. In fact, the ethical stand of Aristotle was based on a kind of relative absolutism as distinguished from an absolute absolutism and any form of absolute relativism. St Thomas Aquinas while upholding absolute and unchangeable nature of the primary principles of ethics always granted room for flexibility in the application of the secondary principles and values of ethics which are derived from the primary principles and are actually practised in concrete moral situations.

God has created the human beings with knowledge, will power, and freedom and thereby placed the human species in a privileged mode of existence which we may designate moral or ethical. The humans have a natural tendency to follow the good which would lead them to their ultimate and overall perfection. Good-minded and well-intended people spontaneously follow the right ethical course of action in so far as they are not deviated by negative forces of selfishness, attachments, concupiscence etc. But there are persons with inborn or acquired vicious tendencies who resist to submit to the dictates of the good or who constantly rebel against the principles of *dharma*. Even such persons may be lovingly coerced to change their ways by a process of moral and spiritual discipline which may at first appearance be seen as a violation of their personal freedom. However, it is a service to humanity when such people are assiduously trained to submit themselves voluntarily to embrace a just and ethical life style which would certainly enhance their own overall happiness and sense of wellbeing. In the long run, they will respond positively to the dictates of a value based ethical life.

In brief, we need to draw a distinction between an ethics which dictates its thoughts and practical ordinances in the direction of common good of all people and of the mother earth, and of all her inhabitants, and a morality which has more to do with the legal codes and practices demanded and enforced by the different caste or religion based sectors of the society. In a pluralistic world, a social situation in which each religious, caste or tribal group having its own independent absolute moral laws obliging the adherents to follow them literally, will necessarily lead to conflict and disharmony in the social matrix which resists to be communally broken into pieces.

The main project of a sound ethics ought to be the greatest possible common good. Ethics elucidates an ideal that the individuals and societies seek to follow. In contrast, morality in the customary sense refers more to the legislated laws and ritualistic practices that the individuals are coerced to follow by virtue of their belonging to communal groups based on caste, clan, religion, political ideology etc. The individuals are persuaded to follow these prescriptions in order to be accepted as following an upright life as per the parameters accepted and enforced in the communal group they belong to. In contrast, a genuine ethics, based on universal values (*sanathana dharma*), underscores a sense of universal justice, human equality and freedom which are deeply rooted in the basic dignity, and goodness of all people. It is driven by the urge "to do good to all" as the right thing to do. It dictates attitudes and activities that propel the progress of humankind. It is different from the status quo morality that is deeply individualistic and personal and not egalitarian. In contrast, a sound ethics will help people to transcend all communalistic interests and to find each one's core identity as a responsible member of the united human family.

In order to build up a new ethical vision by way of providing a spiritual foundation for the reconstruction of the post-Covid 19 world, we need to strive hard to transform and enlarge the scope of the status quo morality. This will inevitably bring in oppositions from the followers of the narrow-minded parochial and communal vanguards. Conflicts with them may engender no beneficial fruit. Instead, we need to open doors of dialogue with them. Moreover, all protagonists of a new united world will have to struggle and suffer against diverse odds. It is this struggle that offers meaning to our life and quickens a sense of undefeatable hope ensuing from the divine source from which we drink the medicine of immortality and continue our endeavours for a better united world.

Christ's Role in the On-going Reconstruction of the World

The true Disciples of Christ believe that the Jesus of Nazareth is the incarnation of the eternal Son of God, the Father and creator of all that exists, and who is continuously re-creating the world through the Holy Spirit, which is the Spirit of Jesus Christ. The Christ, who continuously recreates and redeems the world, is the Lord of all creation and he cannot be delimited to the spatio-temporal features that he assumed in the historical person of Jesus of Nazareth. Christ is the eternal, universal, unchanging Word of God. In the Gospel of John, Jesus clarifies this truth beyond all doubts: "It is the Spirit that gives life, the flesh is of no avail: the Words I have spoken to you are spirit and life" (John 6: 63). Concerning the Risen Christ who has become the cosmic Christ and universal redeemer, St Paul affirms and proclaims: "the last Adam became a life-giving spirit" (1 Cor 16: 45).

The urgent task of the true Disciples of Christ today is to present to the world a Christ who is alive and recreates and liberates the human kind and the earth which is our common home continually until the end of time. The Christ experienced, understood, and proclaimed by the Christian Churches and denominations today is a Christ garbed-tight-fit in some foreign super-impositions whether they be theological, ecclesiastical, liturgical or institutional governed by holy rules and regulations. All these elements were valid dimensions of incarnating Christ in the respective religion-socio-political milieus in which they were developed. However, in the present era, most of the historical accretions and super-impositions on Christ are proved to be hindrances for Christ to be accepted by people at large. Indeed, they impede Christ's universal redemptive and recreating activities in the world.

In India, especially we need to present an Indian face of Christ, not the western colonial face, nor the Hebraic-Syrian face. India is the most ancient land of seekers of Truth, a land of Yogis, who incessantly worked for the unity of mind and body under the spirit within the human person. The psycho-somatic disciplines (*sadhanas*) practised in India from time immemorial, sought union or integration not only with the psycho-somatic fields of man in which the Spirit of God indwells but also unity and integration with fellow humans and with the cosmos at large. A presentation of the living and universal person of Christ as the fulfilment of the spiritual seeking going on in India will certainly appeal to the Indian people. An evangelical profile of Jesus relevant in India is that of a Sadguru, fulfilling the teachings of the spiritual masters of India. At the same time, Jesus needs to be presented as the one who intervenes in our daily life, as a forgiving God, for the salvation of the sinners and as the liberator of the people who yearn for the alleviation of their poverty and for the restoration of justice and peace in life. Such a profile of Jesus will definitely create more space for Christ in the hearts of the Indian Masses. Besides, the Gospel of Christ must be lived in India in an indigenous way avoiding any form of cultural alienation. A Christ delimited and distorted to fit into the vested interests of the present day Christian Churches and denominations renders the universal salvific power of Christ less and less effective and operative to reconstruct the world. In this context, let me quote Pope Francis who in an interview with an Italian journalist, said: "I believe in God, not in a Catholic God. There is no Catholic God. And I believe in Jesus Christ, his incarnation."

The highest mission of Christ is to unite the humans among themselves as members of a universal family. As Cosmic Christ and the Lord of creation, Christ is incessantly working also for the regeneration, restoration and final integration of the cosmos. St Paul attempts a poignant illustration of this in his letter to the Colossians: "For in him all the fullness of God was pleased to dwell and through him to reconcile to himself all things whether on earth or in heaven, making peace by the blood of his cross" (Col 1:19-20). The universal Christ embraces all members of the human family –past, present, and future disregarding ecclesial denominations, religious allegiances, and all other delimiting social structures and institutions like caste, creed, race, tribe, nationality. Christ creates communion and unity always and everywhere.

Christ as a Unifying Force

All those who are called to be Disciples of Christ should seek to transcend their limited and delimiting identities ensuing from their belongingness to their respective Christian denomination or Church. Transcendence does not mean a severing off their existing belongingness to the Church group from which they enjoy a sense of fraternity, wellbeing and social power. However, the true Disciples of Christ should consciously and continuously strive after transcending such limited identities and seek to embrace the universal, unbound Christ who belongs to all and to whom belongs everyone and everything. Unless one learns to relativize one's fractional Christian identity one can never grow into the full dimensions of the universal power and grace of the real Christ, the Lord of all and the Saviour of the world. In fact, every Christian denomination and Church needs urgent interior reform to set it free from the numerous enslaving elements which prevent them from following the real Christ and worshipping Him in Spirit and Truth (John 4:24). All the true disciples of Christ, belonging to the numerous fractional entities of the one body of Christ should dare to begin to think in a way, faithful to the universal Christ and become radical reformers within their respective denominations and institutions, basing themselves on the simple and fundamental teachings of the Gospel, not on the divisive interpretations super-imposed on them by the vested interest of the wielders of power and authority in every Christian group.

The true disciples of Christ, while maintaining their relative belongingness to their respective denominations, need to form local and regional "communions" or fraternities all over the world. Actually, it is already happening under the inspiration of the so many reform movements spread across the world transcending the limitations of relative Christian identities. Every religious institution needs some ritual expressions for their survival and continuity. Jesus himself followed some Judaic ritual practices. But the main thrust of the words and deeds of Jesus was to challenge and to go beyond ritualism and exploitative power structures that nourish and maintain ritualistic structures. Religions based on ritualism have always been exploitative as episodes in the history of the world well attest to. Hence, the Disciples of Christ need to endeavour consistently to withstand the enslaving onslaughts of ritualism. They should be constantly reminded of the truth that ritualism violates the basic dictates of reason and fosters ignorance and superstitions which in their turn are amply used by the narrow-minded and self-centred leadership of the religious groups for exploitation with immunity.

Finally, the reconstruction of the post-Covid 19 era demands a harmonious coming together of all religions. Inter-religious dialogue needs both a theoretical frame work and a practical strategy. The disciples of Christ in their endeavours to reconstruct the world in accordance with the dimensions of the kingdom of God need to be committed to inter-religious dialogue, especially on the local level so as to generate interreligious peace and harmony and to transform all religions into protagonists of peace and welfare of the society, the members of which are all brothers and sisters of a single family inhabiting a single home which we love, honour and protect as our Mother Earth.

---

* **Revd Dr Thomas Kulangara** is a priest of the Syro-Malankara Church. He is the founder of a Secular Institute named 'Missionaries of Unity' and a movement working for peace and unity in the world in collaboration with the Focolare Movement. He is also a Prof. of Philosophy.

20

An Ecumenical Mission for Sustainable Development of Post-Pandemic India

*Swami Gurusree **

"Let the Society be strong with Abundance!"

Till the last century tales of social revival movements had their origin mostly in towns and cities before stretching themselves to the villages, because people who lived in the towns and cities enjoyed the cultural nobility, freedom of mind and leisure to think about life and society seriously. However, today, the same advantages of towns and cities prompt man to be more self-centered, pleasure seeking, and least worried about society or social issues. They foolishly crave for the luxuries of modernity only to become termite domes. They tend more and more to replace the ability to think logically with the ability to memorize more things.

And so the waves of the future social revivals will be the other way: the villagers or the intellectuals of the villages will initiate urges to create a happy, beautiful society, which will echo in the towns and cities. We may call it the return of the Gandhian wave of '*Grama Swaraj*', which was rather discarded by the first rulers of independent India. The recent surge in Gandhian studies all over India, especially in Kerala, is a positive sign of the rising relevance and values of Gandhian view about Indian villages. Gandhiji wished to uplift our villages to be economically self-reliant. And so we need to make our rural areas self-sufficient. But our villages cannot achieve self-reliance and self-sufficiency through the policies followed by the governments, which declare them economically backward and support them with concessions or free kits. Such modes of poverty alleviation are not Gandhian at all, for such aids can only make people lazier and non-productive.

Of course, many a villager is weak, and some of them are really backward economically. And the governments as well as the NGOs think rather foolishly that they can handle it easily to the peoples' satisfaction by distributing free gifts and thus create a welfare society. In fact what they do is to perpetuate the situation of penury among the people. So we need to think differently through the Gandhian eyes. We need to have a powerful vision based on the *Vedantic* vision. We need to encourage the majority of the people to be entrepreneurs equipping them with all the latest technologies to create various products of world standards.

Compared to other cultural, religious sects, and looking from various angles, Christianity may be said to be in a better position most suitable to bring about social change and welfare of the world. In that sense, the leadership of the future world and its renewal rest on Christianity, though we are not able to predict at present when it would take place. It is because the main reason being that Christianity itself has to undergo changes and renewal. Provided that Christianity frees itself so that its unscientific conservatism becomes irrelevant and embraces its own natural, powerful, divine vision and mission, the world would be able to enjoy and experience its divine touch.

As an initial step, the villagers need to be educated of their need to be self-sufficient and self-reliant. Free kits and 'Thozhilurappu' (guaranteed labour) programs will neither solve their problems nor guarantee their welfare more than like crutches. Their minds should be, first of all, freed, as Gandhiji had wished to, from the darkness of caste system and the hangover of Colonialism. And then encourage maximum number of people to enter into some kind of small scale industrial business which can make them self-reliant. This procedure is the only way we can free them from their beggar-mentality and help them to be instead generous minds.

The two usual problems the small scale industrialists, or entrepreneurs in general face are products sales for a reasonable price and availability of raw materials. To make sure of both these aspects, it is inevitable that we have the related fraternities or clubs as well as the supportive legal structures from the part of the government. Together with this, we also need to maintain a system for fixing the prices, quality certification and trustworthiness in dealings. This will help the citizens to develop and possess a royal feeling, and the king or ruler, a godly feeling. The Ten Visions or 'The Decalogue' that follows can throw more light into what we have been saying:

1. THE DECALOGUE

1. **Redemption of Farmers is Redemption of India**: If you want India progress into prosperity, first and foremost, the farmers' woe and cry should be solved. And there is only one shortcut to it, and it is most practical and certain. The right to sell agricultural crops and other products processed from such produces should be reserved to the farmers and to the farmers' co-operative societies only. This reservation will not only put an end to the farmers' woes but will also enhance their profit, joy and pride. Some people who make their living out of selling agricultural products will have to be rehabilitated, and some changes will be necessary in the management of certain large scale industries. Nonetheless, it is definite that this will work wonders in the farmers' history.

2. **Bury the filthy dregs of the British reign and the old Royal politics**: End the usage of the word "Sir" (*Slave I Remain*) to address (government) officials. The society should be educated to address the Collector, "Dear Collector". Instead of the word "Application", "Demand Note" should be made use of. The citizens and the officials should enjoy the same rank and rights. The citizens should possess the privilege to use the same language as that used by the government. Cancel all the unnecessary laws and rules. And the appropriate laws and regulations should always be practiced and upheld. Even ordinary citizens should have awareness of the same. Such idiotic practices like seeing the man of authority as the 'owner' and the citizens as 'slaves' should be stopped.

3. **The bureaucratic stupidity of making citizens beggars should be stopped**: The citizens should have a sense of royalty (*Raja bhava*) and the rulers should possess a god-sense (*Deva bhava*); then only a society can achieve social welfare and progress. To come to possess this sense, the citizens should have mental caliber to look at the people who are richer and more powerful than them as their equals. At the same time, they should have also the heart and nobility to view as valuable those who are poorer and powerless than them and the *jnani* (*sanyasi*). When that happens, a sense of royal feeling will emerge in anyone who possesses them. On the contrary, when the citizens become and behave like beggars, the ruler will become a scoundrel who bulge and bully the beggar citizens. Or a scoundrel needs such a state of affairs, like the corrupt current scenario, in which alone he could retain his power. This fact must be made public. All should take care to put a stop to such social and political calamities. The hopeless atmosphere of religion playing party politics ought to be stopped.

4. **The citizens should be given authority, rights and responsibilities**: The officials should be reduced to the status of the Registrar of births and deaths. The malicious predicament of the governments becoming centres of robbery must be terminated. The arrogant colonial mentality that the citizens are the tenants of land leased by the government should be discarded. The citizens should not be conceived of as surviving at the mercy and generosity of the governments. On the contrary, both the citizens and the governments should know that the government survives on the generosity of the citizens, not vice versa. The status of India in the Happiness Index should be elevated to the front row. For that, the feeling of inferiority complex must be totally eradicated from the minds of the people and ignite their sense of national pride. The filth and arrogance of the caste consciousness "*Chatur-Varnya*" should be thrown out of the minds of all the people. Everyone should be freed from the cobwebs of false notions and the stupid traditional antecedents of divisive forces. All should be equipped with the wings of *Dharma* to soar into the skies and fly freely. And then, true joy will take all to dance.

5. **The need for government permits must be discarded**: Right-Permits should be put into practice. The current corrupt practice of imposing on citizens the need to get various permits in advance for starting constructions, industrial and commercial buildings, service centres, etc. must be taken away. The citizens should be given the right to start any enterprise with an understanding between the owner and the recognized/registered mentors. We do not need the government's permit to be born or to die. Do we? And still, births and deaths are registered unconditionally. Don't they? In the same way, the citizens have the right to live and act justly. The government has no right to deny him that right, especially, within a democratic frame. All the civil laws should be dealt with as if they were

criminal offences. Once a crime of commission or omission has taken place, the government agencies can start the criminal investigation procedure and dictate the punishments. However, the citizens do not require any advance permission from the government for any civil system.

6. **Local Self-governing Bodies should be revitalized as self-sufficient Provinces**: There should be a political decision which allows the citizens to choose the presidents of the local self-governing bodies by themselves directly. Elements like religion and party politics should not be allowed to intrude into such local election process. The presidents of the local governing bodies must be vested with judicial powers. They should have the authority to interfere in all the civil disputes of the locality and execute right solutions appropriately and justly. The local governing bodies should be dignified agencies,who are capable enough of solving all the local problems of the people. They should have the duty and responsibility to involve in all matters of the locality under their authority. They should be vigilant to see that criminals and anti-social elements and activities do not take place or are not sponsored in their localities. To promote such a social vigilance, the local governing bodies must take care to involve all the people of the locality in all its social issues and offer all support creating such occasions and recognitions. And above all, they should initiate industries and production centers suitable to each place. Special importance should be given to A. I., Robotic and I.T. based industries. People should not be left hopeless, jobless and homeless in any case. There should be a political system for occasions or situations when people of a particular place is evacuated for a higher social cause, or their properties legally confiscated, such procedures must be carried out with the permission of the local governing body only.

7. **The Revenue documents should be simplified**: All the Revenue documents and Sub-Registrar documents except the Location Sketch and Survey Plan of a State should be made available online for immediate reference. The Village Assistants should also be official Surveyors. The Taluk Surveyors' only duty should be reduced to gauging the dimensions of government land, land Acquisition, and dealing legal land litigations. The Village resolutions should be speedy and transparent enough as not to be interfered with by the Collector or the *Tahasildar*, who are, of course, the higher authorities, can look into them later on. The authoritative documents like survey plans, litho plans, A.B. Sketches, etc. should be preserved in the Village offices themselves for official reference and communication.

8. **The governments should not create fake conflicts**: Weapons of war should neither be imported nor exported. Commerce of war weapons is reason for internal conflicts as well as looting the wealth of the country. We need to stop this madness. The government should not create enemies and rivalry with the neighboring countries or declare a country its foe. The government should not inject into the citizens such feelings of enmity, hatred and a belligerent attitude. Let them live life thriving in *Dharma* and dynamic in *Karma*. Lie should be considered a serious crime. So ban the citizens from lying and fraud dealings. If the officials in authority commit crimes of lie or fraud, they must be punished tenfold. However, everyone should have the right not to tell the truth.

9. **Profit taxation should be stopped**: Half the wealth of the superrich who have assets worth more than 1000 crores should be reserved for social welfare, after their death. The GST must be reduced to the $1/10^{th}$ system. "*Arthakranthi*" must be put into practice. The mixed economy should be continued. No special concessions or freebies should be

allotted for government institutions. Let them compete with the private sector and thrive. The government should have no monopoly over any service. The private sector should be given equal opportunities in the supply of electricity or such matters. Liquor and drugs must be banned. The government should discontinue its corrupt schemes to exploit profits by way of tax endorsing all immoralities. If tax loss is what worries governments, there are other ways to raise income of the treasury.

10. **Above all, every citizen should have awareness that this is his/her own country**: We can see the unfortunate tendency of maintaining several hostile countries within the same political geography. Such attitudes and mentalities must be suppressed. Caste and political spirits do play their part in it. But such ideological and religious party spirits must not be extended or lead to profiteering attitudes. We should put a stop to the arrogance of government officials who think that the ordinary citizens are surviving on their mercy and kindness. Everyone should be able to live proudly as a *Dharmee*, fearless of such governmental oppression. We should correct the narrow notion that one becomes a criminal all on his own mistakes. Those who dictate the punishment, those who execute that punishment, the government, the society and those who brought him to and up in life are all equally responsible for him. The society should consider these facts also when he is judged. The local self-governing body has also the duty to look into this aspect. You need to understand that in a society where the rich and those in power are considered great and honorable, and give applause and dance for them, justice will not reign, nor will criminals cease to be. As long as the man in power is rich and the rich man is given power and so long as there is a gang to support him, *dharma* will not reign in that society. Justice will

> reign and *dharma* will be victorious only in a society, where ordinary people live a just and honest life.

A political revolution and transformation in India has become inevitable today. Dynamic citizens should come forward to be its staunch leaders. Each and every citizen has the right to take responsibility of this task and duty. None of the diverse political visions India, our nation, has witnessed to date is not objective enough nor is it honest or wholesome. They all lack the vision about the humanity, the majority of which belong to the marginalized villages. Indian politics, especially, party politics, even today roam about in the ruts of the bygone epoch of royal- politics and glued to the erstwhile dirt of the British rule. The nation has, of course, produced many bold and eminent leaders and has several parties and committees and groups, so many congresses and meetings, and plenty of discussions and declarations every day. Still, in no way the society truly progresses the right way. And the reason for this dilemma is that the political parties do not have a definite proper vision of society. As a result, people are not able to enjoy the good fruits of freedom and democracy. Nor do they get the serene and pristine experience of wealth, goods and other natural resources. The governments and the whole of bureaucracy today are like the legendary serpent in the story of St Geevargees which blocked the flow of drinking water of the people of the locality. In order to get their water, the serpent had to move. And to make it move, they had to offer a virgin and edibles to it. Thus the people were frantically more preoccupied with finding virgins to appease the serpent in order to get some drinking water than any other thing in life. While the problem could have been easily solved by killing the serpent, none of them had the courage to do it. Similar and such are the kind of decision-making committees we have in India today. We need to banish this fateful situation. And we can, of course, do it for sure, only if we rise up and unite!

We could, certainly, fight successfully for our freedom, for we had then an enemy to fight against. We could, certainly, unite in the past for there was a man to unite us all, our dear Gandhiji. And we gained our freedom thanks to this unity and also other global factors. Then we fought for freedom from poverty, for which also we had a reason, and we have really succeeded in it to a great extent. But to date, we have not fought for justice of others; we have not craved for true joy in life; we have not raised our voice for self-pride and self-worth, and we have not stood for the motto of "love for the world". The slogan, "Ma-ni-sha-da" found its place in literature but not in our culture. Feudalism and the insecurity, poverty, and, above all, the superstitious beliefs of God-consciousness it created at that time could be the reasons for it. However, today, things have become more or less transparent. Nevertheless, our minds are still filled with filthy outlooks and keep ourselves distanced from dharma. We need to get rid of such attitudes. Today we join together and put up fights only to acquire power and authority, wealth, profit and fulfill our greed. To achieve it, we turn our brothers into our enemies, religions into explosives and tribes, suicidal squads. And we join them and, as fools, plan out shrewd tactics of deception. So it is time we returned to the basic vision proposed by Gandhiji, the Father of our Nation: the vision of Grama-Swaraj.

---

* **Swami Gurusree** is the founder and visionary-in-chief of "Dharmo Devo Trust of Trusts", which aims at activities to build up a prosperous society. Graduated in the science of agriculture, he was employed for some time in the agricultural research department. He could easily carve a niche for himself as a non-partisan college union chairman and as State level organizing panel convener.

He resigned his job and ventured into industrial and commercial entrepreneurship in order to raise capital for social reforms and has been to date an active presence in the social arena. He travelled a three-fourth of the country on foot and wheels in order to make available to the common man the services of *Panchayat Raj* (rule of the village council), which in turn also provided him with opportunities to have a personal experience of the hapless lives of many a class of people in different parts of India. On many occasions, he had to confront personally the haughty bureaucracy at the Secretariat of the State of Kerala. He fought many a legal battle in almost all tribunals and courts of justice up to the Supreme Court. And he was a litigant in the High Court on many occasions. He has also fought for human rights with the authorities of the institutions and ministerial offices of the Central Government.

He was the first person in India to develop the technology and demonstrate successfully how to produce electricity from sea waves and thus also secure the protection of the seashores. He is exceptionally smart, ingenious and has an intrinsically charismatic personality blessed with an insight to distinguish between values and sciences through intense thinking. He is a *karmayogi* (one doing his duty expecting no reward) committed for the welfare of the world.

www.ingramcontent.com/pod-product-compliance
Ingram Content Group UK Ltd.
Pitfield, Milton Keynes, MK11 3LW, UK
UKHW041857190726
13854UKWH00002B/957